THE TURNING POINT

He stood facing the Chief of Staff and the top brass of the U.S. Navy and most of its Army. As the upstart Eisenhower outlined his plan, General George C. Marshall remained impassive.

"The British Isles," asserted Eisenhower, "must be turned into the greatest operating military base of all time, so we can throw the largest amphibious force in history across the English Channel and invade the coast of France. It's the shortest route to Berlin and the complete destruction of Germany."

Now even Marshall seemed to be joining the chorus of disapproval that answered Ike's words.

"*Complete destruction* of Germany?" Marshall demanded.

"Yes sir," Eisenhower answered without hesitation.

"That sounds a little strange," a three-star general interjected, "coming from an officer of German ancestry."

Ike whirled. It was a sensitive point. "That's exactly why I feel so strongly, *Sir,*" he said, his temper flaring briefly. "Adolf Hitler and his Gestapo and S.S. have made it impossible for any decent German to hold up his head. They have to be destroyed."

IKE

Melville Shavelson

WARNER BOOKS

A Warner Communications Company

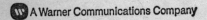

Preface

She was standing on the front lawn, calling out to me, naked except for the bathtowel clutched about her, the sun glinting on the droplets of water in her hair—chestnut then, white now—and the picture is frozen in my memory, never to fade. All of us who lived through that day have a similar photograph.

It was the day our old world died, and a new one began.

"The Japs have attacked Pearl Harbor!" she shouted at me, and I remember I laughed. I was just returning from a script conference at Bob Hope's house, around the corner in North Hollywood, and this sounded like a straight line for Professor Colonna. My wife always confused things she heard on the radio.

I tried to calm her down as I led her into the house, but the bulletins were blaring now. She had gotten it right —for once. On CBS, Artur Rodzinski was conducting the

New York Philharmonic. But this Sunday, as the performance was about to end, the orchestra began to play "The Star-Spangled Banner." And the audience at Carnegie Hall stood and sang the words.

Patriotism was suddenly back in fashion.

At Cornell University a few years earlier, I had almost become a member of the Veterans of Future Wars, a satiric name for the anti-war activists of that time. Now, suddenly, I felt a little better that we had a real army out there somewhere.

I had never heard of Dwight Eisenhower. I doubt that anyone I knew had.

I went to a football game in the Hollywood Stars Stadium that afternoon.

Ike Eisenhower, and ten thousand career officers like him, went to work.

Although I traveled uncounted miles to dozens of army camps with the Bob Hope Radio Show during those early days of America's entry into World War II, I never met General Eisenhower. But he is one of the figures of that period, like Franklin Roosevelt, who were as real to me as my own family.

Ike. The personification of the spirit of a country that had not yet lost its innocence. The good guy in the last war in which you could tell who the bad guys were. Ike. The friend of the GIs. The smile that could not be pretended. The warmth that radiated from a carefully controlled public relations campaign, but a warmth that seemed to be there of its own free will. Ike. The strength that survived the ordeals of D-Day and the Battle of Ardennes. The Supreme Commander who refused to meet with any German generals until after they had signed a complete and abject surrender.

He was something special to our generation—until he became an old man in the Presidency, playing golf and seemingly ineffectual in the political morass he always said he abhorred.

The Ike I knew never became President. He, too,

remains frozen in memory—smiling, waving, parading in victory after V-E Day before cheering millions through the streets of Washington and Abilene and New York, Mamie at his side.

Of course, few of us knew about Kay Summersby then. Now that we do, or think we do, it doesn't diminish either Ike or Mamie. Or, especially, Kay. One thing the new generation has taught us is that humanity is not a crime.

This is not a history. It is a faded photograph of a faded time. Where memory failed or research halted at a closed door, imagination painted the colors.

Exactly thirty-four years after D-Day, it seems to me that it all felt something like this. . . .

Melville Shavelson
North Hollywood
June 6, 1978

PART 1
IKE

I
Awakening

The green blips appeared suddenly on the face of the P-7 phosphor in the radarscope and began to spread across the entire tube. In the eerie glow in the darkened room, Pvt. Joe Lockard pushed his friend Pvt. George Elliot out of the way and sat down to see what had gone wrong. After all, it was 0702 at Kahuku Point and the radar was supposed to shut down at 0700. Lockard had only stayed on because Elliot had wanted to practice on the brand-new electronic gear. He had probably fouled it up.

Lockard checked the hold and synch controls as the blips grew larger and larger. Nothing was wrong. Nothing was wrong except that the largest flight of planes either had ever seen on the scope was 137 miles to the north, 3 degrees east, and heading toward Oahu like a flight of glowing green locusts.

Elliot grabbed up the phone and got through to Lt.

Kermit Tyler, an Air Corps officer in training who was the only one on duty at the Information Center.

"Sir!" he shouted. "Radar shows maybe a hundred planes coming in from the north!"

He listened for a moment. "Yes, sir," he said, and hung up.

"What did he say?" Lockard wanted to know.

The blips were almost as large as the main pulse from the radar and getting closer.

"He said, 'Forget it,' " Elliot said.

It was Lt. Tyler's second day on the job. Also his last.

A hundred Japanese bombers, 40 torpedo planes, and 43 fighters hit the assembled United States Pacific Fleet at Pearl Harbor in the first wave. They had been launched from a Japanese strike force that included 6 carriers, 2 battleships, and 3 cruisers, all of which had sailed undetected from Japan to a position north of Oahu.

Two thousand, four hundred and three Americans were killed, half of them when the battleship *Arizona* was blown up. Sunk or beached were the battleships *Oklahoma, West Virginia, California,* and *Nevada.* One hundred and eighty-eight American planes were destroyed, most of them on the ground.

The city of Honolulu was hit forty times during the attack—thirty-nine of the hits being scored by U.S. anti-aircraft shells.

* * *

It was a sleepy Sunday morning at Fort Sam Houston, in Texas. Even the Commandant, Brigadier General Dwight David Eisenhower, was taking a nap.

So was most of America.

Mamie Eisenhower was seated in the living room, listening to the game from New York—the football Dodgers were playing the Giants at the Polo Grounds. The Dodgers had kicked off, and the Giants had returned the kickoff to the twenty-yard line.

Mamie happily pinned her husband's first star to the shoulder of his uniform tunic. It had been a long, tough struggle for the ambitious young West Point lieutenant she had met at this same Fort Sam Houston all those years ago. America's peacetime army had been kept at minimum strength after the end of the Big War, and promotion came terribly slowly. So slowly that Dwight Eisenhower, now 52 years old and still only a colonel despite his brilliant record, had thought seriously of asking for retirement. Even his first star was something of a disappointment. It was only a temporary rank, because of the Army's expansion with the coming of the peacetime draft; as soon as the "temporary emergency" was over, Ike Eisenhower and hundreds like him would return to lower rank—and pay.

Mamie, growing older herself but still attractive, the bangs that would become famous around the world framing an alert, intelligent face that reflected an inner strength, had hoped for better. An army wife, she had followed her husband from post to post, even into the jungles of Panama and the heat of the Philippines where Ike helped Douglas MacArthur train the new Philippine army. Army life is inbred; the same officers, the same wives, the same officer's clubs, the same gossip—some of it about her, some of it about Ike. There was always that inner conflict, knowing that advancement for her husband would only come quickly at the time of maximum danger—war. She had already lost a son, Dwight Jr.—"Icky" they had called him fondly, a diminutive of Ike. Icky had died of scarlet fever at the age of three, and neither parent ever fully got over it. Now their son John was at West Point; and, if war came, obviously it would involve Johnny Eisenhower as well as his father.

So when the announcer broke into the broadcast with word of the Japanese attack, Mamie was jolted into sudden horror. As an army wife, she was personally and directly involved. As an army mother, doubly so.

"We interrupt this program to bring you a special news bulletin." The announcer's voice was strained, in-

15

credulous, as if he himself could not believe what he was about to say. America, the land of the free and home of the brave, had been caught with its pants down. By some little yellow Japs, for God's sake! Why, we didn't even know they were mad at us!

"The Japanese have attacked Pearl Harbor, Hawaii, by air, President Roosevelt has just announced. The attack was also made on all naval and military activities on the principal island of Ohau."

"O*a*hu, you idiot," Mamie corrected the stumbling announcer. She knew Honolulu well. She and Ike had often visited Hawaii. She and Ike had visited *everyplace,* during his 26 years in the army. She was on her feet, heading for the stairs, before the announcer finished his next sentence.

Brig. Gen. Eisenhower was taking a well-earned nap. The new star and the new position as Third Army chief of staff brought with them the responsibility for bringing an army post only recently flooded with new recruits and armed with outmoded weapons into a military world startled by Hitler's shrieking Stuka dive bombers and the massive, crunching attacks of the Nazi Panzer Divisions with their fast, maneuverable tanks. The modern German weapons—including the psychological one, "Shrechlichkeit," the deliberate use of horror to inspire terror in the enemy—had enabled the Nazi armies to overrun Europe in a matter of months and throw the British army into the English Channel at Dunkirk. Now the Nazis were hammering toward the gates of Moscow and poised for an invasion of England itself. And still America was unwilling to accept the inevitability of its involvement. The sham of "Lend-Lease" had to be used by Roosevelt to transfer desperately needed over-age destroyers from our navy to the British; and Charles Lindbergh, the "Lucky Lindy" who was the idol of America for his daring solo crossing of the Atlantic in the "Spirit of St. Louis," was haranguing jammed stadiums for the cause of America First, a group dedicated to keeping America out of the fighting and to the full support of that glorious patriotic organization, the German-American Bund.

The attempt to bring the new recruits at Fort Sam Houston out of their lethargy and to some state of readiness required all of Ike's energy and organizational ability, morning and night. This Sunday morning, utterly exhausted, he had sprawled on his bed and fallen into a troubled sleep. He was reliving another day and another war. He had faced this same problem in World War I, when an unprepared America had to tool up almost from scratch to enter a major war. Eisenhower had spent most of that war behind a desk in Washington where his talent for organization brought him quick recognition and advancement. But Ike wanted a field command. Finally, he was given command of the Tank Corps Training Center at Camp Colt, Pennsylvania. All it lacked were tanks. But Ike did meet a brilliant young officer named George Patton, and together they planned what they would do when their tanks finally arrived and they were shipped with them to France.

The tanks arrived—just after the Armistice. Ike never got overseas.

Was it all to happen again?

The jangling of the telephone brought him bolt upright, just as Mamie rushed in. The news came simultaneously from both sources. It was the Duty Officer, calling to tell him of the emergency; it was his wife, to repeat what she had just heard on the radio. Honolulu, she told him, they hit Honolulu on a Sunday morning. The bartender's hadn't even had time to put out the hangover remedies at the Officers' Club. She was immediately sorry; the news probably meant that some of their close friends were dead or wounded, and that many, many more of them soon would be.

This was war.

Brig. Gen. Eisenhower stood up and put his arms around his wife. They had had their differences in the past,

17

they would have more in the future; but at this moment of peril, they were closer than they had been in years.

Dwight Eisenhower was too valuable a man to be left to the routine task of preparing the troops at Fort Sam Houston for combat. Col. Walter Bedell Smith phoned from Washington to tell him that the Chief, Gen. George C. Marshall, wanted Ike on a plane for the nation's capitol as quickly as possible. Mamie had him packed and on his way within an hour.

It would be a replay, Ike thought, of his career in World War I.

II
Potomac Fever

America had awakened from its sleep along with Dwight Eisenhower. Senator Cabot Lodge, Senator Arthur Vandenberg, Senator Burton Wheeler, the isolationists who had fought the administration tooth and nail to keep the United States from any involvement in the war, telephoned the President to assure him of their full support. Only Lucky Lindy didn't seem to have a nickel.

On the arm of his son Jimmy, every step on his shrunken, steel-supported legs a moment of torture, Franklin D. Roosevelt made his way to the podium before a joint session of the Congress and began to speak.

"Yesterday, December 7, 1941—a date which will live in infamy—the United States of America was suddenly and deliberately attacked by naval and air forces of the Empire of Japan. Last night Japanese forces attacked Hong Kong. Last night Japanese forces attacked Guam."

Roosevelt's voice, the rich accents that had helped

bring him the Presidency because of the way they projected his personality over the new phenomenon of network radio, remained firm and controlled. The anger in it was doubly effective. This was no time for purple rhetoric. As he ticked off the frightening record of the Japanese successes of the past few hours, it was a factual statement of an account, an account that must one day be settled.

"Last night Japanese forces attacked the Philippine Islands. Last night the Japanese attacked Wake Island. This morning the Japanese attacked Midway Island."

The President raised his head and looked at his audience, and now, at last, the voice rose, changed pitch, betrayed the depth of his feelings.

"With confidence in our armed forces, with the unbounding determination of our people, we will gain the inevitable triumph, so help us God. I ask this Congress to declare that a state of war exists between the United States of America and the Empire of Japan."

The roar of applause that swept through the assembled Congress was carried by short-wave radio around the world. The answering roar from Berlin was almost immediate. Adolf Hitler shouted himself hoarse in front of the German Reichstag for a solid hour, his words brought back to the United States by those same short waves, echoing and re-echoing with atmospherics:

"The German government, under the circumstances brought about by President Roosevelt and the Anglo-Saxon-Jewish-Capitalist world, considers herself as being in a state of war with the United States of America!"

The solid half-hour of cheering that followed this declaration caused the *New Yorker* magazine to print one of its most famous cartoons: Adolf Hitler, on the rostrum, backed up by a thousand SS troops with submachine guns. The caption: "I think I may say, without fear of contradiction . . ."

From Rome, by the same transatlantic hookup, came another, more familiar, echo, Hitler's faithful—for the moment—ally, Benito Mussolini, beseeching the Italian people to sacrifice everything at the side of heroic Japan against the hated United States.

"Italians!" he cried, from his fortified balcony on the Piazza Venezia. "Once more arise! We shall win!"

Since most of his listeners had relatives in America, they knew that Italians, somewhere, had to win this one. Italy, as usual, was on both sides. They cheered Il Duce, dutifully.

By the time Ike Eisenhower arrived in Washington, his country was at war with all of the Axis powers. A large part of America's navy was at the bottom of the Pacific and much of its infantry was drilling with World War I rifles. The Pentagon, that monstrous five-sided monument to militarism, had not yet been completed. The nerve center of the military was the old War State Navy building, filled beyond capacity, officers and enlisted men and secretaries and defense-contract-seekers jamming offices and hallways.

Col. Walter Bedell Smith guided Ike by the elbow through the bustling throng in one of the corridors. Young, tough, energetic, "Beetle" Smith was at the beginning of the career that was to take him through the war at Ike's side and later into the diplomatic world as America's ambassador to Russia.

"They say Japanese submarines shelled Los Angeles last night," he told his companion as they elbowed their way through the crush.

Ike looked at him. "I don't believe it."

"Well, they do in California. There's absolute panic."

"What do you mean by 'panic'?"

"They've cancelled the Rose Bowl game."

Ike grinned. "That," he said, "is panic."

The Colonel knew that Ike's interest in football was more than academic. Ike Eisenhower, one of the smallest men on the team, had been the toughest fullback on the West Point varsity until a knee injury ended his playing career just before the Army-Navy game. It was one of his greatest disappointments.

Later, he was called on to coach teams at army bases all over the United States, but coaching wasn't the same as playing. It was the story of his life. Ike wanted to be Red Grange, but he was destined to wind up as Knute Rockne.

"Everyone's paranoid in Washington, too," Beetle continued. "You were the first friend I called for help."

"If you were really my friend, you wouldn't have called me here at all. I spent most of World War One in an office right in this building. I want to spend this war up front."

"Not a chance, Ike. If the Chief likes you, you're stuck behind a great big desk for the duration."

"Suppose I'm lucky enough to get him to hate me?"

"He'll stick you behind a smaller desk."

"Who the hell do you have to kiss to get a combat command in this army?"

"I don't know," Beetle grinned, "but it's not him."

And he indicated the nameplate on the door in front of them: Gen. George C. Marshall.

The Chief of Staff swung his swivel chair around and stared at the officer seated before him. He was used to the Young Turks who were anxious to go off and get themselves killed, or promoted rapidly, it didn't seem to matter which. But this was an officer in his fifties, balding, slightly gray, and with a reputation as a desk soldier.

"Eisenhower," he began, controlling his impatience. It had been a long day, as all days in Washington were to be for the Chief for the next three and a half years. Years, incidentally, when the whole world learned to call the officer in front of him "Ike." Marshall, who was to be his greatest friend, never called him anything but "Eisenhower."

"Eisenhower," he repeated, "your enthusiasm for combat is highly commendable. But tell me this: have you ever commanded a division in actual battle?"

22

Ike shifted uneasily in his chair. He knew what was coming.

"No, sir," he replied.

"A battalion?"

"No, sir."

"A company?"

"No, sir."

Gen. Marshall was beginning to enjoy himself, but he kept the smile from showing.

"A platoon, Eisenhower?"

"No, sir."

"In your entire career in World War One, did you ever hear a shot fired in anger?"

Ike's temper was rising, but the West Point training still held.

"How could I, sir," he said, the edge of anger barely showing, "when I never left this building?"

Marshall looked at him, coolly. "Eisenhower, your qualifications are impeccable—for remaining in it."

He got to his feet. The interview, as far as he was concerned, concluded.

Ike didn't budge.

"Sir, I've been recommended for a division command by two of my superior officers who—"

It was Marshall's turn to show anger. "General, *I* make the command decisions around here. According to General MacArthur, you've got one of the best minds in the army for logistics and organization. I want you in the War Plans Division, where you'll be useful to me, not up in the front lines stopping a bullet. Good afternoon."

He sat down, expecting the officer to leave. The Chief of Staff had dismissed him. Possibly any other officer in the United States Army would have left.

Not Dwight Eisenhower.

"Sir," Eisenhower asked evenly, "does that mean I'll be stuck behind a desk for the rest of *this* war, too?"

"If I say so, General. *Good afternoon.*"

This time there was no denying Marshall's tone. Reluctantly, Ike got to his feet and started slowly for the door, facing the bleak possibility of his military career winding up in a snowstorm of army paperwork.

"Another thing, Eisenhower . . ." Marshall was studying his man, judging him, testing him. "Even though you may have been recommended for division command, you're going to stay right here at your present rank, and that's that. Don't expect promotion."

The fuse had burned down. Ike's face flushed red; the consequences no longer mattered.

"General Marshall, I don't give a damn! If you want to nail me to a desk where I don't want to be, I'll do my job for my country as long as you insist on it. And to hell with rank!"

He turned and yanked the door open. In that fraction of a second, he realized that he had been guilty of an act of insubordination in wartime to the Chief of Staff of the United States Army.

Ike turned. Marshall waited, expecting an abject apology. Instead, Ike grinned. The Eisenhower grin. The naughty boy.

Marshall stared back at him stonily. The grin vanished from Ike's face. Slowly he stepped out into the hallway, closing the door behind him.

Only then did Marshall permit himself to smile.

Dwight Eisenhower sat behind a desk piled high with papers, burning the midnight oil along with others of the War Plans Division—soon to be renamed Operations—as they labored over the design of the military future of America's armed forces. One of the questions Marshall had posed at their first meeting concerned how Eisenhower would meet the crisis in the Pacific. Ike's answer, delivered to the Chief after a period of intensive study, included a forecast that the Philippine Islands were doomed as an American outpost, and a suggestion that the convoys already en route as reinforcement should be diverted to Australia, which must become America's first line of defense in that part of the world.

Ike's knowledge of Philippine defenses was second only to that of his former commander, Douglas MacArthur, who showed an understanding of the situation by leaving his command in a submarine loaded, so it was reported, with his furniture, his wife, his son, and his dog. Now the last American bastion in the Western Pacific had fallen with the surrender of the fortress of Corregidor; and Ike's plan, which had been seconded by Marshall, had proved to be correct. It was to Australia that Douglas MacArthur had retreated, promising, histrionically, to return.

The young officers in the War Plans Division were now thinking far ahead, to the war in Europe and the desperately complicated problem of transporting sufficient men and material to that theater through an Atlantic Ocean infested with Nazi wolfpack submarines. Eisenhower was in the forefront of that planning.

He was taking a last sip from a cardboard container of stale coffee when Beetle Smith barged in, the bearer of familiar news.

"Chief wants to see us all right away in the conference room."

"Not again!" Ike groaned. "It's after midnight. It's too late to think."

"Not if you have four stars," Beetle informed him. Ike grabbed up his tie and located his electric razor. Marshall insisted that his officers look military, even in the small hours of the morning.

"I didn't spend all those years at West Point to sit in an office watching the old man's army newsreels," Ike complained, running the buzzing Remington over the stubble on his chin.

"Ike, for Christ's sake!" Beetle warned. "Don't give him any arguments this time. He's getting a little annoyed with you. Try to remember you're in the army."

"I know," Ike growled. "Keep your mouth shut, your

powder dry, and your brain in a sling." He tossed the razor back in a drawer. "Ours not to reason why."

The newsreel flickered dimly on the small screen set up in the Joint Chiefs' conference room, but the scenes projected burned their way into the consciousness of the army and navy officers assembled at the long table, watching, George Marshall the most grim-faced of all. These were unforgettable scenes; the American flag being hauled down from a flagpole above U.S. headquarters in the Philippines to be trampled upon by grinning Japanese soldiers; an American general, tense and emaciated after prolonged siege and starvation, facing the well-fed Japanese officers from the tiny, barely understood islands across the Pacific, officers who had humbled the military forces of one of the great white powers of the world. The American general looked numbed by his experience. There is nothing more feared than the unknown, and these little brown men represented a military culture America would never quite comprehend: the kamikaze, the banzai charge, the deification of the Emperor, the glorification of death. The tea ceremony. The chrysanthemum. The sunset. Harakiri.

The Japanese newsreel film had been fitted with a commentary by United States Army News announcers. Their message was stark.

"Japanese forces stormed the fortress of Corregidor in the Philippines and overran its last few American survivors. These films show General Jonathan Wainwright signing the first major military surrender in the history of the United States of America, and the death march of American prisoners captured with him on Bataan."

The scenes that followed turned Dwight Eisenhower's stomach. American soldiers, on the brink of starvation, hands raised in surrender, stumbling along dusty roads, prodded on by Japanese bayonets, falling, dragged to their feet, stumbling. Dying. Nothing quite like this was to be seen again until late in the war, when Ike Eisenhower walked, horrified, through the Nazi concentration camp in Ohrdruff, Germany, the first to be liberated by the Allies and the first actual proof that such inhumanity to man still existed in the twentieth century.

For the moment, Bataan was the worst America had yet seen. Even George Marshall had had enough. He raised his hand to stop the film. The sergeant running the projector was only too happy to turn it off. He had been raised to believe such things could never happen to Americans.

Marshall turned to face the hushed officers lining both sides of the conference table. There was a moment of silence while he brought himself under control.

"Gentlemen," he said finally, "how can we make certain that this doesn't happen again?"

The admiral sitting at his elbow had been waiting for this moment. There was no doubt in his mind as to the course the United States must take after suffering such a humiliating blow.

"Obviously, George," he said, "by doing everything we can to strengthen the navy."

Marshall grunted. No matter what the question, he knew, the admiral at his side would have reacted in the same way. Each service had been trained to think in its own self-interest. This, after all, was Washington.

"I would have been disappointed if you hadn't said that, Admiral," Marshall remarked, but the irony was lost amid a flash of braid and battle ribbons as the admiral got to his feet and crossed to the huge wall map. He picked up a pointer and indicated the West Coast of the United States. This was to be a geography lesson for which he felt supremely qualified. The oceans were his world. The navy was his home. And he had the confidence of knowing he was in the mainstream of military thought at that moment. Around that table were two dozen high-ranking officers who agreed with him wholeheartedly.

"With the fall of the Philippines," the admiral said, "our entire West Coast from Seattle to San Diego is wide open to attack and invasion." He looked to his fellow officers for approval. He got it.

"We must immediately write off the war in Europe and shift most of our fleet from the Atlantic to the Pacific through the Panama Canal—"

Ike was shifting uncomfortably in his seat. He nudged Beetle.

"Four-star idiot," he whispered. Beetle hastily motioned him to relax. But Ike was beyond caring.

"—so we can throw every available ship, man, and weapon to the defense of our exposed Pacific Coast. This is not only my considered opinion, but, I believe, the opinion of every ranking officer of all the services, General."

There was a general murmur of assent around the table. Except at the far end, where the more junior officers were seated. Ike took advantage of the talking to whisper to Beetle again.

His remark was typical. Ike Eisenhower was of the earth, a Kansas farm boy, a soldier, and his vocabulary in private reflected it.

"Bullshit," Ike said.

There was one of those unfortunate lulls at that moment, and Marshall turned, far down the table, to look in Ike's direction.

"Was that your voice I heard, Eisenhower?" he inquired.

Ike flushed crimson. His private self was not for exposure in public, in any way, ever. It was one of the cardinal principles of his career, then and later. Conscious of the raised eyebrows and suppressed smiles of the high brass seated at the table, he retreated.

"Sorry, sir. Just a private opinion."

Marshall's eyes were boring into him. Even at a distance they were enough to chill the marrow.

"Would you care to make it public and give us all the benefit of your one-star wisdom?"

Some amused whispering ran about the table. The top

brass was about to witness, they were certain, the humiliation of a minor officer by an outraged Chief of Staff. What they may have underestimated was the intelligence of General George Marshall; informed insubordination, coupled with extraordinary ability, was something he felt vital to his country's existence.

"Sir," said Ike, "almost every officer in this room is better qualified to speak than I am . . . if rank is the measure."

Marshall couldn't resist the opening. "Eisenhower, you surprise me. You told me yourself you had no regard for rank."

Ike swallowed, at a loss for an answer.

Marshall prodded again, refusing to allow him an escape. "We have these informal discussions to encourage independent thinking. If you have anything of value to contribute, it is your duty to do so now."

"General Marshall, if you put it that way, sir, I have no choice!"

Ike got to his feet, aware that every eye was on him, and strode toward the front of the room, past a blinding array of gold braid and battle stars—the most junior general of all, a sardine in a shoal of sharks.

The admiral waited, condescendingly, at the map. He handed Ike the pointer. "My sword, General," he said, hoping his wit was not wasted.

"I'll only use it in self-defense, sir," Ike said, flashing that smile, and the admiral found himself outpointed, outsmarted, and, above all, outsmiled by a man who was destined to do the same to most of the world's leaders. The Eisenhower grin was to become a trademark, a symbol of the spirit of a nation, as American as Coca-Cola.

Ike turned to face the enemy—the United States Navy. And most of its army. He was understandably nervous.

"May I smoke, General?" he inquired of Marshall. "I think better when I smoke."

"If you thought properly, Eisenhower, you wouldn't smoke at all. But go ahead."

"Thank you, sir." Ike lit a cigarette. He found that smoking eased the pressure, at least temporarily. It was said later that he chain-smoked his way through World War II, using only one match.

Ike crossed to the map and indicated Moscow with the pointer. "If Russia is knocked out of the war, we all better start learning German."

He had pressed the most sensitive button of all without bothering with preamble. Knifing to the heart of a situation without regard for niceties or sham was the keystone of his ability. Only later did he learn, painfully, the circumlocutions of diplomacy.

"Only Russia has enough manpower facing Hitler on the Continent to keep him too busy to invade England and give America enough time to tool up."

He looked defiantly at the brass assembled at the table. Not all, he knew, sided with the navy's viewpoint, but none was willing to risk disagreeing without a better indication of the position of the Chief of Staff.

Marshall's face gave no clue.

That didn't stop Ike. "We have to keep Russia in the war," he insisted, "or a lot of Americans will have to do a lot of unnecessary dying."

He indicated the area of the English Channel and the coast of France.

"Most of the War Plans Division agrees with me that Europe, not the Pacific, is the only front that can be attacked by all three allies simultaneously—the Russians, the British, and us. The British Isles must be turned into the greatest operating military base of all time, so we can throw the largest amphibious force in history across the English Channel and invade the coast of France. It's the shortest route to Berlin and the complete destruction of Germany."

Now even Marshall seemed to be joining the chorus of disapproval from much of the table.

"Complete destruction of Germany, Eisenhower?"

"Yes, sir." Not one moment of hesitation.

A three-star general shook his head, considering the implication. "Eisenhower," he growled, "that sounds a little strange, coming from an officer of German ancestry."

Ike whirled. It was a sensitive point. The Eisenhower family had come to America more than two centuries earlier, to escape religious persecution, but the Germanic traits were still evident. Even the nickname "Ike" had been tagged on him because of them. Eisenhower never ducked the implication; he wanted to be proud of it.

"That's exactly why I feel so strongly, *sir,*" he said, his temper flaring momentarily. "Adolf Hitler and his Gestapo and SS have made it impossible for any decent German to hold his head up for at least a generation. They have to be destroyed."

Marshall was watching him closely now, testing, listening. "Aren't you laying it on a bit thick, Eisenhower?"

Ike tossed his cigarette away. "No, sir! General Pershing sent me to France after World War One to write a history of that war. I learned one vital lesson. If we let the German army surrender *outside* of Germany, as they did in that war, they will claim once more it was the collapse of the home front that did it. If we don't beat the guts out of their arrogant Wehrmacht where their own people can see them beaten, World War II won't be over when it's over, it will only begin again in a few years. That's why the first step must be an overwhelming invasion of Europe."

"A lot of our experienced officers say a frontal attack against the massive fortifications across the English Channel would be military suicide," Marshall reminded him.

Ike was lighting another cigarette. "I'm not advocating an attack tomorrow, sir. But one day soon, America will be mass-producing planes by the thousands."

Ike was pacing now, caught up in his view of the logistics of the future, when America would be one large munitions factory, and Rosie the Riveter and hundreds of thousands like her would be helping Lockheed and Boeing turn out P-38s and B-17s by the acre. The Swing Shift would become a way of life. America's productive capacity was greater than that of all the rest of the world combined; that was her secret weapon. If only she could gain the time to use it.

"The Luftwaffe will be driven from the skies long before the invasion. Our bombers will destroy the railroads, the bridges, the communications of Western Europe. We'll paralyze the movement of German troops. Our paratroopers will drop behind those 'massive' Channel fortifications so we can blow them up and land a million men in Hitler's front yard."

There was a derisive whisper among some of the other officers. What Eisenhower was advocating was dependence upon a kind of air power whose effectiveness was still unproved. They turned to see Marshall's reaction.

"Eisenhower," Marshall said, "the airplanes you are talking about don't exist. Planning for the use of imaginary weapons goes against every military textbook. Your whole idea is visionary."

The others smiled. The Chief had put the junior general in his place.

"Yes, sir," said Ike, staring right back at Marshall. "That's its strongest point."

The shock wave ran around the table. Insubordination again.

"Eisenhower," said Marshall, measuring his words, "what if I said your whole plan was idiotic?"

Muffled laughter. Obviously the Chief was moving in for the kill.

Ike had had enough. The fuse had burned down. "General Marshall," he said, angrily, "war is idiotic."

There was a startled hush.

Marshall looked at Ike, and spoke quietly. "How soon can you leave for London?"

This time it was Ike who was startled. "Sir?" he said. He'd expected a court martial, at least.

Marshall was ready to lay down his poker hand. He

did it with considerable relish, eyeing the group of dis-comfited officers about the table.

"The President and I have been discussing a plan similar to yours with the British. We need an experienced officer to assess our forces in England and recommend a course of immediate action. Are you packed?"

Ike exhaled, the tension gone, savoring the moment. "General," he said, "I never unpack. I'm in the army."

III
This . . . Is London

For most Americans, wartime London had become a living thing, a personal friend in mortal danger. Edward R. Murrow, of the Columbia Broadcasting System, had brought the sounds and the horror of the Nazis' destruction of a brave city into millions of homes from coast to coast.

"This . . . is London," the familiar voice told his listeners, one desperate night in the fall of the year 1940. It was the middle of the Blitz, but you could not have detected it from Murrow's calm, matter-of-fact words.

"Trafalgar Square," he continued quietly. "The noise that you hear at the moment is the sound of an air raid siren. I'm standing here just on the steps of St. Martin's in the Field. It's almost impossible to realize that men are killing and being killed, even when you see that ever-thickening streak of smoke pouring down from the sky which means a plane and perhaps several men are going down in flames. The sense of danger, death, and disaster comes only when the familiar incidents occur. The sight of half a dozen ambulances weighted down with an unseen cargo of human wreckage has jarred me more than the roar of dive bombers or the sound of bombs. But London has gotten used to it. A near miss rocked the cab I was in one evening. The old man slid back the window and remarked, 'You know, sir, Hitler'll do that once too often, once.'"

There was another voice that brought home even more vividly the brutality of the Nazi fire-bombing and the strength of the Londoners who resisted it, many times to the death: Winston Churchill's. In 1940, radio had brought his measured oratory, his rich vocabulary, his bulldog stubbornness, and his contempt for his immoral enemy directly to the ears of the dormant giant across the Atlantic.

"Hitler knows that he will have to break us in this island or lose the war. If we can stand up to him, all Europe may be free and the life of the world may move forward into broad sunlit uplands. But if we fall, the whole world, including the United States, including all that we have known and cared for, will sink into the abyss of a new Dark Age, made more sinister and perhaps more protracted by the lights of perverted science. Let us therefore brace ourselves to our duties and so bear ourselves that if the British Empire and its Commonwealth last for a thousand years, men will still say, 'This . . . was their finest hour.'"

London had survived the Blitz. The RAF stood off the attacks of Herman Goering's bombers, and made the raids on English cities and civilians too costly for even the Nazis to continue. An island nation that many in America had given up for lost fought back and refused to be downhearted. Hanging on through sheer dogged determination, the British, whose defenses consisted of little more than a handful of antiaircraft and machine guns after the disastrous defeat at Dunkirk, continued to exist. And now, with America finally forced to commit herself, the bleak danger of a Nazi invasion began to recede, the clouds seemed to be clearing, and the two great English-speaking powers were ready to start forward together toward the goal of eventual victory.

If they could find some way of working together. Some personality who would weld two jealous, disparate armies into a single fighting force.

* * *

England, an island composed of odd dialects from the Scotch highlands to the Welsh seacoast, had been united by the common danger. Only Ireland stood aloof, or reached out a hand to any enemy of the hated British, including the Nazis. Under the terrible pressures of war, British women joined the men on the battle lines. Women were fire-watchers on the rooftops of London during the worst of the bombing; women were attached to ack-ack batteries, exposed to enemy fire; women drove London's ambulances during the terrible days of the Blitz when every street was a battleground and civilian bodies, some with life ebbing fast, littered the streets, waiting for the ambulances to take them to the overcrowded hospitals.

The British Women's Motor Transport Corps, a volunteer operation, was organized early in the war to create a pool of civilian drivers for the military and to free men for more deadly duty. At first it was an upperclass women's club—a lark, a heady adventure, a uniform to wear. Then it became grim and dirty business, the bloody task of bringing the wounded and the dying to safety.

One member of the Motor Corps in the perilous days of 1940 and 1941 was a strikingly attractive, auburn-haired Irish woman, born Kathleen McCarthy-Morrogh not far from County Cork. Her father was a retired officer in the Royal Munster Fusileers. After her mother divorced him, she took Kathleen and the rest of her family to London in the 1930s. Kay's beauty got her some bit work in British motion pictures; then, for a while, she worked as a fashion model. When the war came, she couldn't endure

37

her sybaritic existence and volunteered to become an ambulance driver along with her sister, Evie. They became known as two of the least flappable, most courageous members of the Motor Transport Corps during the darkest moments of London's ordeal. Kay had married Gordon Summersby, an Englishman who was shipped out to India with the British army when the war came. The constant danger she was in kept her mind from dwelling on their separation.

By 1942, the Blitz was over. London had lost 20,000 civilian dead. The streets remained littered with debris; gaping holes stood where whole buildings had once been. As the Luftwaffe departed in defeat, or crashed in flames, the Ambulance Corps and its women drivers were no longer needed at full strength. Kay Summersby was assigned to the U.S. Embassy. She knew London well enough to be of considerable value to the American army officers visiting the city, since by that time all the street signs had been removed. An American driver, lost in that maze, often pulled his car to the side and hailed a double-decker bus. One of the first Americans Kay drove about London was Capt. Richard Arnold, West Point graduate and engineer—handsome, easy-going, charming. They hit it off immediately. It was a typical wartime romance, including the fact that Dick Arnold was also married.

It wasn't long before they were both arranging to be divorced, so they could marry. War has a way of shaking up lives, disrupting old ways. When death is a hairbreadth away, love and life become almost synonymous. It wasn't only Kay and Dick; it was tens of thousands of others, caught up in the excitement and separations of war, who reached out for affection and happiness to counteract the hate and destruction.

There was a popular vaudeville skit of the time, depicting an American soldier in England, a comely English blonde on his lap, phoning his wife back in the States to inform her he was leaving her for his new British girlfriend.

"What's she got that I haven't got?" the wife inquired petulantly.

"Nothing," replied the soldier, patting the blonde on her ample posterior, "but it's *here*."

For Kay and Dick, it was much more than that. They were deeply and truly in love. Though they had to steal the moments they spent together, they felt as if they had known each other all their lives. They were alike in vivacity, in good looks and youth and intelligence. And now Kay found that her job as a driver at the American Embassy was getting in the way of her romance. This became unendurably annoying.

One morning in the spring of 1942, fuming after having been summoned to the Embassy early in the morning to drive a new-to-London American officer who hadn't shown up, Kay decided, after a four-hour wait, she'd had enough. She whispered to Sybil Williams, the petite blonde who drove the next car in line, that she was taking leave of the American army for a few moments to visit Dick. Sybil was to sound the alarm if the missing Colonial general ever put in an appearance.

Then Kay raced breathlessly through the throng of noontime Londoners and officers in the uniform of every Allied country, down the block to the staid Connaught Hotel, which, along with Claridge's, was the primary billet for American army officers stationed in London. The Connaught looked a little tacky at the moment—sandbags blocked the entrance, windows were taped against bomb fragments and concussion. Only the Connaught doorman, imperturbable in his gray frock coat and black top hat, went about the business of opening the doors of the arriving cars as if there were no bomb crater in the street before him. In London's streets, bomb craters were common, and therefore beneath his notice.

Kay, looking back over her shoulder to see if by any chance her general was coming out of the Embassy a block away, ran full tilt into the doorman and knocked his treasured hat into the dust. Contrite, she kneeled down to pick it up and hand it to him.

"Sorry, dear," she said. "Are you all right?"

When he was on the job, that hat had not been off the doorman's head since 1918, the end of the last unpleasantness. He dusted it off, giving Kay a stiff British stare.

"In a proper war," he said haughtily, "women stay out of uniform."

Unabashed, Kay flashed him a radiant smile. "With any luck, I'll be out of this one shortly. Ta!"

And she was off, racing happily inside the hotel.

Capt. Dick Arnold opened the door of his room, touching the nick on his cheek the frantic ringing of the doorbell had caused while he was shaving, to find his beloved in the corridor. She flung her arms about him.

"Kay! I thought you were working!"

"Darling, I'm AWOL. I've been waiting in my car all morning for some bloody American general and I finally told Sybil I was starving for lunch."

Kay kissed him fiercely. "Oh, Dick," she said, kissing him again, "we have so little time together. I *am* starving."

Gently, Dick disengaged her arms from about his neck. "Sweetheart, I have one rule. I'm not fussy, but not in the hallway."

"Why not? Shake up this stuffy hotel." But she allowed herself to be steered into the room as Dick carefully locked the door.

"The Connaught is the finest hotel in all of London," he said, smiling at her. You couldn't help smiling at Kay. She lifted the spirits, invigorated each moment with her own love of living. Dick touched the piece of tissue he had patted on his cut. "See? They even have real toilet paper."

"Oh, darling!" Kay's concern was immediate. "You're wounded!"

"I don't think there's a Purple Heart for shaving. But that's the closest I've come to combat since I've been here."

"Not true." Kay kissed him again, holding him to

her. "That was a lovely little battle we had last night."
She released him and crossed toward the bed, still un-
made, the Connaught's elegant serving table beside it, the
remains of a breakfast for two still visible. Croissants, jam,
margarine. Not bad, for wartime. She looked back at Dick
invitingly.

"Kay," he said softly, "I want you. I want you very
much. I'm going to marry you. But I have a staff meeting
at one o'clock."

Kay had been searching through the bedclothes. She
pulled out a sheer, lacy negligee.

"There you are, you little beggar," she said, holding
it up triumphantly, "I lost track of you during the night!"

Dick came up behind her. "Did you hear what I said?"
he asked. Kay turned and put her arms about him again.

"My dear Captain Arnold." She brushed her cheek
against his. "Two of my uncles and one of my dearest
nieces have been killed in this bloody war, and they weren't
even in uniform. I'm not going to be cheated. Who bloody
well knows if either of us will be alive tomorrow? We
have exactly thirty minutes."

And, turning from him with the certain knowledge
that all of us, everywhere, are a little closer to death today
than we were yesterday, she began to unbutton her uniform
blouse.

Dick put a hand on hers. "Stop."

She looked up at him, puzzled.

"One of us should say, 'I love you,' " he said.

"I believe it's your turn," Kay said.

"I love you, Kay."

"I love you, Dick. Oh, please. I love you so."

Duty, the war were forgotten—unimportant now. As
she clung to him, Dick deftly removed her unbuttoned
blouse. They moved together toward the bed.

The telephone rang. Reality crashed back about them,
shattering the moment into crystals of tension.

"Oh, God, it's Sybil! I gave her your room number."
Kay broke away and headed for the shrilling telephone.

Dick was startled. "You gave Sybil my *room number?* What the hell will she think?"

"That I'm the luckiest girl in the world," Kay told him, quite honestly. "She's between romances at the moment."

"Don't answer that phone!" Dick warned, agitated. "It could be headquarters!"

Kay smiled at him and covered the mouthpiece.

"I'll tell them I'm forcing you at gunpoint," she whispered. Then she spoke into the phone.

"Hello? . . . Sybil, love, you couldn't be more inconvenient . . . Well, not *quite* yet . . . Oh, dear . . . Yes, I'll be right there, what's his rank, love? . . . A *two*-star? Do you realize I dragged myself out of bed at six a.m. and have been waiting all bloody morning for him to show up? How *dare* he have only two stars?"

She motioned to Dick to bring her blouse. Duty was calling.

"What's his name?" Kay inquired into the phone, and listened incredulously for a moment. "My God, can you spell it? . . . *Eisenhower?* You sure he's on *our* side?" Dick was caressing her as he slipped the blouse on her, and it didn't help matters. "Yes, I'll be right there. If he was a spy, he would have thought of a much better name."

She hung up, distracted, straightened her hair, and searched for her lipstick.

"Can you imagine, Dick, a *two*-star? I was told I was to drive only the top brass. Sybil's getting Hap Arnold—he's got three stars, going on four. I always get the part of the chicken that goes over the fence last."

She gave him a forlorn kiss. "To be continued," she insisted, "as soon as possible."

And she ran for the door, fastening the last button of her uniform jacket. A woman at war.

Dick stood for a moment, unwilling to let the moment vanish so quickly. But he was smiling.

Outside the Connaught, the doorman was just closing the door of a departing Rolls as Kay dashed out of the sandbagged entrance and barged into him. The elegant top hat went flying once more.

"Haven't got time to pick it up this time, pet!" she called over her shoulder. "Put a string on it!"

And she was gone, across the street, dodging pedestrians and lorries.

On the sidewalk outside the American Embassy on Grosvenor Square, an impatient two-star Eisenhower checked his watch. An important meeting was scheduled in just ten minutes at a London hotel; he had no idea where it was located, and the driver the British had assigned to him was nowhere to be found.

Ike's companion was an old West Point classmate, Maj. Gen. Mark C. Clark, whose six feet six inches made him look more like the center for the Boston Celtics than the chief of staff for General McNair, head of the United States Army ground forces. Ike had requested that Clark be sent with him on this mission to survey the situation of American forces in England. He wanted Clark to help him assay the possibilities of the British Isles as a training and staging area for the coming invasion of the Continent.

Gen. Clark also looked at his watch. Punctuality, to the military mind, is often as important as patriotism.

A moment later, Kay came racing breathlessly down the sidewalk behind them and slid to a halt beside her car. The officers turned to stare. Her hair flying, her eyes sparkling, worry flushing her cheeks, Kay Summersby was a moment of casual loveliness in a city ugly with the scars of war.

"General Eisenbauer?" she inquired breathlessly.

"Nice try," said Ike, more concerned with her timing than with her disheveled beauty. "Eisen*hower*."

"Sorry. I'm bloody awful at foreign languages." That didn't help matters, she realized too late.

"I'm your driver, Kay Summersby," she went on, and to make up for everything, she saluted smartly. Or so she thought.

43

"You're bloody awful at saluting, too, Miss Summersby," Ike informed her.

"I'm a civilian, sir."

"And a woman."

Kay eyed him with distaste. "Oh," she said. "One of those." No woman would think of the phrase "male chauvinist pig" until years later. But Kay came close at that moment.

Clark interrupted to break the tension. "I'm General Mark Clark," he said, hoping he sounded pleasant. They needed her car. "You *can* pronounce Clark, can't you?"

He tried a smile. It worked.

"Oh, yes, sir!" Kay smiled back. "A fine British name, Clark."

"Thank you. We're late for our meeting—let's get going."

"Yes, General!" Kay flung open the rear door of the khaki Packard and delivered another of those gestures she considered a salute. Clark got into the car. Kay held the salute, rigidly. Ike, about to step in, paused to stare at her.

"Miss Summersby?"

"Yes, sir?"

"Would you please not salute? I went to West Point." And he stepped into the car.

Kay closed the door. "Bahstard," she murmured to herself. She opened the front door, slid behind the wheel, and started the engine.

"Where to, sir?"

"The Connaught Hotel," Ike ordered.

"Merde!" It slipped out, just as she accidentally released the clutch too fast. The car bucked like a stallion, throwing her two generals against each other in the back seat.

"Sorry," she managed to say, as they straightened up and regained their dignity, Ike eyeing her with growing distrust.

"Miss Summersby," he inquired, taking a firm grip on the passenger strap in the rear of the car, "I hate to ask . . . but you do know where the Connaught Hotel is?"

"Yes, sir," she replied. "This is it."

She braked to a stop in front of the proud little hostelry. The two American generals exchanged a sheepish glance. Next time, they would consult a map.

"For your information, General Eisenhower," Kay remarked, grasping the wheel firmly and looking straight ahead, "I got out of a very warm bed at six a.m. to drive you and General Clark a total of three hundred feet. It is going to be a tough war for you Americans. I am glad you are saving your strength. Sir."

Clark grinned, but Ike was not amused. He leaned forward to be certain his words were heard.

"Miss Summersby," he informed her, "like it or not, we are allies. We are going to have to learn to get along with each other. Since the British nation is our host, I suggest you start first."

He climbed out of the car, followed by Clark, as the top-hatted doorman held the door open. Then Ike leaned into the front of the car, indicating Kay's fingernails.

"And if you're going to drive for us, get rid of that red nail polish. It's unmilitary."

"So is wasting petrol, General."

Clark pulled the angry Ike away from the car and steered him toward the hotel.

The doorman had observed the little exchange with interest. Now he approached Kay, holding carefully onto his top hat. "Begging your pardon, miss, but who are those officers?"

She controlled herself with considerable effort. "I don't know who the tall one is," she said, "but the shorter one is Jesus Christ."

"Gentlemen, *gentlemen!* Take your seats!"

Maj. Gen. James Chaney, chief of the American military mission to England, was standing at the front of one of the Connaught's small banquet rooms, trying to get the attention of his officers. Although the bar had been closed

45

for the occasion, tea and pastries were laid out, and the assembled officers seemed more interested in their stomachs than in the two generals waiting to be introduced. Dick Arnold managed to secure a cup of tea and a chocolate eclair to fortify himself for the coming ordeal.

"Gentlemen!" repeated Gen. Chaney, and this time his voice was loud enough to quiet his subordinates. "May I present our visitors from the War Department in Washington—General Dwight Eisenhower and General Mark Clark." Since none of the assembled officers knew precisely who these generals were, the quest for nourishment continued. Until Ike stepped forward.

"Sit down!"

It had been a long time since they had heard a voice with that much military authority. Slowly, they seated themselves.

"You officers in this room," Ike began, lighting the inevitable cigarette, "are the vanguard of American forces in England, a drop in a bucket that is soon to be filled to overflowing. General Clark and I have been detailed by General Marshall to report your state of readiness for combat against the German war machine—the Wehrmacht, the Luftwaffe, and the SS."

Dick choked on his tea. Although, as a West Pointer, he was aware of the realities of warfare, the months of inactivity in England had made it all seem something remote, a newsreel others were going to participate in; nothing with immediate danger for Capt. Dick Arnold personally. Now something in Ike's voice convinced him everything in England was going to change, very rapidly. The uneasiness that spread through the officers around him echoed his disquiet.

"If what I see here is any indication," Ike continued, "the fate of the free world is in desperate trouble."

Someone snickered.

Ike was not amused. "May I inform you that things are going to be quite different in the immediate future. Many of you may be recalled to the United States. I have heard this operation has been called the Connaught Country Club. That club is now disbanded."

His eyes swept his audience. Few were willing to meet his gaze.

"The Atlantic Alliance was not intended to be formed solely with members of the opposite sex."

The words hit home with Dick; he became aware that a brother officer was signalling, rubbing his cheek. When Dick did not understand, the officer pursed his lips and made a kissing sound.

Horrified, Dick grabbed his handkerchief and tried to rub Kay's lipstick off his cheek. He wondered whether Eisenhower had noticed.

"From now on," Ike continued grimly, "any one of you who fails to do his duty must forever bear on his conscience the certainty that he has contributed, in some incalculable amount, to the agony and the anguish and the sacrifice that lie ahead. Your country expects more of you."

Ike Eisenhower, although sometimes stiff and uncomfortable when speaking in public, had the ability to put his thoughts into forceful words. He had often been called on to write speeches for his superiors in the army. This one he had carefully prepared for himself.

"To each one of you who will remain to participate in the coming inevitable and bloody invasion of Europe, I wish godspeed and good luck. Good day."

His message delivered, he left with Gen. Clark. They made their way through a group of officers suddenly quieted by the weight of their own thoughts.

One of Dick's friends nudged him. "What do you think?" he asked, indicating the departing Ike's rigid shoulders.

"For the first time," Dick said thoughtfully, "I have the strange feeling there's a war on."

His eclair was uneaten and his tea had grown cold. He realized it didn't matter very much.

* * *

Lt. Gen. Sir Bernard Law Montgomery was a small, cocky man with great ability and an ego to match. He was positive, opinionated, and as certain as the Pope of his infallibility. Unlike Eisenhower, he had a distinguished record of combat command; in the eyes of the British and most of all himself, he was one of the Empire's foremost soldiers. The visiting American generals from Washington were invited to watch his troops in training and afterwards permitted to join Sir Bernard at his headquarters, with his staff, where he was most happy to give them a short lecture on their own shortcomings. Dressed, characteristically, in an old sweater and corduroy trousers, carrying a riding crop, he pointed out the obvious on a series of large maps —a schoolmaster instructing the Third Form.

"Our impulsive American cousins," he declared, with what he felt was an ingratiating smile, "must learn the virtue of patience. They will never succeed in shipping sufficient numbers of men and material to this side of the Atlantic to launch any sizeable attack across the English Channel this year, or even *next* year."

Mark Clark looked over at Ike, whose face was taking on the telltale flush that usually preceded a volcanic eruption. Clark motioned a warning to relax.

Montgomery plunged ahead. "In the meantime, they must rely on the British General Staff to lead their inexperienced army and navy on the long and terribly slow road to victory."

Ike was already on his feet. "General Montgomery, don't you think it would be better to join together, rather than have you British lead us and us miserable Americans follow?"

Montgomery stared. He didn't know this chap and didn't much care to. It was not his custom to allow even his own junior officers to interrupt.

"My dear chap," he said, carefully choosing the words that would put this Kansas farmer in his place. "My dear chap, the British army and navy were winning wars when America was inhabited by naked savages."

A murmur of laughter from his staff.

"Well, sir," Ike replied, "now that we've got our clothes on, maybe you ought to let us help." Angrily, he lit a cigarette.

Monty had turned his back as he returned to the map. "We *shall* let you help," he explained, not too patiently. "But the only attack we can mount with any possibility of success in the near future—even with America's eager help—is one directed here, at the German and Italian forces occupying North Africa and"—Montgomery broke off; he had sniffed the offending cigarette. "Who is smoking?" he inquired sharply.

Ike was just seating himself, unaware that he had violated a cardinal law. "Why, *I* am, General Montgomery," he said.

"I don't permit smoking in my headquarters. You will please put it out. Is that an unreasonable request?"

Ike's answer was a growl. "On the contrary, General, it's the only reasonable remark you've made all morning."

He looked around for an ashtray, but there were no ashtrays at Montgomery's headquarters. As Sir Bernard continued his lecture, Ike snuffed out his cigarette with his fingers.

Ten days in Britain had passed all too swiftly. Ike was already formulating in his mind the report that he was going to present to Gen. Marshall and President Roosevelt, a report that was destined to change his own life drastically and influence the course of World War II in ways not even Ike could foresee. Its essence was the appointment of a single commander with authority over all military services, first for United States forces in England, and eventually over the combined military forces of all the Allies. It was a revolutionary idea for the time. Typically Eisenhower, it cut through to basics. It made immediate enemies of most of the heads of the rival land, air, and naval forces of the United Sates, whose authority would be compromised; and it seemed absolutely unworkable to the

British generals and admirals who were their counterparts. Searching in his own mind for a man with the vast knowledge and abilities required for such a gigantic task, Ike thought first of Admiral Lord Louis Mountbatten, Chief of Combined Operations for the British. The thought that he himself possessed the qualifications he was to spell out in his report never occurred to Ike. Or, if it did, it was never mentioned.

The problem was on his mind this morning as he and Gen. Clark crossed to the car waiting at the curb to take them and their luggage to the military airfield from which a plane would return them to Washington. Kay held the rear door open and saluted Clark, but quickly dropped the salute as Ike followed Clark into the car. Despite his preoccupation, Ike noticed.

"Thank you, Miss Summersby," he said.

Kay decided not to reply. She slid into the driver's seat.

"Can you make it to Northfield Airport in forty-five minutes?" Clark asked from the rear seat.

"If your rear end can take the pounding on the back roads, General," she said, letting out the clutch a little too rapidly. She was thinking of Eisenhower's remark. The car jerked forward.

Ike, who had been watching her, leaned forward.

"What have you done to your fingernails, Miss Summersby?"

It was the question Kay had been waiting for. She hit the horn to emphasize her point. "I Americanized them according to your instructions, General." She held up one hand to show him. "Khaki."

Mark Clark grinned. Ike merely grunted, then sat back.

The car weaved through the London traffic and eventually found its way into open countryside, green and beautiful, embroidered with spring flowers on a lovely June morning. The war, outside the car, seemed a million miles away, but inside it Ike was reviewing the problem raised by Montgomery.

"North Africa!" he said. "Ridiculous! We've got to make some sort of strike across the Channel—even if it's a limited strike—and try to open some kind of second front to take the pressure off the Russians, even if there's a chance it might fail."

Clark shook his head. What he had seen of American strength in England had been far from encouraging. "Can't do it, Ike. Monty's right. We won't be able to get any invasion at all launched this year. We can't get enough fighting men over here."

Kay had been listening intently, caught up in a conversation between two Americans that vitally concerned her beloved England.

"What about fighting women?" she blurted out.

Ike looked up, annoyed. "Wipe this conversation from your mind, Miss Summersby," he said. It flashed through his head that she was a civilian; the British were wrong again—his car should have been driven by a soldier, subject to military discipline. "It's privileged, confidential, and not for your ears."

Kay restrained herself. "Yes, sir," she said as the car hit a bump, throwing her passengers against each other. She could have avoided it.

"The British *do* use their women in posts we reserve for soldiers," Clark reminded Ike when they had regained their composure.

"Only because they have no choice, with so many men in the fighting. Women are too emotional for most military jobs."

"That's a stupid male attitude." Kay was angry now, and she didn't care if Ike knew it.

"Miss Summersby—"

The words rushed out. "General Eisenhower, if you persist in holding a privileged conversation in my car, there is no way I can pretend not to hear it. We have been

51

in this war since 1939, and no American is going to come over here for ten days and tell *me* how the good old U.S.A. plans to save the British Empire. We'll muddle through without you, thank you."

It was Ike's turn to grow angry. It was foolish, he knew, for a military officer to argue tactics with a woman, but this stubborn Irish girl had a way of getting under his skin. It was time to put her in her place, once and for all.

"You won't muddle through *this* one," he said with finality. "These islands were invaded by Julius Caesar in the first century B.C. and the Romans ruled your country for four hundred years. The Germans would like to do the same, and without our help they might succeed. The terrible truth, Miss Summersby, is that you and I need each other."

Kay's chin set in a firm line. It was not in her nature to retreat one inch.

"Then for God's sake, be reasonable," she said. "I watched a thousand bombs fall on London in one awful night before Christmas, and the Nazis weren't too particular who they fell on. I saw parts of bodies that could only have belonged to women picked up and placed in those canvas bags and tossed into my ambulance. If my arse is on the line, General, don't tell me a woman can't fight back. No one's throwing *mine* into a canvas bag, thank you. I have other plans for it."

Ike flushed a bit. In Abilene, a woman did not discuss her more delicate anatomy in public. Or private. But Mark Clark, from a less old-fashioned background, had been listening sympathetically.

"You drove an ambulance, Miss Summersby?" he inquired.

"I, and a few hundred other emotional women. Right through the Blitz. You've heard of the Blitz?"

The sarcasm wasn't lost on Ike, but he remained silent. General Dwight Eisenhower had never yet seen anyone die as the result of enemy action. In this area, Kay Summersby outranked him.

She tried hard to keep her emotions in control. They were driving through one of the most beautiful sections of the British countryside surrounding London, a back road for the moment devoid of the lorries and cars and jeeps that crowded the main highways with the cargo of wartime. Here were only the fields, green and blooming—the lilac, the primrose, and the profusion of wildflowers set among cottages and barns, against a background of Turner clouds, so typical of the landscape that has inspired poets from Chaucer to Shelley.

"Somewhere in that lovely English sky," Kay said, so softly that Ike had to lean forward to catch her words, "was the Luftwaffe, day and night. My area was Lambeth, down by the docks and the tenements. They are all burned and shattered now. Some nights it looked as though they were all on fire at the same time. The bombs would be falling like grapes and the ack-ack would light up the sky like Guy Fawkes day at Kew Gardens, and my little ambulance didn't need lights to see the dead and the dying." She paused now, remembering, and even the remembrance was difficult to bear. "Somehow, my crew would get those bodies out of the broken shells of the blasted buildings. Some of them were mangled beyond recognition, twisted and burned. I will never cleanse from my mind the smell of burned human flesh."

Even as she said the words, she could smell the odor: sweet, sickly, cloying.

"And then," she said quietly, "it was over, because some British lads in their foolish planes had given up their lives for the rest of us. And where were the brave men of the United States Army then? Waiting for us girls to get out of our bloodstained ambulances so they could tell us not to wear red nail varnish? What the devil do you think made our nails red to begin with?"

Ike took a deep breath and put a hand on Kay's shoulder. "Miss Summersby," he said gently, "I want you to know you've succeeded in making me feel like the son of a bitch I really am."

53

IV
The Job

EYES ONLY. CHIEF OF STAFF. DIRECTIVE FOR THE COMMANDING GENERAL, EUROPEAN THEATRE OF OPERATIONS.

The report lay on the desk in front of George Marshall, who picked it up and slid it into his briefcase. It was evening, but the summer heat in Washington made an oven out of his office in the War State Navy building. Nevertheless, impervious to heat, humidity, and the continuing series of Allied defeats in a war that had now spread completely around the globe, Marshall wore a tie and jacket.

Eisenhower, seated in front of the desk, beads of perspiration on his forehead, tried to retain his composure. The Chief had not yet revealed his reaction to the voluminous report Ike had slaved over since his return from London.

Finally, Marshall looked up. "Eisenhower," he said, "you've come up with a highly unusual plan for pulling our forces together in time to make a strike across the Channel this year."

Highly unusual? Ike pondered the phrase. Was that good or bad for junior generals?

"The idea of a single unified commander over all our services in England is not standard operating procedure. And you know how the army feels about new ideas." Marshall squinted at Ike. "We're still feeding two thousand mules," he concluded, and relaxed into a smile.

"Most of them wearing gold braid," Ike said, grinning.

"Present company excepted?" Marshall was enjoying the moment. It was a brilliant report. His confidence in Eisenhower had been fully repaid.

"Of course, sir," Ike answered, relaxed now. "Eventually, I believe we've got to have a single commander over *all* the Allied forces. But this is a beginning—eliminating separate commands for the U.S. Army, Navy and Air Service, and putting them under the control of just one man."

George Marshall crossed the room to get his cap. He was still testing this man, a process that was to be never-ending.

"I thought Franklin Roosevelt was Commander in Chief of our armed forces?" he inquired.

"If you'll excuse me, General," Ike said, and it was only half in jest, "what's his training for the job?"

Marshall didn't smile. "Why don't you ask him?"

The ride to the White House was relatively brief, giving Ike little time to worry about FDR's reaction to his report. Instead, he discussed with Marshall who should be the American to take over the new position, if Roosevelt approved. Marshall himself, of course, was Eisenhower's first choice, but the Chief brushed that aside. He had another job to do. Ike was ready with a substitute: Maj. Gen. Joseph McNarney, one of Marshall's assistants.

"We've got to sell him to Roosevelt, sir," Ike told his superior. "He's worked with the British before, he's an Air Corps general and only air power is going to make the invasion possible. He knows our production capabilities and has the tact to work with our allies. He's the one man who can prepare our forces in England for the invasion you are going to lead."

For some time, Marshall had been considered the outstanding candidate to command the European invasion; right up to the end, Eisenhower felt his Chief would be given the job. "McNarney," Ike continued, "will get our men ready for you."

The army limousine turned into the East Gate of the White House, dimly lit in Washington's blackout but still impressive, its graceful columns looming through the darkness.

Marshall was watching Eisenhower as the car pulled to a halt. "You're absolutely sure McNarney's the best man?"

"Not only the best. Outside of yourself, he's the *only* one qualified."

"Eisenhower, I wish I could be as certain of what I'm going to have for dinner as you are about the future of mankind."

The driver opened the rear door. Marshall started out, then paused to throw a final bit of advice over his shoulder. "Don't tell him how to steer his wheelchair," he admonished.

The President was emphatic. "Joe McNarney? Never!"

Seated in the Oval Office on the first floor, the one that adjoined his bedroom so that he could wheel himself in and take up his position behind his desk without aid, Franklin Roosevelt was savoring the meeting. The cigarette holder was held at a jaunty angle as he surveyed the two generals seated before him—one who knew, one who didn't.

"We need McNarney here in Washington as Deputy Chief of Staff," FDR continued. "Didn't General Marshall tell you that I concur with *his* choice?"

Ike looked surprised. "No, sir."

The President smiled, his theatrical moment intact. "Well, then, I am delighted to allow my distinguished house guest to reveal this military secret. He enjoys a good surprise as much as I do." And he indicated his visitor, who stood to one side chewing on his cigar.

Winston Leonard Spencer Churchill, son of Lord and Lady Randolph Churchill, was born prematurely in the year 1874. The rest of his life, by ordinary standards, continued to be premature; he had a gift of vision that made him a stranger out of time. He saw clearly his own country, her allies and her enemies, and because what he saw sometimes made him unpopular with his own countrymen, he was to be in and out of office for decades before England turned to him in her darkest hour. He became Prime Minister in the fateful year of 1940; by 1945, after bringing Britain through her most dreadful war in triumph, he could not help but speak out about her supposed friend, Russia, and was turned out of office as soon as he had accomplished Britannia's rescue. Cherubic, blessed with an impish sense of humor and a formidable intellect, he denied that it was he who had given the people of England the courage to survive Hitler's onslaught. "They already had the courage," he said, "I only focused it."

And focus it he did, the bowler hat and the cigar and the jump suit becoming the image of bulldog British determination. Having triumphed over "the Nazi beast" in the Battle of Britain, he had come in this June of 1942 to visit his great friend Franklin Roosevelt in the White House. Now that the American voter and taxpayer was definitely committed to the war, he and Roosevelt did not have to go through the charade of meeting on a battleship in neutral waters to sign a so-called Atlantic Charter, or promote the "Four Freedoms." Now they were partners in arms, meeting in Washington, committed to the use of every weapon of modern warfare against a common enemy. It was a moment that Churchill, unhappy architect of the British defeat at Gallipoli in World War I when he was First Lord of the Admiralty, relished completely. He would now have the opportunity to vindicate his tarnished military reputation.

After Roosevelt's introduction, Churchill paused, savoring his cigar, one thumb hooked in his vest above the gold watch chain as he eyed this low-ranking American general seated before him. Low-ranking, yes, but with the full support of George Marshall and Franklin Delano Roosevelt.

Churchill cocked an eyebrow. "The last time we British surprised the White House," he reminded the American President, "we burned it down."

FDR laughed, noting in his mind that he would have to mention Gallipoli before the evening was over, to even matters.

Now Churchill turned to Ike. "I trust you won't want to make us repeat that gesture, for by the action your President has taken, with my hearty approval, we may well be placing the future of our island in your capable hands."

Ike sat bolt upright in his chair. He could feel the perspiration starting on his palms.

"*My* hands?" he inquired.

The President reached for a document on his desk and read aloud: "Major General Dwight David Eisenhower is hereby appointed Commanding General of the European Theatre and will command all U.S. Forces now in, or hereafter dispatched to, the European Theatre of Operation." He looked up.

Ike was sitting, speechless, as his Chief of Staff regarded him with a quizzical smile. Churchill took in the tableau, an enigmatic twinkle in his eye.

"What's the matter, Ike?" asked FDR. "Don't you want the job?"

Ike exhaled. "You're damn right I want it, Mr. President," he said.

He knew now he had wanted it all along. The specifications he had drawn up fitted Maj. Gen. Eisenhower perfectly.

"General Eisenhower." Winston Churchill's robust tones tore Ike's attention away from his own feelings. "As His Majesty's First Minister, I will do my best to remember that your authority in joint military affairs is comparable to my own." That had been Churchill's agreement with Roosevelt, and he had no intention of going back on it—yet.

"However," he continued, then paused to draw on his aromatic cigar, "it is only fair to warn you that I will fight you to the death if I happen to disagree on the slightest detail of military strategy, upon which, as you well know, I have often declared myself the world's foremost authority."

Ike realized this was a challenge, however lightly worded. He parried in kind, but in dead earnest.

"Mr. Prime Minister," he said, "if you'll excuse me, there are only two occupations in the world in which the amateur excels the professional. One is military strategy. And the other is prostitution."

Churchill smiled. He appreciated a battle of wit in the heat of serious debate, since he usually emerged victorious. He crossed behind the desk and placed a comradely hand on Franklin Roosevelt's shoulder.

"Ah, but my dear General Eisenhower," he murmured, "it is common knowledge that we politicians must practice both."

Laughter was followed by a moment of silence. What was being done in that room was to influence the course of the greatest war in history, a war whose outcome was, at that moment, very much in doubt.

"General Eisenhower." Roosevelt removed his glasses, wanting this to be as direct, as personal a contact between two human beings as possible. "You will be preparing men for an invasion such as has never been seen before in human history. We have jumped you over three hundred sixty-six general officers in the United States Army who outrank you, even though you have never commanded so much as a platoon in combat, because we need someone with tremendous vision who is not yet hamstrung by the military conventions of the past."

This, Ike thought to himself, is what insubordination sometimes gets you: the chance to prove you are desperately wrong.

"The Nazi armies," FDR continued, "are fighting a new kind of war, and it takes a new kind of soldier to beat them. Under Adolf Hitler's insane leadership, the German armed forces have driven the British into the sea at Dunkirk, forced the surrender of France, and goose-stepped into Mother Russia."

The enormity of the enemy was brought home to Ike again. The images had been seen on every newsreel screen in America: the terrible defeat of the British and French armies; refugees scurrying for safety under the attack of the Nazi planes, their pitiful belongings blown up by the relentless strafing; a Frenchman crying before the Arc de Triomphe as German troops marched down the Champs Élysées; mass murders of Russian civilians. And always, the face of Adolf Hitler, a triumphant mask, yelling, screaming the German victories into carefully positioned cameras and microphones.

"No army in the world," Roosevelt reminded his new commander, "has yet been able to stand up to their Stuka dive bombers and the huge tanks of their Panzer Divisions . . . but we've got to find a way." He looked at the officer he had picked, on George Marshall's word, to bear the brunt of the burden in the months to come, and felt a kinship that bridged the difference in their backgrounds.

"You will have to make many fateful decisions by yourself," the President said softly, "affecting hundreds of thousands of lives. I can't say I envy you. Until this moment, I always thought *mine* was the loneliest job in the world."

* * *

Fort Meyer, Virginia, is an anomaly, a Civil War army post frozen in time and transferred into the twentieth century. The red brick buildings of another day, the stately trees, the broad streets, seem out of place so close to Washington, the world's most frenetic city, visible in the distance, the Washington monument pointing a finger to the heavens as if to remind soldier and politician alike that Big Brother is watching.

Ike was given a house on the post when he was transferred from Fort Sam Houston, and Mamie had followed soon after to set up housekeeping in yet another military setting, this the most prestigious of all.

Dwight Eisenhower loved to cook, in his own fashion. This fashion included having someone else do all the peeling, slicing, mixing, and chopping, after which Ike placed the final result on the flames of the backyard barbecue and watched to be certain nothing burned.

This night, attired in an apron, Ike was barbecuing a tasty steak. He knew it would be tasty because Mamie had prepared the sauce, sliced the onions, marinated the meat, and checked the coals. Chef Eisenhower was now on his own, long barbecue fork in hand, a kitchen towel protecting his middle, his keen soldier's eye watching closely, ready to remove the steak from the fire the moment Mamie told him it was done.

She came out of the red brick house with its Government Issue back porch, carrying a tray. It was a warm summer night, the moon adding a final glowing touch, and Sgt. Hunt and Sgt. Moaney, Ike's two black orderlies (who were to remain with him until after the war—Sgt. Moaney, indeed, remained in Mamie's service until his death in 1978) had been given the evening off. It was just Ike and Mamie, as it had been when he was a newly married second lieutenant at Fort Sam.

Mamie set down her tray, poured two glasses of wine from the decanter, and crossed to her husband, who was busily turning the porterhouse over the coals. "Is it all right to propose a toast to the new Commander of the European Theatre of Operations?" she inquired.

It was their last night together before his departure. Mamie knew he wasn't going into combat in the usual sense, but the battle he was about to engage in was just as deadly, in its own way, to a man's courage and sanity. Few returned from this kind of command unchanged, and no one knew it better than an army wife. It was goodbye to the Ike Eisenhower she had always known. Their marriage had endured many trials; the most difficult one lay ahead. Trial by fire.

Mamie handed Ike a glass of wine. "Only six months ago," she reminded him, "you were just a colonel. Tonight, you're Napoleon. That deserves a gallon of champagne, but this will have to do."

She raised her glass and touched his. "I'm so very proud of you, Ike. This almost makes up for not getting to play in the Army-Navy game, doesn't it?"

Ike smiled and put his arm around her. His football career was one of the many things they shared, the many small things that are part of the intimacy that is marriage.

"Almost makes up," he said, "but I don't know whether I deserve congratulations or condolences." He paused. Then what had been on his mind since the meeting at the White House tumbled out, as most of his troubles did when Mamie was there to share them. "It's a job too big for any one man."

"Frightened?"

"No. Plain scared. Scared to death. I didn't expect it. I'm not sure I'm ready for it."

"Ike . . . do you have to leave tomorrow?"

"Yes. I think they want me to go before I change my mind."

"You'll go," she said. Of course he would. Nothing she or anyone else said could change that. He had always gone, when duty called. Or adventure. She remembered the days when they were about to be married and Ike had characteristically applied for transfer to the dangerous Army Air Corps. Only her father's adamant refusal to allow his daughter to marry a man who insisted on throwing away his life in those damn flimsy planes finally changed Lt. Eisenhower's mind.

"You'll go," she said, "and I'll stay."

Now she had a husband who was a commanding general; she had a grown son at West Point; there was a terrible war on—and she was to be left here, alone.

She kissed him. "Goodbye, Ike. I guess, come to think of it, I'm the best soldier in this family."

V
War

In the short month since Ike had left, London had undergone a rapid change—American uniforms blossomed on the streets, American vehicles jammed into the left-hand traffic. The first trickle of weapons had made its way through the gauntlet of Nazi submarines in the North Atlantic. The clamor for the opening of a second front to aid the failing Russian armies was front-paged in all the newspapers, but the hard fact was that only the United States First Armored and 34th Divisions, and some bits of the Air Forces, had arrived for training in Northern Ireland.

But the future was drawing closer. Lt. General Carl A. Spaatz, Commander of the U.S. Eighth Air Force, had already set up headquarters in Quonset huts at Bushey Park, outside of London. Eventually the fighters, bombers, transports, and gliders for the invasion across the English Channel would total 15,700 aircraft. But in June of 1942, the Eighth Air Force consisted of "Tooey" Spaatz, his staff, a stack of papers, and a few drivers from the British Women's Motor Transport Corps—among them Gen. Spaatz's personal driver, Kay Summersby.

Kay skidded the khaki-colored American car through the traffic in Grosvenor Square and braked to a halt in front of Number 20, Eisenhower's headquarters, where a steady stream of army automobiles was arriving and departing. Kay jumped out and flung open the rear door. Gen. Spaatz made a fetish of speed, and Kay found this exhilarating, especially since he had never objected to her salute.

"Tooey" Spaatz got out of the car and checked his wristwatch. "Twenty-two and a half minutes from Bushey Park," he noted. "Damn good."

"Thank you, General. Although I think I did nip the trousers of that bobby in Trafalgar Square."

"*C'est la guerre,* Miss Summersby." He smiled and started for the entrance.

Kay knew it was now or never. "General?"

Spaatz turned.

"I know this is terribly forward of me, but are you liable to be long?"

"It's my first conference with General Eisenhower since his arrival. My guess would be—yes."

"Sir, my fiancé is a major on staff here, and I understand he has some time free. Would I be allowed to be unmilitary? Perhaps for thirty minutes?"

The general looked at her for a moment. Of course, anyone as beautiful as Kay must have a romantic interest. Or several. But until this moment she had never mentioned it, and Spaatz realized he had been treating her like a chauffeur, monopolizing her days and most of her nights in his headlong attempt to get his Eighth Air Force off the requisition forms and into the air to battle the Luftwaffe.

"Kay," he said, "you've never complained about the hours I work you or the jobs I ask you to do, seven days and seven nights a week. Any time your major is in town, let me know, and I'll stop the damn war for you somehow. Will an hour and a half be sufficient?"

"Oh, yes, sir, thank you, sir!"

"Well, it wouldn't be sufficient for me. But go ahead." He turned and strode into the building.

Sybil Williams, she of the inopportune telephone call to Dick's hotel room some few weeks ago, had been standing by the Packard of another American general, applying her lipstick as she took in the little scene. Sybil was an attractive blonde who saw the sudden influx into London of thousands of stalwart young men as a golden opportunity no patriotic English girl had a right to ignore. There was a quip making the rounds about American soldiers in England: the only thing wrong with them was that they were overpaid, overfed, oversexed, and over here. To Sybil's mind, that was exactly what was *right* with them.

She moved closer to Kay as Spaatz entered 20 Grosvenor Square to go about the dull business of fighting a war.

"Oh, he's a love," Kay remarked. "I can hardly believe he's an American."

"Probably not full-blooded American," Sybil reasoned, "or he'd be like Eisenhower. Did you know Eisenhower has made all the officers move out of Claridge's and the Connaught and into barracks?"

"Oh, *no!* You can't do that to *officers!*"

"Tell that to your spit-and-polish general. They're calling Grosvenor Square 'Eisenhower Platz.' "

It was a name that stuck to the stately square with its graceful trees, mannered buildings, and incongruous, sandbagged defenses, until the end of the war.

Sybil reached inside her uniform blouse and pulled out a key on a pink ribbon.

"Never fear, luv," she told her friend, "Apartment 12-E. Over the greengrocer's in Shepherd's Market."

"Oh, I wouldn't think of taking your apartment."

"It's not mine, dearie. This is war. A group of the

girls got together and chipped in on a foxhole. You bring your own fox."

Thus the privations of wartime are overcome by ingenuity. Sybil and Florence Nightingale had both dedicated their lives to easing the pain of fighting men.

Kay smiled, but politely refused the key. She and Dick had nothing to hide, but Shepherd's Market was just a bit too public, and she—

Dick's shout interrupted her. "Kay!"

He had come out of Number 20, looking for her. He looked harried, but he was still Dick, and her heart leaped into her throat. In an instant they were in each other's arms, beneath Sybil's experienced eye.

"Oh, darling, it's been so long," Kay sighed, holding him. Gently, Dick disengaged himself from her embrace.

"No fraternizing with the natives," he warned. "That order just came through from the Commanding General."

The mention of Ike brought Kay instantly back to earth.

"Darling, can we get married in an hour and a half?" she inquired. "Then that Eisenhower bahstard will have to let us fraternize as often as we want to."

"Slight technicality. In the first place, my wife would insist on our divorce becoming final first . . . and in the second, I've asked for combat duty."

He tried to say it lightly, but the implication was not lost.

Kay felt her throat tighten. She stepped back. *"Combat?* Oh, Dick, have you gone bonkers? Here you are with a nice, cushy job at headquarters—"

"With Ike in charge, combat is the coward's way out."

"Dick!"

"That's only part of it, of course. He's made all of us here feel a little guilty."

It was the truth. All around him in London, Dick was meeting civilians who had survived the worst of Hitler's bombings, soldiers who had been rescued by the little boats and small craft sailed across a bomb-swept English

Channel by weekend sailors to create the miracle of Dunkirk. And, then, of course, there was Kay. And here stood Capt. Richard Arnold, West Point '40, safe and sound at his desk job.

"You've done more than your share in this war, Kay," he reminded her. "It's time I did mine."

"Oh, for heaven's sake—!"

"It wouldn't be fair to you to go through with our marriage now."

"If there is anything I detest," she said, "it is patriotism . . . from Americans!" She looked around helplessly. Passersby had stopped. A sentry at the doorway was listening avidly. "Dick, we really have to talk this over in private."

Sybil, who hadn't missed a word, stepped forward and handed her the key.

"12-E," she reminded Kay.

"Thank you, luv." Kay accepted now, gratefully. She took Dick by the arm. "Come on, if we're going to have a battle, I want to be free to use all of my weapons."

"Miss Summersby?"

Kay turned, startled by the implied command in the voice. A young U.S. captain had come out of the headquarters building—studious-appearing, wearing glasses, the antithesis of the traditional army officer. But there was a certain authority in his bearing that belied his appearance.

"Excuse me," he said, and he had a nice smile, "I'm Tex Lee, one of General Eisenhower's aides. The General wants to see you."

Kay bristled as she released Dick's arm and turned to face this new obstacle to her romance.

"Really?" she inquired, too sweetly. "Does the General know I am a British citizen and a civilian, and not subject to his orders, Captain Lee?"

"Don't be too sure, Miss Summersby. I have it on good authority it won't be long before even the British army, the British navy, and the RAF are under his control."

"Good Lord," murmured Kay, "I may become a nun."

"Too late, dearie," Sybil reminded her.

Kay felt somewhat as if she were on exhibit, as she stood before this American officer who had suddenly been catapulted into a high position she felt he could hardly be qualified for.

General Spaatz, seated uncomfortably at one side of Eisenhower's desk, avoided her eye. Rank has certain privileges, and Ike, with his newly acquired third star, now outranked "Tooey" Spaatz.

"To put it briefly," the Commander of the European Theatre was saying, "my American driver has gotten me lost three times in this city." Ike was in his shirtsleeves, cigarette in hand, lounging behind his desk with an informality no British officer would have permitted himself. "Whatever your faults, Miss Summersby, and you have many . . ." he looked at her pointedly, and she remembered having lectured this American general on women and the Blitz. Well, so be it. He had needed educating, and she had provided the proper lesson.

"You never seem to get lost or flustered," Eisenhower continued. "I have made a trade with General Spaatz for your services."

Kay's face flushed red, her Irish temper threatening to break through the bounds of good manners.

"General Eisenhower, I do not relish being treated like a side of beef. There are certain of my services even General Spaatz is not authorized to negotiate for me."

Spaatz suppressed a smile. He had anticipated Kay's independence. In fact, counted on it.

"If I were authorized, Miss Summersby," he told her gallantly, "I assure you I would have negotiated them for myself."

"Thank you, sir. At least *you* are a gentleman."

She turned to direct her ire at the man who had inspired it. "May I inquire exactly what it is for which

70

General Spaatz agreed to trade me? I'd like to have some idea of my worth."

"There seemed to be nothing of sufficient value to induce the General to part with such a fine driver. So we tossed a coin," Ike replied.

Kay stared at him icily. "Was I heads or tails?"

Spaatz coughed violently to smother his laughter, but Ike refused to recognize the sexual inference.

"Miss Summersby, it may seem like a very small thing, but getting me where I have to go as promptly as possible may be of some aid to your country—otherwise I wouldn't be wasting your time and mine."

"I would be happy to point you in the direction of the Connaught Hotel, sir, if you're certain it will benefit the British Empire." Kay was not conceding one inch.

Spaatz emitted a low whistle and got to his feet. "Come along, Kay," he ordered. "Ike, what did you ever do to her?"

There was no reply, and Kay started to follow Tooey Spaatz out of the office. A sharp command halted her.

"Miss Summersby!"

The authority in Eisenhower's voice shook her; it carried overtones of a firing squad. She turned. Ike reached down behind his desk and brought up a large cardboard box.

"I've been searching all over London for you," he said, the grin he had been suppressing now twitching the edges of his mouth. "I brought this from the United States. Consider it an apology."

And with a flourish, he opened the lid. Crammed inside was an assortment of grapefruit, tangerines, and oranges such as had not been seen in the British Isles since 1939. Ike had spent a full hour in the A & P in Washington, picking out the choicest fruit.

Kay's eyes opened wide. Wartime rationing had almost made her forget the taste of fresh oranges and fresh grapefruit. This was not only a tempting assortment of something she desperately craved, it was a touching demonstration of thoughtfulness and kindness. Ike surely must have had more important things on his mind than his rudeness to a lady.

But, being Kay, she controlled her better nature. "What?" she inquired. "No Hershey bars?"

With a grin of absolute triumph, Ike leaned down, picked up a second carton, and opened it before Kay's astonished eyes. It contained four dozen Hershey bars.

* * *

Chequers, the traditional home of the British Prime Minister, lies in Buckinghamshire, some distance to the south of London. Originally the estate of Oliver Cromwell, it was used constantly by Winston Churchill for meetings throughout the war; its baronial spaciousness and ancient battlements fitted perfectly his sense of his own historical importance. Many times during the war, Dwight Eisenhower spent the night in its cold halls and bedrooms, shivering in its unheated vastness, unimpressed by its place in British hearts. Harry Hopkins, FDR's right-hand man and sometime brain, was once discovered reading in a bathroom at Chequers, wearing his hat and overcoat against the chill, but perfectly content—the modern lavatory being the only room in that medieval structure which boasted an electric heater.

The weather was more congenial on the occasion of Ike's first visit, but the imposing facade of the huge building was enough to daunt the spirit of any but the most fearless soldier. Studying the medieval battlements, Ike nervously lit a cigarette as Kay brought their car to a halt. The procession of limousines behind them also came to a stop.

"I don't mind telling you, Miss Summersby," Ike said, "I feel like a Connecticut Yankee entering King Arthur's Court."

Kay smiled to herself. "I would venture that's precisely the way our Prime Minister wants you to feel," she answered, and got out to open the door.

Observing the scene through a leaded-glass window, dressed in the familiar jump suit he affected because he could simply roll out of bed and zip it on, Winston Churchill smiled a cherubic, knowing smile.

Beside Churchill stood Field Marshal Sir Alan Brooke, Chief of the Imperial General Staff, and an old friend. "Mr. Prime Minister," Brooke muttered, as he followed Churchill's gaze, "what sort of fellow is this Eisenhower chap?"

Churchill chewed the stub of his ever-present cigar. "You'll find the Americans have sent us a clerk," he said, finally.

"With your approval?" Brooke was surprised. The Prime Minister was well known for his unerring choice of brilliant soldiers to carry on the war.

"My *insistence*," Winston growled. "It will be simpler to maneuver him out of our way. In medieval times, we would just lift the drawbridge and let him fall into the moat. Unfortunately, in the twentieth century we are forced to use more subtle means." Grinning, he raised two fingers in the V for Victory he had made famous.

"Rule Britannia," said the Prime Minister.

As Ike and the other high-ranking officers entered the main portal, Sybil, who had been driving one of the other cars, sidled up to Kay.

"Did you notice, dear?" she inquired. "One of mine has *four* stars."

Kay smiled sweetly and raised her hand, which had been hidden behind her. It contained half an orange. Ostentatiously, she began to eat it.

The wood-panelled walls, medieval trappings, huge chandeliers and deep plush furnishings of Chequers, with its tremendous ceilings and vast halls, were enough to impress all visitors, particularly those from the United States. Churchill led his guests, including Ike and Sir Alan

Brooke, Lord Louis Mountbatten and Gen. Sir Bernard Paget, into the grandeur of the fifteenth-century dining hall, pointing out with relish the historical importance of various furnishings which predated the discovery of America. Having made his point several times over, he puffed expansively at his cheroot and turned to Ike, who was carrying a mundane twentieth-century briefcase and trying not to stare at his surroundings.

"Do you have houses like this in Abilene, Kansas, General?" Churchill inquired grandly.

Eisenhower, unabashed, flashed a grin. "I was told there *was* one, Mr. Prime Minister," he said, "but my mother would never let me visit it."

In the laughter that followed, Churchill scrutinized his guest a little more closely. It was not his custom to be outdone in repartee; this was a tougher adversary than he had figured.

"Sit down, gentlemen, sit down," he urged, more businesslike now. They all seated themselves around the huge table, which, in ancient times, must have seated warriors more picturesquely attired in armor. At this moment in history, it was set for tea.

Ike wasted no time. He pulled some papers from his briefcase. "Mr. Prime Minister, I have some recommendations here for the invasion across the English Channel which the American Joint Chiefs feel should take place as quickly as we can—"

"My dear Eisenhower."

It was the tone, not the words, that made Ike look at his host with sudden suspicion, the suspicion that he had walked into a carefully set trap. Winston Churchill was on his feet, pacing. Several times, he walked into the huge, empty fireplace of the dining hall, disappearing momentarily into its vast interior, only to reappear shortly, waving the cigar in an eloquent gesture. Eisenhower was certain Churchill had practiced this startling maneuver often, for he had its timing down perfectly.

"With all due respect to America," Churchill intoned,

"the far-sighted nation which gave the world my mother" —he looked about for the appreciative response he knew this would provoke, and timed his next words so as not to interfere with the laughter—"I urge caution. After the frightening news from North Africa that Rommel and his Nazi Afrika Korps have destroyed our British forces at Tobruk and are once more hammering toward Cairo and the Suez Canal, it seems obvious that the invasion of Europe will have to be put off for at least a year." He emerged from the fireplace, crossed to a sideboard, and poured himself a whisky.

Ike flushed angrily. He got to his feet, almost knocking over a priceless antique chair.

"Mr. Prime Minister! I thought this meeting was called to set the date!"

"Precisely." Churchill was returning, whisky in hand. "The date I propose is next year. June, 1943. Or possibly 1944."

"How about the year 2000?" Ike almost shouted. "That has a nice ring to it!"

"I quite agree. I am willing to wait, if you are."

"Mr. Prime Minister! You promised President Roosevelt—you promised Josef Stalin—that England would help America cross the Channel and open a second front in Europe to draw off German troops from Russia. And, eventually, to smash through into Germany itself. Are you saying England will *never* do it?"

Churchill turned away from Ike and measured his words carefully. This was the crucial point. Ike, as usual, had zeroed in on it immediately. It was a question Churchill did not want to answer. Not yet.

"Perhaps yes, perhaps no," he said, and then plunged on, hoping his adversary would be impressed by his oratory, if not his logic. "When, in my mind's eye, I see the English Channel running red with British blood . . . the beaches of France strewn with the broken flower of British youth . . . I have my doubts, I have my doubts."

Ike crossed to confront him before he could reenter

the fireplace. They stood eye to eye, their weapons only words, but their meaning measured in lives.

"Mr. Prime Minister, I'm just a Kansas farmer and I can't compete with you in flowery oratory, but you *did* promise your allies that—"

So it hadn't worked. Ike was still doggedly on the trail. It was time, Churchill decided, for the truth; something, he had once said, which is so precious in wartime that it must be surrounded by a bodyguard of lies. He set down his whisky glass.

"General," he replied, "certainly, a Channel crossing must one day be attempted. When the Nazi monsters have been bombed into submission, when the risk is low and the reward seems great, we will go along. But if it means as large a sacrifice of British life as we had in 1915"—he paused, thinking of Gallipoli—"England may well win the war and descend to the status of a second-rate power. To that, General Eisenhower, I will never accede."

"If Russia falls, how many British and American lives will have to replace the Red Army?"

"I'm told that you're an expert bridge player, General. You must know that Uncle Joe Stalin has more aces in his hand than he wants his partners to see. I assure you, Russia will survive."

The Prime Minister crossed to the huge globe in the magnificent bay window that overlooked Chequers's historic gardens. He turned the sphere with a practiced hand, rolling it around so the continents moved under his touch. He placed his fingers across the Middle East, drew a line toward the Indian subcontinent.

"Rommel and the Afrika Korps are heading for the oil fields of Arabia. The Japanese army is knocking on the gateway to India. If these two link up, if the Japanese get the fabulous treasures of rubber of the Indies, if Rommel reaches the Arab oil, America and Britain will be cut off. Our tanks and our factories will clang to a halt. We must stop Rommel *now*."

It was time for the supporting cast to make an entrance. At a glance from Churchill, Lord Mountbatten, the adventurous young naval officer who was Chief of Combined Operations, stepped to the globe and indicated the southern Mediterranean.

"If we can land amphibious forces here, on the French North African coast—"

"Lord Mountbatten, you're planning to land in Algeria and Morocco, and they belong to the French!" Ike was fuming. TORCH, the North African operation first mentioned to him by Montgomery, had long been thrown out of consideration. He was certain the British were introducing it now as an excuse to postpone Ike's carefully planned attack on the continent of Europe. "The French in North Africa will shoot back," he reminded them. "They hate you worse than they hate the Nazis. You tried to sink the French fleet after France surrendered to the Germans!"

"True, we made a grave tactical error," Churchill had to agree. The abortive British effort had succeeded in incapacitating only a few French vessels. The rest of the fleet had holed up at Toulon, under watchful German eyes, and England had become an enemy in the eyes of many Frenchmen, especially the Vichy French, led by old Marshal Pétain and his devious second in command, Admiral Jean François Darlan. "But this time, to get their battleships to come over to our cause," the Prime Minister declared, "I will personally crawl on my hands and knees and kiss the arse of every admiral in the French navy!"

"With the French navy it might work," Ike remarked dryly, "but I doubt it."

Gen. Paget, commander of Britain's Home Forces, had joined the group. "What is your estimate of the chances for a successful North African invasion?" he asked.

The question was directed to Ike. Paget was aware that Eisenhower, a soldier who had spent a lifetime in the field of logistics, was better qualified to answer than was a Prime Minister.

Ike began to pace, hands clasped behind his back, head lowered. It was a reflex action when his mind was occupied with difficult problems. He ticked them off with characteristic precision.

"One: we can't strip American forces in England of too many men. We'll have to ship green troops into battle directly from basic training in the United States to face the Afrika Korps. Two: our supply lines will be two hundred times as long as they would be across the English Channel. Three: we'll be short of landing craft, heavy tanks, artillery." He had come face to face with Churchill once more. "I would say our chances of landing and making it stick are less than fifty-fifty."

Military logic made no impression on England's leader. Had he listened to it after Dunkirk, Britain would now be another prostrate victim of Nazi arrogance and terror.

"Then we must land," Churchill said firmly, "and we must make it stick. We have not journeyed all this way across the centuries, across the oceans, across the mountains, because we are made of sugar candy. If we must do this thing because it is the only thing we *can* do at this time, we will do it. The young men of Britain and America will do it."

"How?" Eisenhower was unimpressed, as usual, by mere words.

Churchill had been waiting for this moment, setting up his quarry. Now he moved in for the kill. "I have been in communication with your President," he said, "and he has promised the tools to do the job: weapons, supplies, troops."

It was a surprise, a private arrangement. Eisenhower had not been aware of it.

Churchill made the final lunge. "And," he added, "an extraordinary soldier to fashion the massive assault." He raised his glass in a toast, savoring the moment. "Congratulations, General Eisenhower. I am recommending that you command the coming Allied invasion of North Africa."

He drank deeply. There could be no turning back.

78

As his car wended its way homeward that night through the countryside to the battered streets of London, Ike hunched down in the rear seat and tried to figure out how he had allowed himself to be out-maneuvered. True, he was to command both British and American forces in the North African invasion, the first combined Allied command of the war, a test of his own organizational plan for the invasion across the Channel. But the manner of his receiving the command and the delay of the Channel invasion made him apprehensive.

"Mousetrapped," he muttered to himself.

"Sir?" Kay, driving the car had begun to become accustomed to Ike's habit of voicing his thoughts aloud. It was an indirect compliment that, with Kay at the wheel, Ike could feel safely alone.

"Faked out of England by good old Gorgeous Winnie," he explained, "so he can run the show by himself and postpone the Channel invasion—maybe forever."

"Good Heavens! What makes you so pessimistic?"

"I've just been offered another promotion."

"I don't see why that—"

"My first combat command, in an impossible situation, against the French navy and coastal defenses, the Afrika Korps, and General Erwin Rommel, the best tactician the Germans have. Huckleberry Finn against Alexander the Great."

"Well, then, you intend to turn it down?"

"Hell, no! To use a phrase from American history, I've just begun to fight! Churchill went behind my back to get Roosevelt to agree that—"

The sudden wail of the air raid sirens jerked them both upright. The sound echoed and re-echoed down the London streets, was picked up and repeated frighteningly throughout the sprawling city. In a quick reflex, Kay slammed on the brakes of the Packard and jounced it into the curb, almost throwing Ike out of his seat. All about them, pedestrians had begun to run.

"Good God!" Kay shouted above the sirens. "There

hasn't been a raid in *months!* Underground station at the corner. Closest shelter!"

Horns were blowing as other cars screeched to a stop nearby.

"To hell with shelter!" Ike shouted back. "Get me to headquarters! That's an order!"

"Not bloody likely! Grosvenor Square's the other side of London. It's much too dangerous!"

"Miss Summersby—"

She was already halfway out of the car. "Don't expect me to hold your door open for you, General! It's every man for himself!" And she was gone.

Ike hesitated a split second. It could be a false alarm. Probably was. The Germans hadn't risked a raid in force over London for almost a year. Then the ack-ack guns opened fire in the distance. There was an explosion. Ike had often wondered how he would react in battle. Now he knew. He was out of the car in a flash.

Kay had flattened herself against a wall of the building opposite. Londoners were hurrying by, trying not to show concern as they went about the familiar business of finding shelter against bomb blast and concussion. Beastly annoying, this. When she saw Ike start out of the car, Kay leaped forward, grabbed him by the arm, and guided him toward the sandbagged entrance to the underground station.

The familiar hodgepodge of all classes was crowded onto the stairway leading down into the white-tiled depths. The Blitz had taught that London's subway was the safest of sanctuaries—far beneath the streets, impervious to all but the most massive of direct hits. Sometimes the trains continued to run during the raids. More often they did not, allowing the huddled families on the platforms to stretch out on their bedrolls and sleep, or cook their dinners over bottled gas, night after night. Now, of course, most of the temporary bunks had disappeared. The almost summer-camp atmosphere of the platforms was long gone, and people merely hurried down to take their places in regular rows on the platform, as if waiting for a train. A train that never came.

Ike and Kay found themselves on the stairway, jammed behind a Cockney woman who was struggling to get a pram down the steps and carrying a small, squirming dog under one arm. The baby in the pram was crying loudly, and the woman leaned down to it with a motherly admonition: "Shut up, dearie, or next bombing I'll leave you outside." But she paused to kiss the child before straightening up. "I 'ope 'Itler 'as boils," she said.

Ike was impatient and irritable. This was one occasion when he should have been at his desk, at the nerve center, getting a grasp of how the defenses of London operated.

"If you disobey my orders again," he declared, "I'll have you skinned alive, Miss Summersby."

"Kay. Call me Kay. Next time you leap out of my car, you may not have time for my full name."

Ike's reply was smothered by a loud grumbling from the assembled Londoners as the lights suddenly went out. One more inconvenience. Flashlights appeared from pockets and purses. Lanterns were taken from posted positions, lit, and placed where they would illuminate the station. A city inured to war was enduring another battle—stoically, typically.

"Here, give me your hand," Kay said to Ike, as he stumbled forward in the semi-darkness. "This is my second home. Wouldn't do for you to be falling off the bloody platform." She turned to the woman behind her. "Stop shoving, dear," she said, "we have a general with us tonight."

The woman was unimpressed. "If 'e was out fighting the ruddy war, *we* wouldn't be down 'ere," she said reasonably.

"I've never felt quite so appreciated before," Ike told Kay, his anger receding before the calm of the civilians all around him, most of whom had had more personal experience with warfare than the Commander of the European Theatre.

Kay steered him through the throng toward the wall.

More lanterns were being lit, but the platform was still black and dangerous in spots.

"I come by my disrespect for generals honestly," Kay told Ike. "My father was one, in the Royal Munster Fusiliers."

"That's an Irish regiment, isn't it?"

"Oh, yes, he was Black Irish. So am I. Mum left him because she couldn't stand the Irish weather or his temper. Personally, I didn't think the weather was so bad."

A harmonica was striking up a melody somewhere in the semi-darkness, Noel Coward's "I'll See You Again." Kay leaned back against a War Bond poster and fished out her cigarettes. She offered them to Ike.

"You owe me one," she warned, as he accepted. "They're rationed, you know."

The lights flickered on. Ike turned and was greeted by a yelp. Somehow, the Cockney woman's dog had gotten underfoot. He leaned down, picked it up, and petted it; dogs had always been his friends. This one stopped whimpering. The lights flickered off again.

"Oh, dear." Kay was worried now. No telling what was going on in the streets far above them. "I do hope there's no direct hit. I'm very much in love and I *would* like to get married first, if it's not too much trouble for God."

Ike looked at her. It was the first time he'd heard her mention her romance.

"I'd almost forgotten people still got married," he said.

"I'd almost forgotten people still fell in love." Kay puffed at her cigarette. It had seemed incongruous, in the midst of so much tension and fear, that a new love could blossom so suddenly, so fully. What was it about war?

"My major has volunteered for combat because you've made him feel he had to," she said.

Ike lit his cigarette. That was the difficulty with command: you were insulated from the fighting you had to send others to face. He was never comfortable with the feeling.

"He's so unsuited for it," Kay continued. "I don't think he could knowingly kill a human being."

"Do you feel I could?"

Kay looked up. Eisenhower's eyes were watching her; she knew her answer might be important to him. Being Kay Summersby, she didn't hesitate.

"Yes, I think you could. Definitely, yes. My father actually enjoyed it, he told me. Of course, only if it helped the Empire."

"I don't think I'll enjoy it much, when the time comes." Ike puffed at his cigarette. This was something he had wondered about, thought about, many times. "I keep telling myself this is a just war . . . the Nazis are a sadistic, vicious enemy . . . this killing will be necessary. But my father and mother are pacifists . . . my grandfather was a minister." He shook his head. "My mother cried when I told her I was going to West Point. She never has understood."

Kay had been watching him. She knew this was a rare moment; Eisenhower seldom allowed the real person behind the facade to show through. "I don't understand, either," she said.

Ike tossed away the cigarette and ground it out with his foot. He was still holding the dog, petting it occasionally.

"Kay," he said, and she started at the use of her first name, "I have a son back home. Just nineteen years old. I want Johnny Eisenhower to live his life a free man. Mamie —my wife—and I lost our first child when he was only three . . . scarlet fever . . . and there wasn't a damn thing we could do about it. His name was Dwight, also. He was barely old enough to pronounce it when he died."

Kay offered another cigarette, and he lit it, lost in the remembrance. Even this long after, the hurt was still fresh, the pain still there. Standing so close to Ike, their shoulders nearly touching, Kay could almost feel it herself.

"Johnny's old enough to get into this war; he graduates from West Point in a couple of years. I couldn't bear to lose him, too. How can I send someone else's son to get killed? And I know some day soon I'll have to." He turned to her, to emphasize his concern. "If anything I do should add one extra minute to this fighting, and cost the life of someone like Johnny who didn't have to die, I won't have done my job. That's why I'm not going to let Winston Churchill or anyone else push me around. This is going to be a soldier's war, not a politician's war, so that my kid and other kids like him won't have to do it all over again." The cigarette had gone out, and he tossed it aside. "I didn't mean to turn this into a sermon, Kay. I had to say it to someone, and you were here."

"It's perfectly all right, General," she said softly. "You've made me feel like the son of a bitch I really am."

Suddenly the lights flashed on and the all-clear signal sounded. Talking, laughing, grumbling, people headed for the end of the platform and the stairs. The Cockney woman located them and reached for her dog.

"Sorry, guv'nor, but I'm takin' 'im back now," she told Ike. "Lend-Lease."

VI

The French
They Are A
Funny Race

The problem Ike would face in North Africa was one of the most complicated of the war. After the surrender to Hitler, France retained a semblance of independence, with the pro-German government in Vichy under Marshal Pétain and Admiral Darlan. The Nazis allowed them to save face by restraining German troops from overruning the southern portion of the French nation, which was left under Vichy control.

The situation in French Algeria and French Morocco was less clear. Theoretically under Vichy, a number of the leading officers longed desperately to join with Charles de Gaulle's Free French forces. De Gaulle had begun to organize an army in Africa under General Le Clerc, but was having great difficulty because of the animosity of Franklin Roosevelt. FDR felt de Gaulle was a usurper, attempting to seize power that rightfully belonged to the French people. De Gaulle knew that unless he seized that power now, the

French people would never have an opportunity to express their choice, but would have to take a leader dictated by the Allies. Given the unbending nature and monumental egos of both men, they were on a collision course.

When the invasion of Morocco and Algeria was first contemplated, Roosevelt sent his own private emissary to contact the dissident French officers in Algiers. Robert Murphy was a career diplomat; this was a mission of utmost risk and delicacy. He operated under the noses of the German military in North Africa. His work had to be clandestine, his identity secret.

When the invasion became imminent, Murphy was spirited out of Algeria; he eventually wound up in London under the *nom de guerre* of "Lt. Col. McGowan." Murphy was tall, stoop-shouldered, and looked more like a harried American businessman than a consummate spy. In meetings with Eisenhower, he reported that the second in command in Algeria, General Mast, could be relied upon to swing his troops to the support of the Allied landings. The commander of the Oran Airfield was also friendly, and Murphy was certain he would arrange for the field to be overrun by the Americans without opposition. General Mendigal, the commander of the French air force in the area, and General Bethouart, commanding a division near Casablanca, were also strongly pro-Allies. It was suggested that Ike send someone from his staff secretly into Algiers to meet with all of them and formulate plans for the secret defection of French forces. It would be a mission of utmost danger and delicacy. The United States was to underwrite treason.

Eisenhower selected Gen. Mark Clark for the task. Although outwardly pleased at the thought of the adventure, Clark's first action was to write a letter to his family which his old friend Ike was to mail if he didn't return.

Mark Clark and his party were taken by submarine to a position off the North African coast. In the dead of night, they left the submarine and paddled canvas boats to the rendezvous point with General Mast and the dissident French officers, who led them to a blacked-out villa nearby.

In a tension-packed meeting, the details of the invasion and the cooperation of the French were worked out, but Clark discovered they were all far from unanimity. Most of the officers still held the old hero, Marshal Pétain, in great esteem; they would not move except by his orders. Others were suspicious and jealous of Charles de Gaulle. While the wrangling was going on, Clark excused himself to go to the bathroom. When he returned, he was startled to see French generals leaping out of windows in all directions. Someone had betrayed the meeting place to the pro-Vichy French police, and a police raid was in progress. Capture meant death.

Somehow, Clark and the others in his party made it back to the canvas boats, despite intermittent firing. Hastily, they stripped off their clothing and placed it in the boats. They were about to follow when a burst of machine gun fire sent them diving underwater, capsizing the boats. Clark lost not only five hundred dollars in gold that was in his pants pockets, he also lost his pants. The story later made headlines in the American press. As Clark described it, six feet six of frightened general swam bare-ass back to the waiting submarine and made the return journey to England in borrowed underwear.

Plans for the invasion had proceeded secretly in England. Shipping was being mobilized, and troops were sent to training bases for undisclosed reasons. There were hasty departures, hasty goodbyes on packed railroad platforms. While it was a welcome change from all the inactivity (in some nine months since Pearl Harbor, the United States had not yet been able to mount a single offensive action), there was the usual grumbling and complaints of inefficiency and snafus—a World War II acronym for Situation Normal, All Fouled Up. ("Fouled up" was itself a euphemism for something considerably more vivid.)

At a railway station somewhere on the outskirts of London, a huge jam of GI's crowded the platform between two troop trains, preparing for departure. The platform was illuminated only by blue blackout lights, which gave every face a ghostly appearance and added to the unreality of shadowy figures moving about loaded with rifles, bayonets, and field packs, shoving their way past the Red Cross women serving coffee and doughnuts.

She had come up the jammed stairway from the underpass beneath the tracks and was looking desperately about, when Maj. Dick Arnold saw her.

"Kay!" he called. "Kay!"

He started toward her, the unaccustomed battle gear banging against his shoulders. In a moment, they were in each other's arms, oblivious to the mass of khaki-clad bodies all around them.

"Oh, darling!" Kay was out of breath, almost in tears, the fear that she might have missed him having frightened all the arrogance out of her Irish nature. "Things got so hectic! I broke every traffic law—lucky I have the General's car, they wouldn't dare to stop *him*." She realized something on his chest was holding them apart. She looked down. "Gas mask?"

Dick nodded. "I tried it on once and almost suffocated." Something in his voice told her of the fear within.

"Dick, where are they sending you?"

"You're not to worry. Whatever happens, I've decided to surrender."

She clung to him. He was trying so hard. She hoped he hadn't seen the tears.

"Don't do anything foolishly brave, do you promise? I want you back in one large, delicious piece."

"Kay, I'm only going to Scotland."

She pushed away from him, suddenly rigid. "Scotland! Oh, my God."

Something in her voice chilled him. "Do you know something I don't know?" He tried to make it sound light, but it didn't come out that way.

"I know *everything* you don't know."

It was true. They had often joked about it. He was a major now, but Kay, a civilian, was the trusted confidant of the Commanding General. Only Winston Churchill, she had once told him, knew more of the secrets of the war than she did. And she wasn't too sure about Churchill.

"What's in Scotland, Kay?"

"I can't tell. Not even you. Oh, this damned war!"

He didn't press her. It wouldn't have done any good, he knew. She put her arms about him, the tears beginning again. His lips brushed her hair. Down the platform, the train whistle blew mournfully. A sergeant was shouting for his platoon to get the lead out.

"Kay." He had to say it; this might be his last chance. "Kay, I've changed my mind."

She looked up at him, wondering. He continued quickly, the train whistle echoing again over his words. "Honey, if I happen to get through whatever I'm headed for . . . and if my beloved wife ever comes through with the divorce her lawyer is charging me for . . . I'm going to marry you even if we have to live in a foxhole in Siberia . . . unfurnished."

He kissed her.

"Will you do me one favor, darling?" she whispered.

"What?"

"Always hide behind something." She tried to smile.

He held her close for one final moment, then turned away. Without looking back, he climbed aboard the train. The wheels began to turn. The whistle wailed again. The train began to pull slowly out of the station.

Kay stood and watched it leave, the cars jammed with their cargo of soldiers.

And I'm the only one here who knows where they are going, she thought. Then, echoing the train wheels: the only one the only one the only one. . . .

Telegraph Cottage was Eisenhower's secret hideaway near London. Searching for a place where Ike could be safe from prying eyes and relax from the terrible business of running a war, Capt. Harry Butcher, Ike's naval aide, had found the unpretentious little cottage hidden away in ten acres of woods—and adjoining the thirteenth hole of the Little Coombe golf course, which sold the cottage immediately to Ike. Butcher and Ike were old golfing friends. Harry Butcher had been a vice president of the Columbia Broadcasting System, and was exceedingly well qualified to run the public relations operation that made Ike the darling of the press in World War II. Butcher's wife became Mamie Eisenhower's hotel roommate and confidant in Washington during the long wait for their absent husbands. While it was somewhat strange for a naval officer to be the aide to an army commander, Ike had wangled it for his friend, and Butcher became one of the most important members of Ike's little private family, which also included Capt. Tex Lee, Ike's orderly Sgt. Mickey McKeogh, and Sgts. Moaney and Hunt. And, eventually, Kay Summersby.

Telegraph Cottage was a perfect place. It had five bedrooms, spacious lawns, a rose garden, and it rented for $32 a week. A little steep, but worth it for the Commanding General.

Kay, at the wheel of Eisenhower's olive drab Packard, sped down the bumpy country lane that led to the cottage. Capt. Lee sat beside her, unhappily holding a tiny Scottie puppy on his lap. Tex had an aversion to dogs that was heartily returned by most of the canine population.

"What makes you think Ike wants a puppy for his birthday?" he asked Kay unhappily. The puppy was nuzzling his chin, evidently unaware of Tex's reputation. "This one can't even salute."

"I've noticed the General pets every stray dog he sees, and I've been hunting for days for the right one for him."

"I thought you didn't care for American generals?"

"Don't pry," Kay said, and braked the car to a halt in the driveway of the picturesque cottage, set like a Tudor dollhouse in the midst of the woods and flowering shrubs. She picked up the package she'd gone to so much trouble for, got out of the car, and lifted the puppy from Tex's hands. He looked so relieved that Kay couldn't help smiling.

"All right, Tex," she explained, "I need a favor from General Eisenhower. A big one."

"Thank God," he told her. "The war is confusing enough. I like my bitchy women to stay in character."

They started up the walk to the cottage.

One of the joys of the Little Coombe golf course was that it was so little used. Most of the male members of the club were more suitably occupied in such places as El Alamein and Burma. Ike found it possible to sneak out the back way from Telegraph Cottage, take the little path, and play the twelfth and thirteenth holes without being noticed.

Today his impromptu threesome included Gen. Mark Clark, just returned from his mission to Algeria, and Beetle Smith. It was as private a place to discuss military secrets as Ike knew of—and it helped him perfect his iron shots.

"Who tipped off the Germans about your meeting?" he asked Clark, as he lined up a long putt on the edge of the green.

"It wasn't the Germans shooting at us. It was the French police."

Ike was to learn later never to be surprised by anything the French did. "The French *police?*"

Clark nodded as he stepped up to address his ball. Ike's putt had stopped 3 feet short. "Most of the police are pro-Vichy. And some of the Army officers I met are pro-de Gaulle. Some are anti-de Gaulle. A few are pro-Nazi. But one thing is sure—all of them are anti-British."

His shot rimmed the cup and Beetle stepped up to take his turn, humming under his breath, "The French they are a funny race, *parlez-vous . . .*"

"We've got to arrange somehow for the French to hold their fire during our landing," Ike said, the worry evident in his tone. This was not something that could be arranged through military strength; it required diplomacy, an area in which Ike had no experience and less inclination. "Is there anyone in the world the French will listen to? Other than de Gaulle, whom Roosevelt can't stand?"

91

"General Mast spent most of the meeting telling us the only one who can unite all the French officials is General Henri Giraud."

"Giraud?"

Clark nodded. "Hero of the two World Wars. Refused to go along with the surrender to Hitler and wound up in a Nazi prison. Koenigstein."

Beetle sank his putt. "He escaped, didn't he?" he inquired.

"Yes. His third prison break. He's somewhere in southern France now."

"Anyone who escaped from a Nazi prison camp has the kind of guts we can use," Ike said. The golf game was forgotten as he considered the possibilities. "If the French open fire on our ships with their coastal batteries, if they attack our troops when they hit the beaches, we're going to lose a lot of lives in a senseless battle. If Giraud can swing them to our side, he's worth two divisions. We've got to get him out of France and fly him to invasion headquarters on Gibraltar." He bent to pick up his golfball. "I'm going to have to have a grandson some day," he mused, "so I can tell him that once upon a time, Grandpa commanded the Rock of Gibraltar." He glanced at his watch. "Let's go. Time for my surprise party."

Beetle looked at him, startled. "How did you know we were giving you a surprise party?"

The Eisenhower grin was real and deeply felt. The little triumphs were so much more heartwarming than the big, difficult ones.

"I've broken your code," the Commander told him.

A fire was blazing merrily in the fireplace of the small living room of Telegraph Cottage, a welcome glow of warmth against the fall chill. Sgt. Mickey McKeogh was lighting the candles on the birthday cake Sgt. Moaney had baked; Sgt. Hunt was setting out the liquor and glasses. Tex was supervising the operation, taking care that all the presents were carefully placed to one side, and warning

92

the guests to observe complete silence. Since the guest list included Sybil and other women of the Motor Transport Corps, the warning was needed, but before it could take effect, the door flew open and Ike strode in, smiling broadly and shouting, "Surprise! Surprise!"

Everyone turned, startled.

"Well, there goes another military secret," Tex muttered, crestfallen.

"General, you've ruined the whole party!" Sybil complained.

Ike dipped a finger into the cake's icing and tasted it. "Sorry, Miss Williams," he said, "but I understand you're having your own party later, over the greengrocer's."

Sybil's face grew red at the laughter that followed. "Good Lord!" she murmured. "Everybody's a spy."

Mark Clark and Bedell Smith had followed Ike in. Now all took their places around the table as Tex handed Ike a dress sword.

"For the cake," he said. "I have an idea it may need it."

"*Three* candles?" Ike inquired.

"A little belatedly, in honor of your third star."

"That leaves me outranked by General Montgomery and half the British General Staff," said Ike, a little wryly. It seemed that every time he received a promotion, the British were always given one to match or exceed him.

"Make a wish and blow 'em out, sir," said Sgt. Hunt, anxious to get the party going.

Ike took a breath, but he was interrupted by the yelping of the Scottie puppy, who burst into the room dragging a small parachute behind him, pursued by an irate Kay Summersby.

"Come back, you bloody little wretch!" Kay called. "You've ruined everything!" She managed to grab the parachute and bring the chase to a halt. Then she picked the tiny culprit up in her arms and crossed to Ike.

"Sorry, General," she said, "I went to so much trouble to get this ruddy parachute made for him, then the

93

little rotter decided to bail out." She handed the fluffy creature to Ike. "Happy birthday! This one is definitely *not* Lend-Lease. He's for you to keep."

Ike was already fondling the puppy, pleased beyond words. It was the ideal present for someone whose world was becoming much too complicated. "Thank you, Kay," he said, "I'm truly touched. How did you know I wanted one?"

"Everyone needs a dog to kick around, sir. I thought he might take the pressure off the rest of us."

"You may be right." Ike smiled.

"Better blow out the candles, General." Sgt. Moaney was growing worried. "They're melting my icing, and we can't get no more sugar."

"And don't forget to make that wish," Mark Clark added.

Ike set the puppy down on the table, hesitated a moment, then blew out the candles in one quick breath. There was mock applause for the effort.

Kay was curious. "May I ask what you wished, General?"

Ike turned to her. "That all the dying that is about to happen will be worth it," he said.

There was a sudden hush. For a moment, Ike felt exposed, embarrassed.

"Jesus! That lousy mutt just ate the General's cake!" Sgt. Moaney shouted, and the tension was broken.

Later, Eisenhower wandered into his study, holding the Scottie under his arm. The birthday party was in full swing, the phonograph playing Glenn Miller's "Little Brown Jug," but Ike was impatient to get on with the pressures of war. At least, now he had a companion.

He set the puppy on the desk on a stack of papers, found his glasses, and searched for a sheet of stationery. Under the Scottie, of course. He lifted the dog up, removed the papers, and set the puppy down again.

"At ease," he ordered. He picked up his pen. There

94

was one thing he had to do before he turned his attention to the problems of North Africa.

The door opened behind him, and Kay peered in. "General?"

Ike looked up.

"I'm terribly sorry. Am I interrupting some very hush-hush correspondence?"

Ike nodded, smiling. The dog and the girl had become connected in his mind. Two friendly creatures with whom he felt at ease.

"Top secret," he said. "Classified. I'm writing a letter to Mamie." He removed his glasses and rubbed his eyes. "What is it you want, Kay?"

She closed the door and started toward him. "I want to go to North Africa. Oh, dear, that didn't come out the way I meant at all. I intended to plead."

"You could never plead, Kay. Argue. Order. Shout. But never plead."

"I know how busy you are and how it must sound, but you see, there is this young man of mine, the one I told you about, Major Arnold. He was shipped to Scotland last night, and being here I can't help knowing that means he's going to be in your invasion of North Africa."

Ike got to his feet. "Kay, you've been cleared for sensitive information, but you must understand that whatever you hear is not to be repeated."

"I didn't think there was any harm in telling *you*," Kay said, and Ike couldn't help smiling again.

"I wish," he told her, "your Prime Minister felt the same way." He placed his hands on her shoulders. It surprised him to feel that she was trembling. Kay? This major must mean a great deal to her.

"Now, just what do you expect me to do for your young man? Have him transferred out? I can't and won't do that."

"No," she said, "Dick would hate me if he thought I'd done something like that. But last night he asked me

95

to marry him. Or I asked him. I'm not exactly certain. He's asked me before, many times, but last night was definite. We were both perfectly sober and fully clothed."

Her voice had softened at the mention of his name. Her eyes were moist. Dwight Eisenhower felt more than his 52 years. The memories of his youth came rushing back, and for a moment he envied the young major, whoever he was.

"Yes," he agreed gently, "that does sound definite."

Kay leaned over and picked up the puppy. She held it to her cheek, caressing it.

"This isn't some wartime roll in the hay, General," she said, feeling for some reason the necessity to *explain* to this man, almost as if he were the father she never truly knew. "Dick and I have both been married before. My divorce has come through, and as soon as his wife takes him for every cent he's got, then his will, too. When it does, I'd like to become his bride before he stumbles into a booby trap or something equally foolish. If I'm in North Africa, I might have a chance of bringing it off."

"But you're a civilian, Kay. I can't order a civilian into a combat zone."

"I'm not terribly civilian, you know that," she pleaded. "And you *will* need a driver over there. Generals never walk." No, that wasn't the right thing to say. "I do love Dick so very much." Her voice was betraying her now. "So now you know why I gave you this bloody expensive puppy, sir."

Ike took the little dog from her. "For a bloody expensive puppy, this one's not very well housebroken." It was true. The puppy had disgraced himself earlier, in the living room.

"He'll learn, General," Kay said, petting the tiny creature. "He's very bright. I'll explain things, and I'll set him a good example."

"I'm sure you will."

Kay turned away from him, the game having gone far enough.

"Please, General Eisenhower," she said shakily, "I'm tired of making girlish small talk. Yes or no? Don't force me to resort to tears, it's so undignified."

Again, Ike remembered how it had been when he was younger.

"Tomorrow," he said quietly, "I'm going to have Tex take you out to one of the firing ranges and teach you how to handle a pistol until you can knock the buttons off a German uniform at twenty yards. I wouldn't want anything to happen to you, where you're going."

"Oh, General, thank you!"

It was over now, the dreadful worrying, the scheming, the hoping. She threw her arms impulsively around the neck of the Commanding General of the European Theatre of Operations and kissed him, happily, warmly, gratefully. Suddenly, realizing, she drew back. "I'm sorry, sir. I know that was unmilitary. But I thought you'd prefer it to my salute."

"You're absolutely right," Ike said. He turned abruptly, busying himself with his papers.

Kay waited a moment and then, when there was nothing further from him, she crossed toward the door. As she opened it, Ike said without looking up, "Tell your major to be careful. I wouldn't want to have him on my conscience."

Slowly, Kay closed the door, leaving him alone.

VII
The First Battle

In the darkness of the night of November 7, 1942, General Dwight Eisenhower stood on a headland of the Rock of Gibraltar with others of the first combined Allied combat command, watching the shadowy hulks of a convoy of warships and troop transports slip silently into the narrow strait, sitting ducks for any of the German JU-88 bombers that had been sighted on patrol earlier. These were the ships destined for the amphibious attacks on the ports of Oran and Algiers in French Algeria; somewhere in the darkness farther to the east, the huge convoys from America were nearing the end of their transatlantic journey, preparing to attack simultaneously at Casablanca, on the coast of French Morocco, under the command of Ike's old friend, Gen. George Patton. Incredibly, neither convoy had met serious opposition from German submarines or aircraft; only the USS *Thomas Stone* had been torpedoed, with a battalion of American troops aboard. Obviously the convoys had been sighted, but the Germans must have believed they were another attempt to reinforce the island of Malta in the Mediterranean, and were refraining from retaliation until the ships came closer to the umbrella of German planes based in Sicily.

Eisenhower had a fairly good idea of what the Germans knew because of something code-named "Ultra." Before the war started, British Secret Service had been contacted by a Polish mechanic who had been pressed into work in Germany at a factory manufacturing a brand-new, presumably uncrackable, code machine for the Nazi high command. The British managed to get him out of Warsaw and over to Paris; here, startling everyone, he produced, from memory, a wooden mock-up of the machine he had been working on. And there they were thwarted. The German machine was an incredibly complicated device for random coding—that is, the changing of a code at random intervals many times during a single transmission. All known methods of cryptography were useless. The German dubbed the code "Enigma."

But Britain had overcome the impossible many times during the war, and the German coding machine was no exception. At Bletchley Hall, an isolated manor house outside of London, the British had gathered the best mathematical and scientific minds in the free world, whose sole aim was cracking the German code. What was built at Bletchley Hall was, in essence, the world's first computer; it covered thousands of square feet, and at first worked imperfectly. But it could take a randomly coded message and run it through an incredible number of combinations. And it could recognize the right combination from all the variations.

The first coded German messages took weeks to decipher; later, Ultra was to operate in seconds. Enigma was the highest code in use by the Nazis, and was reserved mainly for messages between Hitler and his top generals. Fortunately for the Allies, it was also the method for communication with the Nazi submarines operating in wolf-packs in the Atlantic. It was Ultra that saved the convoys of American goods on their way to Britain and eventually helped turn the tide of the war, so much so that Eisenhower was to write a tribute to the scientists at Bletchley Hall when it was over, crediting them with a major contribution to victory. Later in the war, Ultra kept George Patton informed of concentrations of German armor during his savage, lightning advance through France. At this moment, it told Eisenhower two things: one, that Rommel was in desperate trouble fighting Montgomery in Libya and was appealing to the Fuehrer for reinforcements; two, that the German High Command had not been alerted to the possible destination of the Allied convoys.

Satisfied that men, ships, tanks, guns, and landing craft were making their way safely into the Mediterranean, Ike returned to Combined Allied Headquarters deep in the bowels of Gibraltar. Half a mile inside the Rock, a war room 30 feet high had been cut out of solid stone. Huge maps hung on the walls. Here and in his underground office, Ike awaited the arrival of the one man he considered to be crucial to a successful invasion of French North Africa: Gen. Henri Giraud.

Giraud was living his own suspense story. He had supposedly made good his escape from France to a submarine, but no word had been received to confirm this. A garbled message arrived from the PBY amphibian sent to pick him up from the sub, which confused matters further. It was not until the PBY landed at the Gibraltar seaplane base with Giraud aboard that his arrival in time to be of help was certain.

The tall, gaunt Giraud, with a two-day growth of beard, weary and dishevelled in the civilian clothes in which he had made his escape from France, still had the imperious bearing of a commanding general of the French Empire when he alighted from the British command car with the officers who had brought him to headquarters.

Ike, anxious to show every courtesy to a brilliant and

courageous soldier and new ally, met him at the entrance to one of the endless Gibraltar tunnels.

"General Giraud!" Ike said warmly. "Welcome to freedom!"

He held out his hand, but Giraud ignored it preferring the French custom of greeting one's host with a kiss on each cheek, a ritual that Eisenhower was to go through many times after that, always with a slight sense of shock.

"It has been a long road," Giraud told him, through Col. Julius Holmes, of Ike's staff, who served as interpreter.

Eisenhower and Giraud started the walk down the long tunnel, heading for Eisenhower's war room, accompanied by the others. "I assure you," Giraud continued, "I am ready to take over full command immediately."

Ike was startled. He looked questioningly at Mark Clark, who had met Giraud at the seaplane base. Clark shrugged helplessly and told Ike he had tried to explain the situation, but in all the excitement it had obviously lost something in the translation by Col Holmes; Clark had thought it best not to try his own enfeebled French. The explanation, therefore, rested on the shoulders of the commander.

Giraud, not understanding the rapid exchange in English between the two, continued with his own thoughts. "Naturally," he said, "the first landings must occur near Marseilles. Then we must move quickly up the valley of the Rhone and split the Nazi forces in two. Then—Paris!"

Col. Holmes did his best to translate for both generals, perspiring as he realized he had become the focal point of a giant Franco-American misunderstanding.

"General Giraud . . ." Ike chose his words carefully, trying not to show his impatience. "You have been out of touch with the military situation. The landings will occur at dawn tomorrow. But not in France. In French Morocco and French Algeria—at the ports of Oran, Algiers, and Casablanca."

Giraud stopped short and stared at him in disbelief.

"Unbelievable! You are attacking neutral French possessions! The French Army and navy will resist you to the death!"

"That's exactly why we need your help." Eisenhower's tone was conciliatory, but he was finding it difficult to maintain his composure. Giraud's belief that he, himself, would be in command of whatever Allied operation was in progress bespoke an ignorance of Ike and his abilities that bordered on contempt.

They entered the war room, followed by the others.

"General Giraud," Ike explained, waiting impatiently for Col. Holmes to translate his words, "I understand your feelings. I, too, was in favor of an immediate landing in France. But we don't have the strength to throw ourselves at Germany's throat. Only here, in North Africa, where the Nazis and their Italian allies are weakest, can we get military superiority."

"America is not yet strong enough to attack in Europe? It speaks of poor planning."

"Whatever it speaks of, we have a chance right here to stop Rommel's drive for the oil of the Middle East and win the first major victory against German arms in this war. But you must order the French army and the French coast artillery in Morocco and Algeria not to fire on our landings. We are your allies."

Giraud's answer was immediate. "I must refuse. It is impossible."

"But, General Giraud—"

"I will take command only to return with a liberating army to the soil of France herself. For this reason I am here, for this reason only!"

"For God's sake, you've been rotting in a Nazi prison camp! Certainly you know *they* are the enemy, not us! You *must* broadcast an order to the French not to shoot at us. You're the only one they'll listen to!"

Giraud hesitated a moment, watching this upstart American commander closely.

"What will be my authority?" he inquired.

"I will immediately appoint you commander of all French armed forces in North Africa. You have my guarantee." Ike felt this was more than generous; it meant that de Gaulle would be bypassed.

"And what will be *your* authority?"

"Commander in Chief of the Allied forces in this theatre."

Giraud turned away so that he could hide his feelings. While he had no true idea of what Eisenhower was, this American had shown he hadn't the slightest knowledge of Giraud's place in the history and the hearts of the French nation. It was time to enlighten him.

"You do not understand," he said, his voice husky with suppressed emotion. "My country, my family, will not allow me to assume a subordinate command. I am Joffre. I am Foch. I am Giraud."

He turned now to confront this poorly informed American, one finger pointed heavenward. "I," he declared, "am France!"

"Well, dammit, I'm Ike Eisenhower!" Ike had turned red, his patience at an end. "I'm the toughest goddam Kansas farmer you ever tried to throw horseshit on!"

"Ike!" Clark was trying to flag his commander down, but it was like trying to stop an express train.

"You don't have one French soldier to command in this invasion except for the poor stupid bastards who are planning to shoot the wrong way! Your country surrendered to Hitler while most of its fighting forces were still intact! You've got a whole navy getting ready to blow the arms and legs off American kids who think all Frenchmen are like Lafayette. You've got a government in Vichy helping to ship French Jews to German concentration camps! And don't try to tell me you're God, General Giraud, because I know you're not. Charles de Gaulle is God—he told me so himself! Now you're going to get a microphone and tell the French navy and the French army we're trying to free your country, not hurt it, or by Christ I'll break you to Civilian, Second Class!"

104

There was shocked silence when Col. Holmes finished translating, but translation was hardly necessary. Ike's explosive anger had transcended language.

"Never have I been so outraged." Giraud was trembling with emotion. "General Henri Honoré Giraud is second in command to no one!" He stalked to the door and made a grand theatrical exit.

Suddenly, like the air going out of a balloon, all the antagonism drained out of Ike and he sagged into a chair.

"Dammit, Beetle," he said to his white-faced chief of staff, who realized, as Eisenhower now did, that there would be no broadcast order of a cease-fire to the French before the attack, "you've just seen a lesson in Kansas diplomacy. When am I going to learn to keep my mouth shut?" He sighed, out of deep weariness. "But by God, it felt good!"

Then he grinned, but only for a moment.

In the dim light of dawn, off the coast of Algeria, the fleets of Allied battleships and cruisers protecting the troopships drew within firing range of the coastal artillery. Off Morocco, the convoys from America reached their positions near Casablanca too soon, and circled in a formation 20 miles wide, awaiting the order to head for the beaches. By coded broadcasts, the French officers friendly to the Allies had been alerted that the invasion was imminent; but others, not so friendly, were soon to find out for themselves. At the prearranged moment, the convoys launched their landing craft, the troops climbing hand over hand down the cargo nets into the ungainly LVPs and LSTs.

"Citizens of France! This is General Eisenhower."

It was not, of course. It was Col. Holmes, speaking Eisenhower's words in French over the radio. "At dawn today, combined American and British forces began a landing on French North African territory. We come as friends. Our aim is to drive the German invaders not only out of Africa, but eventually out of France as well!"

The guns of the huge Casablanca fortress had now been alerted. The tricolor was run up the flagpole as morning light began to break through the mist. And now, from the radio, came a more familiar voice, Winston Churchill speaking in French, a language he liked to believe he spoke like a native. He didn't. *"Français!* Join hands with us against the Nazi beast! Men of the French navy and the French army—hold your fire! We are your allies! *Vive la France!"*

But the voice of Gen. Henri Giraud was silent.

The massive French cannon in the harbor fortifications opened fire, whistling huge shells 8 miles out to sea to explode beside the American and British war vessels and landing craft. The big guns of the Allied warships immediately opened up. The battle was joined, ferociously, the first time Frenchmen had fired on Englishmen since the days of Napoleon, except during the brief and abortive attack on the French fleet at Oran two years earlier.

In the war room, the nerve center of the Gibraltar fortress, Ike paced nervously, puffing at his cigarette as his night-long vigil continued. Mark Clark was stretched out on an army cot, trying to catch a little rest; Tex Lee was cat-napping on top of a desk. The room was almost silent as the enlisted men manning the radios listened in vain for reports of the battle. The few that did come through were often garbled in transmission; even the decoding machines could make little sense of the messages. The British were as helpless as the Americans. Adm. Sir Browne Cunningham, commander of the fleet in the Mediterranean, came in occasionally from his own office nearby in search of information, only to be told there was none. His chief of staff, Cdr. Royer Dick, stayed at Ike's side throughout the night.

The two radiomen, hunched over their command sets, held the key to the progress of the landings. Listening intently on the frequencies reserved for battle traffic, the dit-dah-dit of the Morse code occasionally breaking through the background noise in their earphones, the radio operators shook their heads in frustration. In this, the first large-scale offensive action for American troops, communications were proving to be just one more snafu in the job of shaking untested men into life-or-death situations. This was not NBC reporting the World Series; this was World War II, and it wouldn't be over in seven games.

For the tenth time, Ike crossed to the radioman with red hair, who kept his earphones tightly clamped to his head with his hands, as if that would help him to hear in the electronic silence.

"Are we ashore?" the commander wanted to know.

"No word yet, sir."

Ike could see that the radio operator took it personally, as if the failure of the ether to speak was his own fault.

Tex had been watching one of the chattering teletype machines. They were connected to London by cable and, unlike the radios, they were seldom still.

"Ike," he said, "take a look at this!" He rolled off the desk on which he had been resting and tore a dispatch off the machine, handing it to Eisenhower. "The British are already planning for the next six months. Reinforcements will leave regularly."

"I hope they can swim."

It was just like the methodical British. In a war where the next thirty seconds were in doubt, they were already certain of what should be done next June.

"There's even a message to us from Kay." Tex pointed to the dispatch. "She'll be leaving on the *Strathallen*, British troopship. Sometime next month."

"General!" The red-haired radio operator was halfway out of his chair. "The French at Casablanca fortress have opened fire on our ships!"

It was the first definite word to reach Gibraltar, and it was ominous.

"Damn!" Eisenhower had hoped against hope that even without Giraud's orders, the French would have sense enough not to resist.

"They've scored a hit at fourteen thousand yards!" It was the second operator, from British Signals, adding one more distressing note; 14,000 yards was beyond the range of many of the big guns of the convoys.

"Three of our paratroop planes shot down, sir!"

The reports were flooding in fast now, the CW signals chirping through the headsets as fast as the operators could write them down.

"Where the hell is George Patton and his task force from the States?" Ike demanded.

"We've lost contact with his ships, sir," the redhead said.

"Heavy firing in Algiers harbor, General. More French batteries shooting at us!"

"The French they are a funny race, *parlez-vous*." Mark Clark was still sprawled out on the cot, his long body hanging over the ends. Now Clark leaned over and turned on the broadcast radio, hoping for some news from the BBC.

"What a waste!" Ike said. "What a terrible waste!"

French and American soldiers were killing each other, and Hitler would dance another jig. What had gone wrong? Why hadn't he been able to sway the French? And where were George Patton and the huge convoys from America? They had been due to attack Casablanca hours ago.

"Oran Airport on fire, sir." The radio reports weren't helping.

"Ike!" Mark Clark indicated the broadcast radio, from which an aged French voice could be heard through the static.

"Marshal Pétain, broadcasting from Vichy," Clark explained. "He's ordering the French army and navy to resist us to the death!"

Ike leaned over to listen to the emotion-filled voice of the heroic soldier of World War I who had, tragically, helped his nation become the victim of Nazi tyranny.

"The poor old man," Ike said. "He's speaking with a German accent."

"Sir!" The soldier with the red hair was scribbling

furiously now on a message pad, the code signals resounding in his earphones. "General Patton radios he's ashore in force at Casablanca and kicking the hell out of the French!"

Eisenhower was at his side in a bound. "Good old George!" He fought back his emotion. American troops, green American troops, fresh out of basic training, were battling their way ashore, against heavy fire, on the continent of Africa.

"The frogs are throwing down their arms and coming over to our side!" shouted the operator.

That was even better news. The French officers who had offered their support were making good on their promises.

"Get a signal to Patton," Ike said. "Their guns are to be returned, and they are to be treated as allies, not frogs!"

"Yes, sir," the redhead answered, but his words could scarcely be heard over the pandemonium that had erupted in the office. British and American officers were pounding each other on the back. An Allied invasion—the first ever —and it was succeeding!

A sentry opened the war room door. "General Giraud," he announced.

The room quieted. They all turned to witness the entrance of the tall, haggard figure in the worn civilian suit. The sleepless eyes were burning with an emotion the proud old soldier had never before known—shame.

Giraud advanced directly to Eisenhower.

"It has been a terrible night," he said. "For France. For me. For you." He saluted. "General Henri Giraud places himself under your command."

Slowly, Ike extended his hand.

Slowly, Giraud took it.

VIII
North Africa

It was the first joint Anglo-American victory of the war. But it was scored over Frenchmen, not Germans. After the landings on the North African coast, Giraud had been flown into Algiers to exert his influence on the French military to bring about a general cease-fire. To everyone's surprise, including his own, none of the French paid any attention to him. Giraud was from another time, another war, another generation.

The cease-fire came from an unexpected direction. Admiral Darlan, second in command to Marshal Pétain at Vichy, was by chance in North Africa, visiting his son in an Algiers hospital. Darlan was taken into custody by Allied troops. Ike made a quick, military decision: deal with the devil. Darlan was made Chief of State in North Africa, in return for signing an order to the French to stop fighting. That ended it. But it also brought Ike the heaviest criticism of his career—for dealing with a known

French traitor, a lackey of the Nazis. The attacks in the American press were heavy; there was talk that Eisenhower might have to be replaced.

Dwight Eisenhower stood by his guns. The Darlan deal had saved lives.

But it wasn't enough. The Germans retaliated, massively. Reinforcements were flown into French North African airfields; the French, friendly and unfriendly, were thrust aside. Nazi troops brutally invaded all of southern France, ending the myth of Vichy independence. Hitler moved toward the French fleet in the harbor of Toulon, and the French scuttled most of their vessels. And as the Allied forces under Ike's control struck toward Tunisia and the port of Tunis, which would give them control of the western Mediterranean, they found themselves halted only 15 miles from the city by heavily reinforced German and Italian tanks, planes, and infantry. They had hoped to link up with Montgomery's forces attacking the Axis armies from the other side, in Libya.

The only good news came from Russia. The Nazi armies were retreating from Stalingrad.

In an effort to protect Rommel and the Afrika Korps from being shoved back in Libya by Montgomery and the British Eighth Army, Hitler ordered an increase in German submarine activity against Monty's supply lines in the Mediterranean. The subs, acting in wolfpacks as they did in the North Atlantic, began to take a heavy toll of Allied shipping; only Ultra, with its advance information on submarine locations, made it possible to deal effectively with this threat. But some of the German subs slipped through.

On the night of December 23, 1942, a German wolfpack penetrated an Allied convoy heading from the strait of Gibraltar toward the North African coast. The U-boats rose silently from the bottom to periscope depth, levelling out just below the surface. In the cross hairs of his periscope, a German submarine officer carefully lined up the hull of an unsuspecting British troop transport zigzagging its way through heavy swells. He was close enough to read the name on its side: SS *Strathellen*.

In Kay's tiny cabin belowdecks, she and her bunkmates—Jane Armstrong, a pretty British nurse, and Mary Vance, an American WAC officer—had made a pathetic attempt to put up some Christmas decorations. They were all exhausted. For five days the ship had been battered by storms with waves over 60 feet high. Some of the furniture had to be roped down. One night the piano in the lounge broke loose and slammed across the floor into the wall with a crash of mahogany and a twanging of piano wires that Kay had dubbed "The Lost Chord." But tonight the seas were calm, and the women were preparing for bed in a mood of suppressed excitement—tomorrow morning they would be landing at Oran, and Kay knew that Dick Arnold was somewhere in the area. Before climbing into her bunk, she opened her steamer trunk and showed the other girls the little trousseau she had gotten together for the moment when she and Dick could manage a wedding. She held up the sheer nightgown made of silk, so rare in wartime she had had to use all her connections from her modeling days to secure just enough. Kay wasn't going to be cheated of a proper honeymoon; the nightgown was—

A tremendous blast knocked her off her feet, rolled her companions out of their bunks, and sent a shudder through the length and breadth of the *Strathallen*. The lights went out. Steam hissed from the shattered boiler room. The entire ship shuddered like a sick whale.

"Don't panic! Don't panic!" Jane Armstrong shouted at the top of her lungs, scrambling for the door.

"For God's sake, Jane, act British and shut up! Who's got the torch?" It was Kay, unflappable Kay. Mary Vance found a flashlight and lit it.

"Grab the bloody lifejackets and let's get to our stations!" Kay ordered as the alarm siren wailed. Another explosion staggered the ship. The cabin tilted to one side.

"Oh, God, please!" Kay implored. "Not yet, not till I've had a chance to wear my gorgeous nightie!"

She clutched it to her as Jane threw open the cabin door, to be met by a flood of water from the companionway. "We're drowning!" Jane wailed again.

Kay shoved her through the door. "Get your bloomin' arse up on deck!" she instructed, and they fought their way above.

The scene on deck was a nightmare. Fire had broken out; half-dressed soldiers and nurses were struggling through choking billows of smoke to find their boat stations. Ships nearby were hurling depth charges after the submarines, sending fountains of water skyrocketing into the air. All about them machine guns chattered and cannons barked.

Kay and Jane and Mary found their lifeboat. They were joined by frightened nurses in odds and ends of clothing, and by Margaret Bourke-White, the photographer from *Life* Magazine with whom Kay had struck up an acquaintance. Margaret had managed to save two of her cameras, all that really mattered to her, and she lamented the fact that there wasn't enough light to shoot pictures of the half-dressed, barefoot nurses fighting their way past her into the lifeboat. As the crew started to swing the boat out on the davit, a nearby window exploded from the heat of the fire, showering them with broken glass. Some of the girls shrieked in panic and leaped to their feet, almost capsizing the lifeboat against the side of the ship. Kay grabbed two of the girls and hauled them down.

"Sit down!" she shouted. "You fools must learn to obey orders! Discipline, dammit, *discipline!*"

Her sudden vehemence frightened them into obedience.

"Good God, Kay," Jane told her, "you sound just like that bahstard Eisenhower!"

Kay looked at her. "Thank heaven *somebody* does," she answered. And for the first time, perhaps, she understood.

There was another explosion somewhere amidships, and the ship heeled violently, almost throwing them into the water. Fire shot out of the hull. The tiny boat disappeared into the smoke. Another ship had been hit, somewhere over the green water, and the sea was dotted with sailors and soldiers crying out to be pulled aboard the boats. The firing from the warships continued, but the enemy could not be found. That was the most frightening of all. They had come out of nowhere, disappeared into nowhere. Silent. Deadly.

Gen. Bedell Smith ripped the dispatch out of the decoding machine and started through the communications room in the St. George Hotel, Allied headquarters in the city of Algiers. It was late at night, but there were no office hours during wartime. The teletype machines clattered away; radio operators flipped rapid-fire Morse through their Vibroplex bugs; messages to and from the various fronts crackled over the air; the decoding machines were worked to their limit.

Beetle hurried into the office where Eisenhower and some of his aides were marking the latest battle lines on a map.

"Ike!" he called.

Eisenhower recognized the urgency in his chief of staff's voice. Beetle was a professional soldier, given to underplaying the most critical moments; now, however, he seemed genuinely disturbed.

"There's a report here from the British navy," Beetle reported. "Four ships have been torpedoed heading for Oran. One of them is the *Strathallen*."

For the moment, it didn't register. Ship losses were almost too common in this war of supply. But the *Strathallen?* Why did that ring a bell?

"That's the troop transport Kay Summersby is aboard." Gen. Smith hesitated. "*Was* aboard."

Ike's face went white.

"They're picking up survivors," Beetle said. "That's all we know."

"Let me see that!"

Ike took the dispatch from Beetle's hand and read it carefully. He could not explain the feeling that went through

115

him. Many men he had known, many officers he had been close to, had been killed in the landings, and somehow he had found a way to harden himself against it.

This was different. He hadn't realized how much this arrogant, auburn-haired, stubbornly Irish girl with her open laughter and warm heart had come to mean to him in his overpowering job. The thought that she might be in a tiny lifeboat somewhere on the open sea, or tossing in the freezing waters in a lifejacket, or fighting for air in the bulkheads of a sunken ship that would never surface again, made him sick with guilt, with the overpowering knowledge that her death, if it had come, was his sole responsibility.

Ike crossed slowly to his desk, where Telek, the puppy who had been his birthday present at Telegraph Cottage, leaped from the floor to greet him. He waved the eager animal aside and sat down, still holding the dispatch. The war had become an intensely personal thing.

"I could have arranged to have her travel with us by air," Ike said. "I brought the dog."

It was true. Telek had been taken to Gibraltar, then flown to Algiers in a transport plane along with Tex Lee and Mickey McKeogh.

And some office furniture.

The lifeboat floated until dawn, picking up survivors whenever possible. The girls helped the Lascar crew at the oars—the Lascars were kitchen help, from Portuguese Goa, not much given to rowing. With the first light, Margaret Bourke-White started to take pictures, bracing herself against the gunwales of the pitching boat. One soldier was dying, having been dashed against the side of the *Strathallen* while trying to escape; a nurse had a broken leg, which her friends set as well as they could. Kay did her best to keep spirits up, loudly ordering breakfast in bed in the morning —"Two eggs, sunny side up, and no yolks broken," as Margaret would later report in *Life*.

A British destroyer hove into sight after dawn, and soon they were all aboard, searching for friends they had feared drowned, laughing and crying when the friends were found. They landed finally at the port of Oran.

Kay had somehow salvaged her lipstick and did the best she could to make herself look presentable in case, improbably, she should find Dick in Oran.

She was just climbing from the destroyer's gig onto the dock—her hair a mess, barefoot, wearing a huge great-coat loaned her by a sailor—when, to her utter shock, she saw him. He was Lt. Col. Arnold now, and he had come down to the port to check on survivors. He hadn't the slightest notion Kay was anywhere but in England—and then she came flying into his arms.

"Kay! How the hell did you get to North Africa?"

"Oh, Dick, Dick!" She was almost sobbing with happiness. "It's too long a story, much too long." She kissed him frantically. "I was torpedoed! It was wet and awful— all that matters is that I'm here and that you're here!" She searched in the paper bag she was carrying and pulled out the silk nightgown. "I carried this bloomin' nightgown with me all the way for our wedding night—and now that your divorce is final, I don't want to wait one minute!"

It was true. Dick had written her that his wife had finally consented to a settlement.

Kay held up the tattered nightgown for him to see. "We hauled the wounded into our boat," she explained, "and we had to tear some of the nightie up for bandages, but I only tore it where you won't miss it—and oh, darling, you know what you can do for me right now?"

"What?" Dick inquired nervously, eyeing the group that had gathered about them.

"Get me a dreadful American hamburger, please!" Kay pleaded.

Gen. Dwight David Eisenhower arranged for Kay to be brought from Oran to his headquarters in Algeria. The relief in his voice when she had telephoned him was so un-like him that Kay was to remember it—and wonder.

On February 22, 1943, the photographs Margaret

Bourke-White had taken, and her description of "General Eisenhower's pretty Irish driver," appeared in the pages of *Life*.

The stir they caused was to haunt Kay Summersby the rest of her life.

XII
Kasserine Pass

On Christmas Eve of 1942, Adm. Jean François Darlan was assassinated in Algiers. The intrigue surrounding the assassination involved the Chief of Police of Algiers and the Free French forces of Gen. Charles de Gaulle. No direct connection was proved, but the fragmentation of the French in North Africa continued. Gen. Henri Giraud was persuaded to take over for Darlan. Since no one seemed to listen to Giraud anyway, he was the perfect man to assume control of the uncontrollable.

It was the beginning of a series of setbacks for Ike Eisenhower that brought his career to its lowest ebb since the start of the war. It was a period of despair and frustration that affected him, personally, far beyond what he allowed those around him to see. Only Kay Summersby was to become aware of its full meaning.

First came the rains and the mud, bogging down Allied motorized equipment in quagmires so deep it sometimes took four men to push a single motorcycle to firm ground. Ike assumed command of the battlefront and stationed French troops in the center of the lines, between the Americans and the English. The French, using antiquated World War I artillery, proved the weak link in the line Eisenhower had extended toward Tunis. Then Erwin Rommel, thought to be so weakened by Montgomery's forces that he could only retreat, suddenly wheeled his Afrika Korps tanks around and smashed through green American troops, giving them one of the worst defeats in American military history at a place few Americans had ever heard of before—Kasserine Pass. Rommel's tough, experienced Nazi fighters completely out-maneuvered and overwhelmed the Yanks, leaving the battle area littered with bodies and burned-out tanks. Rommel and his men took no prisoners. They were heading for the coast and a link-up with the forces of Gen. von Arnim, a link-up which would cut the Allies in two and possibly force them out of North Africa. The Desert Fox had again proved his mastery of armored warfare.

Eisenhower, although he had only recently recovered from a bout with the flu, was on his way immediately to make a personal reconnaissance of the situation. With Kay at the wheel, he drove through the ancient city of Tebessa toward the headquarters of Gen. Ward Hoffenberg, commander of the Kasserine salient. He was accompanied by Maj. Gen. Lucian Truscott, whom Ike had placed as his representative at a forward command post in the area.

The devastation was all around them. American armor and infantry streamed along the road in a sea of mud, moving up to new positions, passing the burned-out tanks and guns that marked Rommel's deepest penetration. Away from the road, on top of a hill where an American tank unit had made a last-ditch stand, Ike saw something that chilled his blood. He ordered Kay to stop the car and picked up his fieldglasses for a closer view.

Arab men and women from a wandering tribe had descended on the battlefield en masse and were looting the dead, stripping the bloody American bodies of shoes and clothing, of anything saleable in the bazaars, then loading the loot onto camels.

"Goddamit!" Ike said. "Where the hell are our burial details?"

"Hate to say it, Ike, but they're overworked in this area." Truscott was just as disturbed, just as helpless.

"Can't we get some guns trained on them up there and drive those vultures off?"

"No guns to spare. Besides, it's too touchy. Can't antagonize the Arabs, we need 'em."

Ike lowered the glasses wearily and motioned Kay to drive on. "I know," he said. It was the political half of his job that he hated most. "There was hell to pay when I made Darlan get rid of those anti-Semitic laws the Nazis put in in Algeria. The Arabs sent a delegation to me to protest. Know what the leader said to me?"

Truscott shook his head.

"He said, 'What a pity it is the Eisenhower family is Jewish.' "

"My Lord!" It was Kay, from the front seat. "What did you say?" She too had heard the propaganda from the other side.

"Oh, I just said, 'No, sir, what a pity it is that we're not.' " Ike smiled grimly. "After that, they made all their protests to the British."

There was a sudden warning shout from some infantrymen nearby. Out of the heavy clouds, a lone German fighter plane on a reconnaissance mission plummeted down toward the armored column, the machine guns in its nose blinking death. Everywhere Americans dove for the protection of the mud and the ditches, and tanks tried desperately to swing their guns around on a target that was zigzagging at them at hundreds of miles an hour. Kay swerved the car off the road, and they leaped out into a confused mass of soldiers diving in all directions for cover. The plane passed overhead, bullets kicking up the mud at the side of the road.

It was gone so quickly that there was barely time to realize what had happened.

"Good God!" breathed Kay. "That was too dreadfully close for comfort!"

"He's coming back!" Ike called, watching the plane as it swerved over the mountaintop. "Hit the dirt!"

Truscott dove instantly into a muddy ditch. Kay hesitated a fraction of a second, then felt something hit her heavily from behind, driving her head first into the mud. It was Ike, throwing his body over hers as the Messerschmitt roared over them, bullets kicking into the road and clanging off the side of a nearby tank. A moment later, the plane had vanished into the clouds.

Infantrymen dragged themselves out of the ditches; tanks swung back onto the road. Ike got to his feet and helped Kay to rise. The mud had streaked her from head to toe. She was dripping, angry, her clothes and hair a mess.

"This is the only decent uniform I have left," she cried. "I have to get *married* in it!"

Ike turned away from her. "I'm sorry, Miss Summersby," he said quietly and climbed back into the car.

Kay was instantly contrite. It had been a reflex reaction; she hadn't meant it quite the way it sounded. But she *had* said it—there was no taking it back.

"I forgot to say, 'Thank you,' didn't I?" she said.

Truscott threw her a meaningful look. "You bet your stupid ass," he growled, and joined Ike in the car.

They drove up to a sandbagged, concrete-reinforced structure that had been blasted out of the solid rock of an Algerian mountainside. A myriad of Army Engineers labored to complete it, in the midst of hurried military activity all around. Kay brought the car to a halt on the crushed gravel of the carefully constructed driveway, a contrast to the mud and ruts of the surrounding mountain roads.

Ike rose to his feet in the command car and stared

at the building in disbelief. "What the hell is this?" he demanded of Truscott.

"General Hoffenberg's command post. A whole company of combat engineers has been working night and day to build it. It's bombproof."

Ike stared at the massive structure, and his jaw hardened. "Until now," he said. He leaped from the car.

Everything was shiny new, right out of the crates from the U.S.A. Desks, lamps, maps. Hoffenberg's underground headquarters contained a complete communications setup, kitchen, bath, some carved objects of North African art. It also contained Gen. Ward G. Hoffenberg, wishing desperately that he were anywhere else. He was the object of the kind of chewing out Dwight Eisenhower was to become famous for; in wartime, Ike had discovered, the fact that an officer had attended West Point was no guarantee he was not an idiot. Ike's toughest job was to rid his command of old friends who had fouled up; or, tougher still, had not *yet* fouled up, but showed evidence they were on the way.

"Dammit, Ward, your troops controlled the passes, you had the artillery, and you let Rommel's Panzers surprise you! Now there are fifteen hundred American boys lying dead in the Algerian mud, being picked over like hogs in a slaughterhouse!" It had been Ike's closest contact with the horror and reality of war. His voice shook.

"Ike!" Hoffenberg was not in a mood to admit mistakes; his command might very well hinge on this confrontation. "The French wouldn't take orders from me, the British wouldn't take orders from *anybody*, and—"

"Why the hell should they, when you're sitting here in your mink-lined foxhole seventy miles behind the front, getting the battle *phoned* in?"

"My communications functioned perfectly, and I find being away from the front gives me perspective."

"That's a new word for chicken shit!" Ike had no time for niceties. "Ward," he said, trying to hold his voice level, "within twenty-four hours I want you to launch an attack against Rommel with everything we've got!"

"It'll take a lot longer than that just to perfect our defenses."

"You didn't hear me, Ward." Ike had lit a cigarette, and now he was pointing it at Hoffenberg, emphasizing every word. "I said: 'attack'. I'm taking full responsibility. Now, where's the best place to hit, and with what?"

Hoffenberg felt his confidence returning. He had planned for a period of regrouping, but the attack plan was already worked out. He picked up a pointer and crossed to a huge map of the sector.

"Right here on the Fondouk-Sbeitla road," he said, indicating a crossroad. "We'll start with the 18th Armored and the 26th Infantry."

Eisenhower drove straight for the jugular. "Have you personally seen the terrain at the Fondouk road? Have you looked over the Fourth Armored's tanks?"

Gen. Hoffenberg picked a sheaf of papers off his desk. "I have all the reports right here, and you can——"

Ike snatched the papers out of his hand and threw them on the floor. The veins in his forehead stood out; his anger was barely under control.

"Erwin Rommel wrote a book once, Ward. I memorized almost every word, because I knew I'd have to fight the brilliant son of a bitch some day. He said, 'Nothing can take the place of the Commander at the front. Let the men see you. The higher the rank, the greater the example of the Commander on the men.' "

"In that case, Ike, maybe *you* should go." Hoffenberg's anger had gotten the best of him. This was close to insubordination, and he knew it. But he wasn't going to be lectured in front of his own men. Many of his staff were present; there were enlisted men at the radios pretending to be listening to their headphones. He could see the exchange of glances.

"Okay, Ward." Ike picked up his jacket and helmet,

and motioned to Truscott. "That's exactly what I will do. And if you screw up again, I'm kicking your tail back to the U.S. and putting George Patton in command here. Get me a jeep and a driver, and tell him to get me as close to the front as he can." He started for the entrance, then paused. "And Ward," he added, "if Rommel attacks, I'll phone you. Don't let it ring more than once."

Night had fallen by the time Ike, Truscott, and an escort party had bumped their jeeps up a rocky, muddy trail to the top of a mountain, where a camouflaged American artillery unit was hurling shells into the darkness, the huge guns bucking like steers on the recoil, the muzzle flashes lighting up the area. A grimy gun crew, stripped to the waist, was feeding shells into the maw of the hungry cannon. The young lieutenant in command turned as the jeeps approached, then suddenly snapped to attention.

"Jesus!" he said. Men in Hoffenberg's command were not accustomed to seeing high-ranking officers in exposed forward positions. "It's Ike! Cease firing!"

He saluted. The gun crews paused, a shell halfway to the breech of the closest gun.

Ike leaped out of his jeep. "Keep shooting," he ordered the lieutenant, "I'll feel a lot safer."

He started forward, followed by Truscott. The lieutenant signalled the men: business as usual. The shell was slammed into the breech, it clanged shut, a sergeant yanked the lanyard, and the gun blasted another charge of steel and TNT into the night sky.

Ike had paused beside a shattered tree. Below him stretched the dark mountainside, and beyond that the Algerian desert, dotted with occasional blossoms of fire from enemy guns.

Truscott pointed. "That's the Fondouk road down there. Rommel's HQ is just the other side of that rise."

Ike raised his glasses to look. "He's close enough to the front to holler 'Charge' without leaving his tent," he said. But he knew Rommel's method involved continuous movement. He wouldn't stay in that tent long. "Question is," Ike mused, "can our tanks move in that mud?"

He lowered the glasses and turned away. Nearby, several crews were working over tanks damaged in the previous attacks; the men were sweaty, grimy, laboring feverishly. Ike crossed to the closest tank. Beside it, a battered private was stretched out in the mud on his stomach, working with wrench and hammer on the treads.

"Soldier?"

The private looked up, dropped his wrench, and started to scramble to his feet.

"Don't stop," Ike ordered. "I just want to find out how these machines are doing."

The private picked up his wrench and banged on the damaged tread. "If this was a woman, I'd kick her outta my friggin' bed. Sir," he added.

Ike kneeled beside him, took out his cigarettes and offered one. He had found this the best way of breaking the barrier between officer and enlisted man. The borrowed cigarette was to become another Eisenhower trademark.

"What's wrong with it?" Ike wanted to know. He slipped on his glasses to inspect the armorplate.

The private squatted on his heels and lit up. Ike's natural warmth made such questions sound honest, his interest real. The enlisted men opened up to him in a way they did not to other officers. Ike's manner, Ike's grin, Ike's soldierly attitude, cut through the bullshit. For the moment, he was one of them.

"Listen, sir." The private was still cautious. "You just makin' publicity, or you really wanna know?"

"It's my ass as well as yours."

That did it. The private banged the side of the tank with his wrench. "It's a friggin' coffin, sir. Got a 37mm gun couldn't put a scratch on a whore's tit."

An interested group had gathered about them now. A grimy sergeant spoke up. "Supply give us training ammo, sir, instead of armor-piercing."

"Why was that?"

The Sergeant shrugged. "All they had." He indicated the tank, pockmarked with the evidences of battle, and stuck his fist into a hole in the armor. "Krauts are using stuff goes right through the plates. What the hell, I guess back home they need all the good steel for Cadillacs!"

A corporal, standing in the open turret of the tank, swung its machine gun around. "Ever fire one of these guns, General?"

"No."

"Belt boxes so loose, they jam if you spit on 'em. And you gotta open the hatch like this to fire at a plane. If a Stuka dives, it's 'Goodbye, Charley.' "

Ike knew that American tanks were inadequate opponents for the heavily armored German Tiger Tanks with their 88mm guns. But, at the time, they were all the United States had been able to ship. Bigger, heavier, better-armed machines were now being loaded at East Coast ports.

"New Sherman tanks are on their way," he assured the corporal.

The soldier turned slowly, pointing. "Four of my buddies are on their way, sir," he said. "They're bringin' them in now."

Ike looked. There, on the far side of the burned-out tanks, a burial detail was carrying in battered bodies from lower down on the hillside, placing them in neat rows. The scene was lit fitfully by the flashes from the artillery nearby. Some of the bodies had been stripped naked. One, incongruously, still had his boots on, but that was all. Another was missing the ring finger on his right hand. A medic moved down the line, checking for signs of life, pulling blankets over the faces of those beyond hope.

Eisenhower moved slowly toward them. He stared down at the bodies, most of them bloody, eyes staring sightlessly into space. All of them seemed desperately young. After a moment, he turned abruptly away from the sight and strode angrily back to where Gen. Truscott stood watching him sympathetically.

"Goddammit, Luke!" Never before, never again in this awful war, would Eisenhower allow anyone to see him with wet eyes. But now he was too angry to care. "This is all my stupid fault! I gave the order to take a long-shot gamble to capture Tunis before we were ready. I was too damn stubborn to admit we'd failed, and I didn't order a pullback. I was wrong and that smart son of a bitch Rommel saw we were overextended and took advantage of it."

He turned to look back toward the line of stretcher-bearers, still climbing the hillside from below, then continued. "So thousands of green troops die in the mud while their green commander in chief is still alive and sitting behind a stupid desk."

"You didn't get much help from your commanders in the field, Ike."

Ike whirled on Truscott.

"Who picked them?" he demanded. "*I* did. The commander is always responsible, Luke. You know that. I'm responsible for this whole horrible mess."

He turned to look at the young, crumpled bodies. A medic pulled a blanket over the face of the soldier nearest him.

Ike took off his glasses and wiped them. "I've never seen men die in battle before," he said huskily. "I wish to hell some of those poor kids would close their eyes."

IX
The End of
the Beginning

The tide turned. Ike sent Gen. Hoffenberg back to the United States. West Point ties were still strong; the official reason given was that Hoffenberg's battle experience was needed in the training of new troops. Rommel moved again, seizing Faid Pass in a lightning action, but his supplies were running low, and Ike's reorganized forces kept him from breaking through to the Mediterranean coast. Montgomery counter-punched from the East, broke the Afrika Korps defenses and drove them 30 miles beyond Tripoli, continuing the assault without letup. Tens of thousands of Axis troops surrendered.

Shortly after the battle, a camouflaged RAF observation plane circled Tulergma airdrome on the outskirts of Algiers. As the graceful aircraft touched down and the pilot cut the engines, a jaunty figure in an old army sweater and shapeless corduroy trousers vaulted from the rear cockpit, Field Marshal's rank visible on his beret—Sir Bernard

Law Montgomery in battle dress. An honor guard of American desert troops was drawn up on the dusty runway behind Dwight Eisenhower and another officer whose uniform sported a blaze of decorations. He wore riding breeches and a polished nickel-plated helmet; a brace of white-handled revolvers was jammed into holsters on his belt. Gen. George S. Patton never traveled incognito.

"Ike, old chap!" Monty called out cheerily, as he crossed toward them. "Devilish good to see you again!" It was, for Montgomery. His forces had won another smashing victory; Ike had barely survived the defeat at Kasserine.

"Monty!" Ike extended his hand. "My congratulations on breaking through the Mareth Line." That had been the Afrika Korps's main defense, running along the Tunisian border. Montgomery had massed a thousand artillery pieces and an overwhelming force of tanks and infantry in a night attack that had finally smashed it.

"As you British say," Ike added with a grin, " 'Good show!' You've really got Rommel on the run."

"That's when he's most dangerous—as you learned to your sorrow at Kasserine. I could have predicted that."

Ike's grin faded. "Too bad you didn't," he said. Obviously, Monty was still Monty. He turned and indicated Patton. "I've relieved General Hoffenberg of his command. General Patton here is taking over for him."

Patton and Montgomery eyed each other. From now on, they would be allies in combat, but deadly opponents in the battle for headlines. Even now, as the group of photographers gathered for the occasion got into position, Monty was maneuvering to display his best side.

"George is our leading tank expert and the best commander we have for the job," Ike continued.

Monty extended his hand toward Patton, one eye on the cameras. "Delighted," he said. "I've heard so much about you General. Up until this moment, I didn't believe it. Pearl-handled, aren't they?" He stared at Patton's gleaming pistols.

"Ivory," Patton growled. "And I use them. Let's cut the bullshit, General Montgomery. Just remember we're all butchers here. Our job is to kill krauts, and I can't wait to get on with it."

He posed, hands on revolvers, chin tilted at an angle, awaiting the photographers' flashbulbs.

"George, you can relax." Ike grinned at his old friend. "I think they're out of film." He waved the photographers off and motioned the other officers to follow him out on the tarmac, where they would be out of earshot. There was no time for the formality of a meeting at headquarters; the war pressed in on them. They walked through the dust, side by side. Behind them, combat planes took off with a roar, circled, then headed for the battle lines.

"Ike, old chap," Montgomery expounded, "if I may suggest a course of action to capture Tunis quickly: you Americans just hang on to your present positions. My British Desert Rats are tough, experienced fighters. They will do the work better if there's no one cluttering things up."

Patton exploded like a grenade. "The hell they will!" he shouted, his face reddening.

"George, shut up!" Ike knew this had to be a joint Allied operation; there was no point in antagonizing Montgomery now.

Patton didn't even hear him. "Once we get our tanks and armor out of the hills and into the open desert, we're going to kick your British tails out of our way and shove the krauts up to their ass in the Mediterranean!"

"George!" Ike was angry now. "We stopped fighting the British in 1812!"

"Well, I wasn't there," Patton growled.

"A good thing, I dare say," Monty smiled.

Ike took him by the arm and tried to steer him away from Patton. "Monty, this coming attack must be a joint Allied effort," he explained. Soothingly, he thought. "I want American troops bloodied in battle so they'll be ready—

131

God help them—for the real show to come in Europe. With General Patton in command of our men and our tanks, American forces will win their share of battles to come, I promise you."

"You told me the same thing about your famous General Hoffenberg."

It was Ike's turn to grow red. "I got rid of Hoffenberg, and I'll get rid of anybody else who can't handle his job!"

"That's fascinating, Ike," Monty murmured. And then he added pleasantly, "By the way, if your inexperienced American troops are defeated again, who, may I ask, gets rid of *you?*"

* * *

With Montgomery and Patton vying for victories, Allied forces completed the rout of Rommel and the Afrika Korps in a few weeks. The Germans deserted their Italian allies in the middle of the desert, taking all the Italian armor and transport with them. The Italians immediately surrendered to whoever was nearest—including, the story went, a couple of passing camels. (There was also a report that the Allies were dropping leaflets to the Italian infantry, promising free transportation to the United States. Ike's remark, when he heard it, was typical: "I hope they weren't signed.") Finally, the Nazis caved in. Ultra had helped betray their supply ships, their submarines, their plight, their isolation. So many Germans surrendered that Ike complained that West Point had never taught him how to handle 300,000 prisoners of war. It was a victory matching the one the Russians had just scored at Stalingrad.

The triumph inspired Winston Churchill to another of his moments of memorable oratory. He told the British Parliament, "Due in no small measure to General Montgomery's brilliant strategy, Allied forces have caught Rommel's vaunted Afrika Korps in a giant pincer of tanks and armor. The Nazis have received back again that measure of fire and steel they have so often meted out to others.

Now this is not the end, nor is it the beginning of the end. But it is, perhaps, the end of the beginning."

The Allies celebrated the occasion with a huge parade in Tunis which included everything from American fighter planes to the white Arabian chargers of the French colonial troops. Kilted Scots slow-marched to the music of bagpipes; Sherman tanks rolled by the reviewing stand with a clanging of steel treads; British Tommies, American GI's, and French troops of various loyalties marched by in separate units—for the French were still divided among themselves.

Eisenhower, in full dress uniform, stood at the front of the reviewing platform, receiving the cheers of the crowd and the salute of the marching men. Beside him stood the proud, ramrod-straight figure of General Henri Giraud. Conspicuously missing was the equally imposing figure of General Charles de Gaulle, who, at that very moment, was battling to have Giraud removed from command.

At the height of the ceremony, Giraud, in a gesture whose significance caused Ike to tense with an emotion only a soldier could appreciate, removed from his own tunic his faded World War I Croix de Guerre and pinned it on the breast of the American commander he had at first opposed: Dwight David Eisenhower.

As the dignified French commander kissed him on both cheeks, Ike seized the moment.

"General Giraud," he said quietly, "I am deeply moved and deeply grateful. I would be even more grateful if you and General de Gaulle would settle your differences and move forward together for the glory of France."

The old soldier understood. The war might well be shortened by days, by weeks, by months, if all the French combined against the hated Germans, dropped their petty differences for the common good, if Henry Giraud stood shoulder to shoulder with that other great Frenchman, Charles de Gaulle.

Giraud did not hesitate. "Never!" he said.

The band struck up "La Marseillaise." Gen. Henri Giraud snapped to salute.

At Ike's insistence, Kay and Tex had been included in the group on the reviewing stand. It was the first major Allied victory over German arms, and he felt they deserved to witness the celebration.

This had been a grand show, Kay thought—the kilted Scots, the beautiful horses. Lovely, that's all war should be, parades, uniforms. She paused at Ike's side as the group on the platform was breaking up at the conclusion of the ceremony.

"I'll get the car, General," she said, and delivered one of her patented salutes. This one was only medium sloppy.

Ike grinned. "You're learning," he said. "Slowly."

She laughed and moved off into the throng of spectators and soldiers crowding the street. It was warm and sunny, victory was in the air, and the war itself had been pushed out of this corner of the world. There was time to think of things as ordinary as love. And marriage. She smiled to herself. Dick had been promoted; he was now a full colonel. With the fighting over, there might even be time for a honeymoon before his division was reassigned. Kay was sure she could wangle sufficient time off from Eisenhower. He seemed to have given Kay a special place in his official family; they were bridge partners often, since bridge was one of Ike's passions and Kay was a good player. He sometimes talked to her of his fears, his plans, his problems. She had come to admire him for his honesty, his openness, his quick grin, and his ready understanding; rank meant little to him except in the strictest military sense. He was nice, he was comfortable, and she enjoyed being around him. Especially since she knew that, when necessary, she could be feminine enough to twist him around her little finger. A week off for a honeymoon? Two? How about for the duration? Kay laughed aloud, then caught herself. Two French soldiers were staring at her as if she were out of her mind. Well, the whole world had gone crazy, why not Kay Summersby?

Tex Lee, who had waited patiently on the platform until Kay was gone, now pushed his way through a little knot of officers to Ike's side.

"Sir," he said. His voice was choked, strange.

Ike turned.

"Didn't want to spoil the celebration." Tex handed Eisenhower a teletyped message. "Came through this morning."

Ike stared at the matter-of-fact list. Name, rank, serial number. KIA, that was the official abbreviation. KIA. Killed in action.

She was still bubbling as she drove the khaki Packard, with Ike in the rear, up the winding road to the picturesque villa on top of the hill overlooking Algiers. The Villa dar el Ouad, it was called, and it had been commandeered for the Commanding General. Despite his protestations that he didn't want to live in anything so plush. But he had gradually overcome his objections; the villa had an extensive stable and some excellent riding horses. Ike, the Kansas farm boy, dearly loved to ride.

He seemed unnecessarily glum, Kay thought, after that smashing parade; perhaps this was not the right time to approach him about taking off for the honeymoon. First, she'd better cheer him up.

"Lovely parade, General," she said pleasantly, as the car halted for the sentries to open the gates. "I adore those Arabian horses. It's like being at a circus. Without any of the candy floss, of course."

She drove through the ornamented Arabic gateway to the courtyard of the villa. A peddler was leading a camel across. Some of the Moroccan women on the household staff, barefoot and veiled, were sweeping off the huge porches. It was, Kay felt, like something out of the Arabian Nights—if the Caliph of Baghdad had driven a Packard.

"Do you ride, Kay?" It was Ike, startling her out of her reverie. In the rear-view mirror, she could see that his expression was grim.

135

"Good Lord, I told you my father was in the cavalry. Had me on a horse before my diapers were dry."

Not a smile.

"We have Arabian horses here at the villa. Would you like to ride with me this afternoon?"

She was surprised. She'd never been invited to ride before. "Oh, I'd love to, but I have no riding clothes, no scarf, no nothing. No, thank you awfully, I really couldn't."

"You'll ride in what you have on."

"But, General—"

"That's an *order*."

His jaw was set. Kay knew better than to protest further.

The stables were at the rear of the villa, and the trail from them led into the valley below. After the heavy rains, the Moroccan hills had turned green; they were dotted with the short-lived flowers that would soon burn off in the heat of spring and summer. Ike had selected two of the white Arabians for them to ride. Kay thought she had never seen such splendid animals—sleek, newly curried, spirited. She walked with Ike from the stables to the mounting block, where she prepared to swing herself into her saddle. She had managed to scrounge a pair of trousers at the villa, and although they were GI and she felt she looked a little foolish, at least they were more practical for riding than her uniform skirt. Ike had scarcely spoken a word since they had left the car; whatever was on his mind must be terribly important. Perhaps he was going to tell her that another landing was going to take place, possibly in Italy or France, and that he couldn't spare her any time at all for the honeymoon. Well, she would fight that. She had earned her time off, and she would damn well insist on having it, war or no war.

"Kay," he said. At his tone, her head turned sharply. "I have to give it to you straight."

Her heart sank like a stone. Suddenly she knew exactly what he was going to say.

"It's Dick," he told her.

She had known. But she heard herself saying, "No. Please, no."

Ike took her hand in his.

"You were so right about him, Kay. An engineer, yet, he didn't see his own trip wire. Fighting was over. Walking through a minefield, well marked."

She was frozen, unable to utter a sound.

"The Captain who was with him is in a field hospital. He'll recover. Dick—Colonel Arnold—was killed instantly."

Kay sucked in her breath, the hurt almost too sharp to bear. She pulled her hand out of Eisenhower's grasp. It was a general's hand; she didn't want to feel the touch of a general's hand again, ever.

" 'Sorry' is such an inadequate word," he told her. "I hope you understand how I feel."

Very quietly, Kay said, "How *do* you feel, General, now that you've killed him?"

"Kay!" He held his hand out to her again, and she slapped it away, all her emotions tumbling loose at once.

"You killed him! You and the other filthy merchants of death, with your parades and your bugles, pinning medals on each other!" Kay Summersby, unflappable Summersby, who had endured so much, finally could endure no more. "Poor Dick, poor gentle Richard, he wouldn't hurt a fly, but he wanted to play with the big boys, and so you taught him all you knew, and you thought he was listening and he didn't understand, he never really could understand!"

Ike stood in silence, feeling a sorrow for her that was almost matched by the sorrow for himself.

Kay was trembling uncontrollably now, clutching the reins of the horse in one hand, as if she were trying to hold on to reality.

"Dammit, I've seen blood as close up as you have, pulled a body from the Blitz and had an arm come off in my hand, had the gore soak through my blouse and my brassiere, and at night when I undressed I tried to wash it off my breast with soap, and soap won't do it! What do *you* use, General?"

She grabbed him by the arm, her nails digging into him, and still there was nothing he could do, or wanted to do, but let her get it out.

"It's all for power and for politics," Kay cried, "and I won't play your bloody man's game any more! I won't, I won't! For King and Country! Well, to hell with the King! To hell with the Country! You killed him! All of you! You killed him!"

Ike slapped her, hard. "Kay! Get hold of yourself."

She slapped him right back. "Bahstard!" She threw herself into the saddle, lashed out at the startled horse with the reins, and dug into his side with her heels. The stallion reared, then turned and headed straight up the hillside, galloping in huge strides across the flowering fields toward the crest. Kay urged him until they were at the very top, then she let the reins slip out of her hands. The horse slowed to a halt. Kay sat for a moment, erect, silhouetted against the sky. Then, slowly, her head dropped. She clung like a child to the horse's mane, leaned against his powerful neck, smelled the strong, horsey smell that recalled her childhood—and at last, let the tears start.

Far below, at the bottom of the hill, Dwight Eisenhower stared up toward her.

He looked very tired, and very old.

X
Kay

It was to be a routine press conference, one of those arranged periodically by Ike's public relations staff whenever the newsmen became insistent about hearing directly from the Commanding General. Tex led Ike through the corridors of the old St. George Hotel toward the conference room, a bit apprehensive.

"They want news," he warned. "They'll try to trap you into spilling something you shouldn't, so better walk on eggs."

"Why do I have to talk to the press at all right now?"

"Because if you don't, they'll murder you with the home folks. Sending their boys into battle and refusing to answer questions." Tex opened the door to the conference room. "Feed 'em, 'Our glorious troops triumph again' and tell 'em it's off the record, so they're sure to print it."

"Tex, why do I have so much more respect for the integrity and intelligence of newspapermen than you do?"

"I used to be one."

Tex relaxed on the platform as Ike conducted the briefing. The newspapermen were restless, but they were used to being left out in the cold as far as hard news was concerned. Whatever went wrong with the war was protected by the cloak of military secrecy; what they did manage to discover was prevented from being transmitted home to their newspapers by the ever-present military censorship. Only on their infrequent trips back to the United States did they have a chance to print what they had learned. The intensely personal human interest stories about the enlisted men of the United States Army offered by Ernie Pyle in his columns, the closest view the folks back home got of what war was really like, had little to do with actual strategy or tactics.

"Our glorious troops have triumphed again," Ike was telling the assembled journalists. The forty reporters in the room represented some of the most important newspapers in the world, Tex recalled; the last thing they should be given was news.

". . . after they were humiliated at Kasserine Pass in one of the greatest defeats in American military history, a defeat which was largely my fault," Ike continued.

Tex choked on his cigarette. Generals never admitted defeat. Or if they did, they never admitted it was their fault. What would the folks back home think?

"I've learned a valuable lesson," Ike said. "The M-3 tank the GIs called the Purple Heart Box has been scrapped. Basic training has been extended in the United States so that American troops won't have to get on-the-job instruction from the German army. I would like to thank General Rommel, but he's escaped to Berlin and left General von Arnim to hold the bag."

The newsmen made dutiful notes. All of this information had been printed before. One of the correspondents rose, in a forlorn attempt to elicit something newsworthy.

"General Eisenhower, why did you refuse to accept von Arnim's surrender personally?"

Ike focused cool blue eyes on him. "The Nazi armies," he said, "in Russia, in Poland, in France, in North Africa, have violated every rule of human decency. Not until the last Nazi general has signed the last surrender will I meet with one of them face to face."

Tex was instantly on his feet. That was a good finish. No sense letting Ike hang around on the platform, He might think of another defeat he was responsible for.

"Thank you, gentlemen," Tex said, and started to steer Ike off the platform. The newsmen, grumbling, closed their notepads.

One British correspondent made a final attempt. "General Eisenhower," he said, "the British press is claiming that only General Montgomery's smashing victories in the desert saved you and the American forces from your own disastrous mistakes."

Tex had taken Ike by the arm. He felt Ike tense.

"Where did they get that information?" Ike wanted to know.

"From General Montgomery."

There was a ripple of laughter from the other correspondents. They waited, hoping for an explosion, hoping for *something*.

"That's interesting," Ike said calmly.

The British newsman tried again. "Montgomery also hinted he wouldn't be opposed to taking over command of the invasion of France, whenever that is to be. Do you have a reply?"

There was a hush. Tex prayed inwardly that Ike wouldn't rise to this obvious bait. He needn't have worried.

"General Bernard Montgomery," Ike answered calmly, "is one of the finest gentlemen and most capable soldiers it has ever been my good fortune to meet. We are allies in the fullest sense of the word."

"Good day, gentlemen!" Tex said quickly, urging Ike toward the steps which led from the platform.

"General Eisenhower." The voice had a flat New York accent. Another correspondent had risen. He wore horn-rimmed glasses and a look of utter disgust. "Why do you have so little faith in the news media that you cut off any more questions after feeding us this unadulterated bullshit?"

There was a startled murmur. Ike pulled his arm free of Tex's despairing grasp and turned to face his inquisitor. "What newspaper are you from?"

"The *New York Times*."

"I didn't think they knew that word."

"You're teaching it to us."

Ike turned to Tex. "Sit down." Slowly, Tex returned to his seat. There goes the old ball game, he thought.

Ike picked up a pointer and crossed to a military map on a stand on the platform. He indicated Sicily.

"Combined Allied forces will assault Sicily the second week in July with the Seventh Army under General Patton attacking the southern beaches here, and the British Eighth Army under General Montgomery attacking the beaches here, south of Syracuse." He pointed out the exact targets of the coming Allied invasion. Tex felt as if he had been shot. The newsmen, writing feverishly in their notebooks, scarcely believed their ears.

Ike lit up a cigarette. "We are already conducting the preliminary air campaign, but we are doing it in such a way as to lead the enemy to believe we will attack the western end of the island. We will use airborne troops in the operation on a larger scale than has yet been attempted in warfare."

Ike turned from the map to face his startled audience.

"It's a risky amphibious operation whose success will depend upon complete surprise. You are now in possession of information that could lead to the loss of thousands of Allied lives. I hope you have some idea of how I feel every night. Good afternoon."

He started off the platform. The reporters rose to their feet in silence, the responsibility of the information they had just learned already weighing on them. Tex hurried to catch up with Ike.

"Keep this up," he whispered to his commander, "and I think I can get you the Iron Cross."

Outside the St. George, Kay was waiting for them beside the Packard. It was a different Kay—subdued, unkempt, uncaring, mechanically living her life and her duties, submerged in the grief that had shattered her. Her subconscious had learned that she must keep working, must keep busy, or she would have too much time to dwell on what might have been. Better to live in the unreal world of a wartime headquarters. Only at night, in the rooms she shared with four other women, did it seem to be too much. She and Dick had known each other only a short time, if love is measured in minutes; she hadn't realized how much they had become part of each other. One half of her had died, and that half was trying to drag the other along. Only because it was Kay's instinct to fight, to cling to life, did she have enough presence of mind to keep working.

As he reached the car with Tex, Ike's eyes couldn't help taking in the sloppy uniform, the neglected fingernails, the hair desperately in need of a comb. She was a child, he felt, a child who had been deeply hurt. It had been his place to tell her about Dick Arnold, and she had taken that necessity and turned it into hatred. As the messengers who brought bad tidings in ancient Greece were put to death, on his shoulders had fallen the punishment for her lover having been slain. But still, she had remained on the job. A soldier at her post. His heart went out to her. Here, so many thousands of miles from his own family, she was the closest thing he had. To what? A daughter, he told himself.

"Kay, did I ever remember to thank you for staying on the job?" he asked as he climbed into the car.

"No, sir." No expression.

"Thank you, Kay."

"Yes, sir."

Well, that had been a big help. Ike slid into the seat next to Tex as Kay took her place behind the wheel. Obviously, he thought, kindness wasn't the method.

"What have you done to your hair?" he asked sharply.

"Nothing, General."

"That's what's wrong with it. Do something about it. And put some polish on your nails. *Red* polish."

"Yes, General." Quietly.

"Dammit, Kay, don't agree with me! It makes me uncomfortable!"

"I'm sorry, General." She started the motor.

"And don't, for God's sake, be sorry! The past is past, Kay. You're not going to change it by brooding about it. Now, when you're not driving, I want you to come into my office and take care of my mail. Can you type?"

"Oh, God."

"Answer my question!"

"Naturally, since I'm a female, I was born typing."

Ike suppressed a smile. For the first time, he had produced a reaction. The corpse showed life.

"That's a hell of a lot better, Kay," he said. "You are now my secretary, and I hope you hate it."

For answer, Kay released the clutch too quickly and the car bucked forward, throwing her passengers against each other.

"Just like old times," Tex remarked as they straightened up.

The small victories are always the most important, Ike told himself. Kay's face in the mirror was flushed, angry. A child who had been forced to eat spinach. It made him feel good all over.

When she wasn't driving, Kay came into Ike's headquarters and answered his mail. She made a conscious effort

144

to improve her appearance. There wasn't much she could do about her typing, which was atrocious. The deep hurt was still there, always there, but there was less time to feel it. She had to face others continually—the constant flow of military men in and out of Ike's office, an occasional visiting Congressman, the pulse of life as usual in wartime. She and Tex had adjoining desks, and he learned not to treat her gently. It was the last thing she wanted. There was a war to fight; she could no longer blame it all on Eisenhower—he hadn't made the bloody world. But she guarded her inner self carefully; Dick lived there, and she would admit no one, no one at all. Even the puppy, Telek, was unable to worm his way back into her affections. She treated him distantly, even punished him for occasional transgressions, which he took personally, not understanding that he represented a part of her life she was trying to submerge.

Sicily was invaded, and George Patton came into his own as his tanks sliced through the Sicilian countryside and headed for Palermo in a race with Montgomery's Eighth Army. All Europe was waiting for the next move.

Ike was working late in his study at the villa one evening when Gen. Bedell Smith burst in.

"Better turn on the radio, Ike! They're relaying a broadcast from Rome."

Ike switched on the small radio on his desk and waited impatiently for the tubes to warm up. "What's happening?"

"It's King Victor Emmanuel. He's making a speech."

And now the radio warmed into life. The thin voice of the little Italian king was heard, over a welter of atmospherics, and then the voice of the British announcer, translating.

"In brief, the king is telling the Italian people that he has summoned Benito Mussolini to the Palazzo Venezia and demanded his resignation. Mussolini has been placed under arrest."

Ike looked at Beetle, startled. It wasn't until much later that all the facts became known. Hitler had refused to send more troops to save Sicily or Italy itself. He wanted to withdraw all German forces north of Rome and sacrifice Italy and the Italian armies for the safety of the German Fatherland. He urged the Italians to keep fighting to the death. Mussolini had agreed, to save himself, but nineteen of the twenty-five members of his Fascist Grand Council had refused, and the King had finally gotten the courage to act. In the streets of Italy, mobs were celebrating Il Duce's fall and German troops were firing on them. Mussolini was finished.

"Humpty Dumpty just had a great fall!" Beetle exulted.

"That shows how well we've been doing in Sicily!" Ike's eyes were gleaming. The landings had worked; surprise had been achieved. Now they were reaping the fruits. Soon Allied troops would be on the continent of Europe. "I just received a signal from Patton—his tanks have already passed Mt. Etna!"

"How about Montgomery and the British Eighth?"

"Still stalled near Catania. Patton's going to be the first Allied commander to reach Palermo with his American tanks and troops . . . and Monty may swallow his mustache."

The advance was so rapid it could only result in swift capture of much of the German and Italian forces and armor on the island. Only the Strait of Messina would separate the Allies from the toe of the Italian boot.

"One good push," said Beetle, "and Italy's out of the war!"

Ike switched off the radio and sank back in his chair. "If George Patton keeps moving like this," he mused, "I'm going to give him command of the invasion of Italy, instead of Montgomery." He sighed wistfully. "Dammit, George is doing everything in this war *I* wanted to do."

* * *

Brig. Gen. Frederick A. Blesse was Surgeon General of the United States Army in North Africa. One evening, the Adjutant General of the United States Army telephoned Harry Butcher, of Eisenhower's staff, and informed him that Gen. Blesse had something secret to report; the information must be delivered, personally, to the commander within the hour. Since it was evening, Gen. Blesse was told to appear at the Villa.

When the Surgeon General showed up, bearing a briefcase and an extremely grim expression, Kay went to find Ike. She stepped out into the courtyard, gleaming in the North African moonlight, the shadows of the sculptured gates and iron work making arabesque patterns in the sand. Gen. Eisenhower was exactly where she knew he would be, at the newly constructed dog run for Telek and his recent bride, a young female Scottie named Caacie, an acronym for "Canine Auxiliary Air Corps." The honeymoon had been in progress for over a week, but today Telek, obviously hopelessly in love, had defended his bride against a passing camel and been kicked in the side for his pains.

Kay found Ike kneeling near the kennel, holding the wounded hero in his arms. For Ike, it was a necessary respite from the demands of a war that was proving overpowering; no one who has not experienced it can understand the loneliness of command. Ike had suffered tremendous blows to his own confidence. Now, with the invasion of Italy at hand, he knew the Allied leaders— Roosevelt and Stalin and Churchill—were to meet in conferences at Cairo and Teheran. A final decision would be made on a commander for the attack across the English Channel, an attack Ike Eisenhower had long championed, but he was no longer the leading candidate for the job. There was no one he could confide his disappointment to, except possibly Telek, who could be trusted to keep his mouth shut.

"General?"

He looked up. Kay was standing beside him, the moonlight haloing her hair. She looked cool and lovely and very distant. "The Surgeon General is here," she said.

"Tell him I'll be right in." Ike got to his feet, still holding the dog. As she turned to leave, he said, "Kay?"

She stopped. She had never heard Ike's voice quite like that. He seemed unsure of himself. Gen. Dwight Eisenhower was seldom unsure of anything.

"You're nails look better, and your hair is passable. I'm glad to see you've had your uniform pressed."

Puzzled, she said, "Thank you, General. From you, that's the equivalent of two battle stars."

"But you're still looking worn and tired and tense. I understand there are some lovely beaches near Tunis, where we've established R and R for the troops. Why don't you take a week off, and I'll have orders cut to send you there?"

Kay turned away. "I'm through crying, General," she said. "You don't have to give me any more lollipops." She would not, she told herself, allow him to atone for the guilt she still felt was partly his. Not that easily.

Ike petted Telek, who licked his face in response. "Dammit, Kay," he said, his voice tense, "stop hitting back. Can't you accept a little kindness? Do I have to spell everything out?"

She didn't understand. Truly, she couldn't imagine what he was driving at. Only when she turned back and saw his eyes did she get an inkling. And she didn't believe it.

"Spell what out, General?"

Ike flushed. Of course, it had been the wrong moment. He wasn't certain what had impelled him to leave himself so vulnerable.

"Kay, this foolish dog is smarter than you are," he said. It was all he could manage.

Kay's eyes widened. My God, she thought. My God! She turned away again. "I'm still desperately in love with Dick." Her voice was unsteady and she did not trust herself to say any more. Anyway, it was all dead within her, there would never be another spark, certainly never another fire. And above all, God in heaven, not this soon.

"That doesn't help either of you any more," Ike said. "I don't want to sound cruel, but we all must learn to live with death. It's all around us here." Couldn't she understand what he meant? Didn't she know how difficult this moment was for him? "I can't compare my grief with yours. But it's just as real." There. That was better. Better than nothing. Stubbornly, Kay refused to face him. Her emotions were in turmoil. Let him finish, let him struggle, let him get to the point. Then, perhaps, she could sort out her feelings. Not yet.

"You—you've lost someone you love dearly. And I—well, every day of this war I have to send more kids I never knew to an early grave."

Suddenly, she realized what it must be like for him. What was it she felt? Pity?

"Dammit, Kay." Ike's voice shook now. It was, she sensed, his final appeal. "There are moments when everyone needs affection and compassion. Even a general."

Oh, my God, she thought, he's *said* it! What would they ever think in Abilene? A married man! His torment, his trial by fire, must be terrible indeed to wring this from him. He was crying out for help, under the pressures of war. He was, then, only a man. She had been so wrapped up in her own terrible pain, it never occurred to her a commander could suffer too. Poor Ike, she thought, you aren't even allowed to cry, are you? You're scared stiff I might run from you, right now, in shock, in hatred, and you would be left embarrassed and embittered and alone.

She turned now to look at him. He stood stock

149

still, watching her, waiting, the terrible doubt written all over him. Had he made himself ridiculous? He was, after all, almost old enough to be her father. She had recently lost someone young and handsome; there was no doubt they had truly loved each other. He had never had any indication of any sort that Kay felt any affection for him. At least, he thought, I hope she doesn't laugh.

"General Eisenhower," Kay said softly, "I would be simply delighted to accept that week off."

They looked at each other then, unabashedly, openly. The worry vanished from Ike's eyes. "That's better," he said.

Kay took a step toward him. A telephone rang, somewhere in the villa. She stopped. "I'll tell the Surgeon General you'll be right in, General." She turned and walked slowly away.

In the little reception room in the villa, General Blesse had been waiting impatiently. Kay opened the door to Ike's study and directed Blesse inside. Then she crossed slowly to her typewriter and sat down, her thoughts a million miles away. She slipped a sheet of paper into the typewriter and started to type. Anything.

Tex, at the next desk, had been watching, curious. "What's wrong?" he asked. "You look as if you're in shock."

"Please shut up," she managed to reply.

"I was just going to point out that you're typing on your tie," he said gently.

Kay stared down. It was true. In her reverie, she had leaned too far over when she put in the paper. She retrieved the tie and tried to pretend the world was the same as it had been five minutes ago.

It wasn't.

Ike appeared and entered the study, without a word or a look. A buzzer summoned Tex. Kay heaved a sigh of relief. At least, for the moment, there would be no more questions.

Ike was pacing the floor when Tex entered, with General Blesse seated uncomfortably on a chair nearby. As usual, Ike plunged right to the point. "Tex, how do we handle this with the press? General Blesse tells me he has a report that George Patton has just slapped some soldier in a hospital in Sicily."

Blesse pulled some reports out of his briefcase. He was a methodical man, a doctor turned accountant by the enormous paperwork of wartime. "Actually, *two* soldiers," he corrected Ike. "Enlisted men, hospitalized for battle fatigue. Started to cry while Patton was passing through." He paused. "The General slapped them, calling them deserters and cowards. He said brave men don't break into tears and that there is no such thing as battle fatigue. One of the soldiers had malaria and a temperature of a hundred and two." He indicated the reports. "Chief Surgeon at the hospital made this report."

Tex thought quickly. "General, were any newsmen present when Patton slapped those soldiers?"

"No, but there were plenty of witnesses."

"They were military," Tex said. "They won't talk." He heaved a sigh of relief and turned to Ike. "Bury this. Forget the whole thing. The press boys love you now; I'll get them to kill the story."

"Tex—!"

"If you don't, they'll blow it out of proportion and you'll have to get rid of one of your best generals just when you're giving him command of the next invasion. And Monty will take Italy single-handed, with fourteen photographers at his side."

"I can't just overlook something like this!" Ike said.

"You appointed General Patton to his job. If they hear of this, the bleeding hearts in America will raise such a stink, Roosevelt might have to get rid of *both* of you."

Ike pressed the buzzer to call Kay.

"Look at it this way, Ike," Tex continued. "Patton

only slapped those soldiers. Knowing George, you're lucky he didn't shoot them."

Kay entered, carrying her notebook. She had seized an opportunity to apply her lipstick and she hoped now that her rapid pulse was not evident. Good Lord, she thought. What an old, old story. Secretary and boss.

"Kay, can you take shorthand?" Ike inquired sharply.

"No, General," she admitted.

"War is hell," commented Tex, and she threw him a look.

"But I *do* write terribly quickly," she told Ike hopefully.

"Get it down any way you can, and I'll do it over later. Just take out all the four-letter words."

"I'll do my best." She took a seat in a chair near his desk and opened her notebook. As if nothing had happened—nothing at all.

Ike was pacing angrily now. "Letter to Patton. Dear George." He turned to her impatiently. "No, strike that. Dear General: I am attaching a report that is shocking in its allegations. I am well aware of the necessity for toughness on the battlefield—"

"Slower, please."

Kay was writing furiously. Ike eyed her, annoyed, but slowed the pace of his words. "—but this does not excuse brutality, abuse of the sick, or exhibition of your goddam temper."

"Is 'goddam' considered a four-letter word?" Kay eyed Ike. It was all gone, forgotten, what had passed between them, she felt. The war had surged over him, as it always had, always would. Had she imagined what he meant, read more into his words than there really was? Probably.

"Strike that last," Ike said. He resumed pacing, lighting up a cigarette. "If there is any semblance of truth in the enclosed report, I want you to line up your entire Second Corps and apologize right down to the last dogface private for being one stripe below a Mongolian idiot!" He turned to Kay. "Strike that last."

"I already have, General."

Ike grunted, and continued. "I assure you such conduct will not be tolerated in this theatre, no matter who the offender may be. If the report is proven accurate, my next action will be to remove you from your command. Period. Have you got all that?"

Kay looked up from her scribbling and brushed back a strand of hair which had fallen into her eyes. "I don't have any of it, actually," she admitted, "but I'm certain I'll remember every word."

Tex shook his head. "It would be better if you didn't," he told her. "If Patton makes a public apology, the press will print headlines that may mean curtains for both George Patton and his Commanding General!"

Ike whirled on him. "I don't give a damn! There are a lot of things more important right now than Ike Eisenhower or George Patton. The enlisted soldier is doing most of the dying in this war for all of us gold-braid generals. He deserves better than a slap in the face, and I'm going to see that he damn well gets it!"

He signified the meeting was over and crossed to his desk to sit down. Blesse and Tex headed for the door. Kay was about to follow, then changed her mind. She waited for the door to close, then turned.

"General?"

He looked up.

"In defense of General Patton," she said, "we're all under tremendous pressure here. Sometimes we do and say things we don't really mean. I'm sure you have. I know I have."

Ike had risen to his feet. "Now, what the hell—!"

"It's no good, General. I will not allow either of us to make a damn fool of himself. Or herself. Why don't we just chalk it up to battle fatigue?"

"General Patton says there's no such thing."

153

She knew he was hurt. She was also sure she had taken the only course possible. Two married men in a row? No, thank you.

She turned and left, her heart pounding.

Ike stood still. In his mind's eye, he could see her on the crest of the hill, her head lowered in sorrow, clutching the horse's mane.

I don't even have a horse, he thought, and sat down at his desk again, feeling very foolish and very empty.

* * *

Events tumbled so quickly upon each other that there was little time for Kay to cry over spilt milk, had she been so inclined. Ike's attitude toward her became almost stiffly formal, as if he were unwilling to risk another rebuff.

The invasion of Sicily ended in complete Allied victory after only 17 days of fighting, and Montgomery led the first troops onto the Italian boot. George Patton had been relieved of his command and sent to England. King George paid North Africa a surprise visit, and Kay had the honor of driving him and Ike during his stay. Preparations for the coming summit conference of Allied leaders went forward feverishly.

One evening, after driving back to the villa from the St. George Hotel, Kay and Ike encountered a surprise visitor in the driveway—a smiling Winston Churchill, waving his cigar, overjoyed at having pulled off his arrival without the commander having been made aware of his coming. Another victory for Britain.

Ike went immediately to his study to complete the necessary preparations. The guard at the villa must be doubled during the Prime Minister's stay; his plane was to be carefully checked over before its flight to the Cairo meeting. As long as he was in North Africa, Churchill was Ike's responsibility.

Kay was sent off to check on Telek, who had had another unfortunate encounter with a creature somewhat larger than he was, this time a mule. Ike had been understandably concerned. Telek was still in the process of becoming a father, and nothing must interfere with the performance of his marital duties.

Kay returned to Ike's study to make her report. She tried to be as noncommital as possible, returning to the General all the formality that he was inflicting upon her.

"I wish to report that Telek ate his dinner tonight with his customary ferocious appetite and bad manners, and then piddled magnificently on the living room carpet. Apparently, he has survived. May I have permission to go home now?"

Ike looked up at her. She stood rigidly before his desk. Like a plebe at West Point, he thought, trying desperately not to look him in the eye.

"No, you may not have permission," he said. "I would like you to stay and join me at dinner with the Prime Minister, and possibly a game of bridge. We haven't played bridge together for a month."

"I've lost all interest in cards, General. I prefer to go home."

Ike got to his feet. "Dammit, that's both impolite and childish! Now you're going to stay and have the honor of dining with Winston Churchill, or I'll see that you're transferred off my personal staff!"

"That might be an excellent idea!" Kay snapped back vehemently. She turned and started for the door.

"Miss Summersby!"

There was something in his voice she had never heard before. She stopped, but didn't turn.

"Dammit, Kay," he said, "I have nothing to offer you. Except that I need you."

Good Lord, she thought suddenly, I'm crying. Why in the world should I be crying?

She turned toward him slowly, no longer caring that her eyes would give her away. She had fought it long enough.

Ike stood beside his desk as if rooted there, unable to move, unwilling to risk another defeat. Kay moved toward him. Without a word, she put her arms about him and kissed him.

"Kay—" he began.

"Shhhh. Don't say you're sorry, or I'll kill you."

"I was going to say, 'Hello'."

She looked up at him. He was trying to smile.

"Hello, General. I'm not in love with you."

"I know."

"I couldn't be. Not so soon. Possibly not ever. But I do need tenderness, in the midst of so much horror, and so do you, and that I can furnish. Would it be acceptable that we should not be in love . . . but just in tenderness with each other, General?"

"Goddammit, everybody calls me Ike."

"Goddammit, Ike." Her arms went about him again.

There was a knock at the door and she backed away hastily.

"On with the war," she said, and straightened her blouse.

"Come in!" Ike called. He went back to his desk.

Tex entered. "The P.M. would like to see you in his room," he told Ike.

"The P.M.?"

"The Prime Minister. We've gotten very chummy over a bottle of claret. Maybe it was two. Behind all that historical rhetoric lies a brother wino."

"I'll be right there. And tell Mickey there will be three of us at the private dinner I had planned for this evening—myself, the P.M., and Miss Summersby."

He went out. Tex turned to stare at Kay. "What do you have to do around here to get invited to a private dinner?" he wanted to know.

Kay looked at him calmly. "Your guess is as good as mine," she said.

The guest suite at the Villa dar el Ouad was vast and luxurious by any standards, even those of an Arabian prince. The door stood ajar when Ike arrived. He knocked and peered in.

"Mr. Prime Minister?"

There was no answer. Puzzled, Ike stepped into the huge living room, all pillows and pink upholstery, and tried again.

"MR. PRIME MINISTER?"

"In the w.c., Ike!" called a voice that was familiar to the entire free world. "Come in!"

Ike threw open the door to the bathroom and was greeted by a cloud of steam. The bath was a triumph of money over taste—huge mirrors, elegant tile, gilded fixtures. From a marble tub, six feet long, filled with a bubble bath, protruded the head and shoulders of Winston Churchill, cigar in mouth. He was washing himself with a huge sponge. An ashtray and a brandy snifter were balanced precariously on the tub's edge.

"Good God!" Ike was fighting the steam. "Where are you, Mr. Churchill?"

"Right here," said the First Minister of the British Empire, "in this concubine's swimming pool." He motioned Ike to approach. "The only reason I come to Morocco is to take a decent bath, General, you must know that." He applied the sponge. "With the bloody water rationing in London, it's illegal to fill the tub, and with the fuel rationing, it's impossible to heat the water." He squinted through the steam at his visitor. "Given that combination, my wife sends me abroad at monthly intervals in the interest of self-preservation. Hers."

"I can wait until you've finished the purification ceremony, Mr. Churchill," Ike said, and took a step back.

"No, no!" The Prime Minister waved his cigar. "We're going to have a battle, firing broadsides right and left, and as former First Lord of the Admiralty, I feel more at home afloat. Have a seat, and let's have at each other."

Ike looked around for a chair. There seemed to be nothing but pillows on the tiled floor. Rather than suffer that, he chose what he thought was a lesser indignity. The Commander of Allied Forces in North Africa sat down on the ruffled toilet lid.

"Open fire," he told his guest.

Churchill picked up a long-handled scrubbing brush and applied it to his back. "I want to enlist your aid to convince that stubborn Roosevelt that he is absolutely wrong on a major decision. What I am referring to is the timing of Overlord, the invasion of Europe across the English Channel. Don't you agree next spring is too soon?"

"Absolutely not!" Ike was on his feet immediately. "I'm not the same hick you outslickered at King Arthur's Court! I've learned to spot which shell you put the little pea under!" He crossed to the tub, staring down at the chubby figure half submerged in the foam, who removed the cigar from his mouth at this point to sip the brandy. "You're still trying to renege on your promise for a massive assault against the coast of France, which I feel is absolutely necessary to win the war!"

Churchill set down the brandy snifter. "My dear Ike," he said soothingly, "you cannot ignore the solid military realities. Italy is on the verge of surrender. Mussolini, that buffoon from the Commedia dell' Arte, has been driven from the stage by a boot in his ample rear, and the soft underbelly of Europe will soon be within our reach." He picked up the sponge again. "Any parallel to my own anatomy at this point would be uncalled for," he remarked as he applied the soap.

"That, Mr. Prime Minister, is a matter of opinion." Ike attempted a smile.

"Well, then. Forget the Channel. I suggest instead a strike northeast from Italy into Yugoslavia and on to Vienna and Berlin."

Churchill washed the soap from his glistening body. "Would you hand me the towel, General?"

Ike brought the huge, blanket-sized towel from its rack, controlling his temper with difficulty.

"Mr. Prime Minister," he said, "that's a political, not a military strategy, to keep Stalin out of Western Europe!"

"General Eisenhower, mark my words: if the Red Army reaches Berlin first, Russia will hold half of Europe in its iron fist and will never relinquish it."

He draped the towel about his ample figure as he climbed out of the tub, cigar firmly clenched between his teeth.

"You don't win wars by betraying allies!" Ike almost shouted.

He was finding it difficult to make his point strongly enough; Churchill was standing in front of a full-length mirror, drying his body vigorously. "Unless Overlord takes place next spring, *as you agreed,* Mr. Prime Minister, I'm informing the Joint Chiefs that I will be no part of it!"

"My dear General, that may be the best solution of all." Churchill was almost purring now as he toweled himself. "The leader of the invasion of France, if it is to take place, will be selected by President Roosevelt and myself at our conference in Cairo. If you persist in your stubbornness, if the invasion is not postponed, I have it in mind to give its leadership to that brilliant soldier, Field Marshal Bernard Montgomery." He reached for his robe.

"Dammit, you know you don't have the authority to do that alone! You have to get Roosevelt's approval first!"

Churchill smiled cherubically at him. "My dear Ike," he said, "do not fret. I have no doubts as to my own powers of persuasion." He reached for his brandy. "In all her wars, Britain and her Prime Ministers always win one battle—the last."

And he raised his glass in silent toast—to Winston Spencer Churchill.

* * *

The Cairo and Teheran conferences marked another turning point in the war. Actually, there were two conferences in Cairo, one before and one after the meetings with Stalin in Iran. Ike was called on to attend the first, and it seemed the most natural thing in the world that Kay should go with him. Some of the other women on the staff were invited also; Abilene was still a large part of Ike's makeup. But there were moments when he and Kay could be almost alone, in the shadow of the moonlit pyramids, or investigating the Valley of the Kings.

It was a brief vacation from battle for both of them. It was over all too soon; in a few days they were back at headquarters. Ike had been given no inkling as to whether Churchill had blocked his appointment to the one job in the war he wanted above all others. Every day of waiting increased the tension. Every day there was a new rumor.

The grin, the jaunty cigarette holder, the fedora waved in the air, were the visual symbols of an undaunted human spirit, despite the wheelchair to which his body was confined.

Franklin Delano Roosevelt waved to the troops assembled to greet him before the cargo hatch of the Air Force Transport plane that had brought him from Cairo. The band struck up "Hail to the Chief," and he was wheeled down the ramp to meet the Commanding General. Ike greeted him warmly; he had developed an admiration for the tough warrior who had prepared his nation against its will for a war it thought it would never have to fight. They drove from the airport in Ike's new olive drab Cadillac, and Eisenhower filled the President in on the military situation, trying not to reveal the tension within him. He knew very well that the fateful decision affecting his future had been made but dignity and protocol dictated that he must wait until the President spoke.

The President did not speak.

The next morning, the buzzer at her desk summoned Kay into Ike's office. There had been a mixup at the airport with the Secret Service, who were concerned about

160

a woman driving the President of the United States, and Kay had been shunted aside.

Kay entered the office briskly, businesslike, pad and pencil ready. But the moment the door closed behind her, she relaxed and smiled at Ike. Their understanding of each other had become so strong that words were an impediment. Besides, words were dangerous; the walls had ears.

"The President of the United States," Ike told her with a grin, "has officially requested that you drive our car this afternoon on a tour of some of the battlefields." He got to his feet and crossed to her.

"Please thank him for me, Ike," she said. "He's such a brave figure, with those poor, helpless legs." Gently, she placed her hands on his shoulders and kissed him. The telephone rang and Ike stepped back.

"Sometimes," he said, "I wish I were half as brave." He picked up the phone, listened, barked an order, then hung up again.

"Has the President given any hint about who will command Overlord?" Kay wanted to know.

Ike shook his head. "No. Except to mention several times his great admiration for General Marshall."

Kay groaned. Scuttlebutt around headquarters was that Marshall had been picked and was already on his way to England. She felt Ike's disappointment as keenly as if it were her own.

Ike stooped to pet Telek, then picked the dog up in his arms.

"Let's go, Kay." He smiled at her. "We're having a picnic."

"A picnic! Oh, that sounds lovely! I haven't been on a picnic in years!" Happily, she put her arm about him as they moved off. "Who's going?"

"Just you, me, the dog, the United States Secret Service, a military escort, and Franklin Delano Roosevelt."

"Alone at last," Kay smiled.

They had reached the door. She took her arm from about him.

The convoy wound through the Algerian desert, bristling with truckloads of armed troops and carloads of Secret Service men; the President of the United States was in a war zone, and everyone but the President himself was nervous. It was a burningly hot day. The long morning of formal troop reviews and visits to the battle-scarred areas, still marked by burned-out tanks and guns, had wearied them all. Only Franklin Roosevelt, happy to have escaped from the stifling atmosphere of wartime Washington and the prison that was the White House, seemed to be enjoying himself.

To the surprise of the rest of the convoy, Roosevelt ordered Kay to turn the Cadillac into a tiny desert oasis, an unscheduled stop that unnerved the Secret Service man traveling with them. "But, Mr. President!" he protested. "We've prepared a guarded area ten miles ahead!"

"Nonsense!" the President scoffed. "The closest enemy soldiers are in Italy. This grove of palm trees is as safe as Pennsylvania Avenue."

"He *is* the Commander in Chief, you know," Kay informed the discomfited officer as she brought the car to a halt in the grove. Roosevelt smiled. He was growing fond of Kay's forthright attitude toward the world. As soon as they were parked in the shade of a date palm, soldiers poured out of the trucks to form a cordon around the car.

Ike got out to set up a small folding table. Kay climbed into the back for the basket of sandwiches. The President, for obvious reasons, was to picnic in the car. He patted the seat beside him.

"Sit down, child," he said. "I'd like to talk to you."

Kay looked up, surprised.

"Go ahead, Kay." Ike grinned. "I don't think that was a proposition."

"How disappointing," she said, and Roosevelt chuckled. "General Eisenhower tells me he may lose you," he remarked.

Kay was startled. "I beg your pardon?"

"This suggested business about no more British drivers for the American military."

"Oh. Oh, yes."

She had picked up Telek and was holding him on her lap to prevent him from consuming the food. Ike reached in and took the picnic basket from her. Outside the car, he began to unwrap the lunch.

"Why don't you join *our* army?" FDR inquired.

"The WACS? Oh, that's impossible. I would have to become an American citizen first. That takes years."

"Not if it's by Executive Order, I've been told. There are some things I'm allowed to do without the approval of the Secret Service."

"That's awfully kind of you, Mr. President, but—"

"Come, come. But what?"

"There are some of us in this world who are proud of being British. No, thank you, Mr. President."

Roosevelt looked a bit ruffled.

"I told you she'd be difficult, Mr. President," Ike said, leaning in to hand out sandwiches. Kay was Kay. No President, no King, no Emperor, could sway her loyalty to the little island empire that was her home.

"Don't you see *any* merit in becoming an American citizen?" Roosevelt inquired.

Kay hesitated. "You *do* make better coffee," she conceded finally.

Roosevelt laughed, and at the same moment Telek began to whine. Kay knew that signal all too well.

"Oh, dear!" she said. "Even Presidents must wait while Telek goes to the loo. You'll excuse us?"

"I doubt if I have much choice," FDR answered as Kay picked the dog up and carried him out of the car. Ike offered Roosevelt some punch.

"You can never win an argument with a woman, Mr. President," he said.

"I know. They're exactly like Congress. Of course, I could have demolished her female stubbornness in an in-

163

stant, if I permitted myself the indiscretion of violating the Official Secrets Act."

"What do you mean, sir?"

Roosevelt looked Ike squarely in the eye. "I could have explained to her," he said, "that there *are* reasons for being proud of being an American. Proud that we are about to help launch that massive assault across the English Channel this spring to save Miss Summersby's precious British Empire, and perhaps the entire free world. And proud that *all* Allied forces in that assault will be under the command of one American—General Dwight D. Eisenhower."

In spite of himself, Ike dropped the glass of punch he was holding. It hit the running board and rolled off into the desert sand.

Roosevelt chuckled. "I'm sorry, General," he said. "I suppose I should have saved that revelation for an official order. But I can never resist a good surprise."

Ike was still savoring the moment, trying to analyze his own feelings at having secured, finally, the prize he had been dreaming of.

"You are about to command the largest military operations in the history of warfare." Roosevelt was awed himself by the size of the event that was, for better or worse, to change the history of the world. "Now, what the devil shall we call you, to properly impress our British friends?" He thought for a moment. "How does 'Supreme Commander' strike you?"

Ike hesitated. "Pretty frightening, Mr. President," he said at last.

"I know."

They exchanged glances, two human beings burdened with superhuman responsibilities.

"Congratulations, Ike. The honor was long overdue." Roosevelt extended his hand.

Ike grasped it. "Thank you, Mr. President. I hope you won't be disappointed. You know I'll do my damnedest."

And then he asked, "But how did you change Churchill's mind?"

FDR smiled, the cigarette holder at a jaunty angle between his teeth. "I did *my* damnedest. And that's pretty good, you know." He looked around. "Is there any dessert?"

XI
Auld Lang Syne

"Should auld acquaintance be forgot
   An' never brought to mind—"

The voices of the staff in the next room at the villa, welcoming in the fateful year of 1944, echoed in Ike's office, where he sat holding a piece of paper in his hands. How fitting, he thought, the words of a Scottish bard, bringing to a close this episode which had begun with the training in Scotland of the men who had fought and died in the invasion of North Africa, on beaches only a few miles away.

He looked at the orders in his hand, stamped "SECURITY CONTROL" and "SECRET." From the Combined Chiefs of Staff, directed to General Eisenhower:

"1. You are hereby designated as Supreme Allied Commander of the forces placed under your orders for operation for the liberation of Europe from the

Germans. Your title will be Supreme Commander, Allied Expeditionary forces.

"2. Task: you will enter the continent of Europe and in conjunction with other United Nations, undertake operations aimed at the heart of Germany and the destruction of her armed forces. The date for entering the continent is the month of May, 1944."

So it was here. All he had planned, all he had hoped for. A blueprint for either victory or defeat, and the outcome might well lie in his own abilities. He folded the document carefully and placed it in the wall safe with the other confidential papers, including the orders that were to take him from the continent of Africa.

In the next room, Kay was singing with the rest, her arm linked to Tex Lee's. The liberally spiked punch had brought a glow to her cheeks. Good Lord, how many New Year's Eves had there been already in this bloody war? Five? And still no end in sight. Oh, well, what to do?

"We'll tak' a cup o' kindness yet
For auld lang syne."

A cup o' kindness. What a lovely name for Scotch whisky! The kindness that made it possible to forget the bad and to remember only the good. She was letting Tex refill her glass when she felt Ike's hand on her shoulder. Turning, she saw something in his manner that did not go with the revelry of the moment, the singing and the camaraderie of the men and women of headquarters staff.

She moved with Ike to one side of the room, the others barely noticing.

"My orders just came through. I'm leaving Africa tomorrow morning, Kay." He didn't know how to soften the facts. He knew she understood. I'm a soldier. I'm leaving. Goodbye. We may never see each other again.

Of course, she had known the moment would come. But she hadn't expected it so abruptly, so soon. And now the others had turned and were watching them, and there was nothing she could do, nothing she could say.

Just, "Happy New Year, Ike."

168

It was midnight, and now they were all shouting the same words to each other and hoping they would be alive to greet the next New Year the same way—amid friends.

"Should auld acquaintance be forgot
An' days of auld lang syne?"

A procession of military vehicles made its way along the rutted roads to the airport. The morning had dawned clear and soft; the sun was groping its way through the clouds to bring the clammy heat of afternoon. It was New Year's morning, and the year was now 1944. No one in the convoy taking Eisenhower to his destiny had any doubt that it was to be the year of decision. Only Kay knew that there was more than one decision to be made.

Her hands trembled as they grasped the wheel of the General's Cadillac. Ike was in the rear, holding Telek on his lap, another goodbye that had to be said.

Kay kept her eyes carefully on the road and tried to keep her voice casual. "You will take care of yourself and not smoke so many cigarettes, and not let the Germans shoot your plane down?"

"There won't be any Germans." He could see her face in the mirror. "I'm heading for Washington."

He saw her eyes flicker, and then she was watching the road again.

"And your wife." It was not a question.

"Yes, Kay," he said. "And my wife."

"It's been a hell of an affair, this one," she said. "The Virgin Mary at Armageddon."

He almost smiled. Summersby was still Summersby.

"You've never said anything to me you couldn't have said while saluting," Kay said.

"I'm not good at that sort of thing."

"I'm very good at it. I miss it." Kay braked the car to a stop. "Oh, God," she said, hoping she wouldn't be idiot enough to cry. "It's happened. I promised myself it wouldn't. I promised. I know I'm going to be hurt so terribly. Again."

Hastily, knowing he had heard, she got out of the car.

169

She opened the rear door for Gen. Dwight David Eisenhower. And his dog.

Gravely, he handed Telek to her.

"Goddammit, Kay, salute me," he said.

"You know how terrible I am at it."

"That's what I want to remember."

Her hand shook a bit, but she did salute—terribly.

Ike returned it with West Point precision and turned quickly away.

You poor man, Kay thought, suddenly feeling sorry for him. That salute was the most romantic gesture you've ever permitted yourself in public. How must it feel to be a prisoner of your own importance? She hated herself because the tears had started, in spite of her effort at control. She hoped fervently he wouldn't look back.

He did.

There were all the formalities of departure—the honor guard, the brass band, the handshakes and good wishes. Mickey and Harry Butcher were going along, as well as two of the puppies Telek had sired by Caacie. The puppies were to be presented to Mrs. Eisenhower and Mrs. Butcher, both of whom would get rid of the pups as soon as Ike and Harry went back to the war zone. Didn't their husbands realize that a Washington hotel is not a dog kennel?

Gen. Bedell Smith was the last to shake Ike's hand, as the honor guard stood at attention near the open hatch of the C-54 which would take Ike first to Terceira in the Azores, then on to Washington.

Ike hesitated a moment before his old friend. "Beetle," he said at last, "in the years I've been fighting for the Channel invasion, I never once considered what to do if it failed. My God . . . there could be half a million of our boys dead on the beaches of France."

"Every battle is a risk, Ike. That's war."

"But I'm the one who insisted the responsibility for the entire enterprise must be given to one man . . . alone."

He turned and entered the plane. This time he didn't look back.

The huge motors started up, belching black smoke as they backfired before catching, then roaring into life. The slipstream struck Kay and Telek as they waited on the tarmac near Ike's car, and the dog struggled in her arms.

"Oh, no," Kay said firmly. "If *I* don't get to go, *you* don't get to go." She deposited the dog in the front seat, through the open window. Telek whined pitifully, looking out with his paws on the door. Unable to resist, Kay plucked him out again and held him against her cheek. Together, they watched the plane lumber down the runway, picking up speed, then bounce into the air to leave North Africa and Algeria and Kasserine Pass behind forever.

The C-54 headed into the cloud-filled sky of the dawn of the new year, and Dwight Eisenhower's rendezvous with destiny.

Far below, Kay put Telek back into the car and climbed in behind the wheel. She would go back to Algiers and clean out the office. And then she had some shopping to do.

And then she had the rest of her life.

PART 2
IKE

XII
Home

Dwight Eisenhower returned to an America he barely recognized because it had changed so little. The stores were well-stocked, the restaurants crowded, and food plentiful. The war talk was about the Pacific and the hated Japanese. The Mediterranean? Where was that?

Ike's C-54 had touched down at the airport in Washington at 1:30 a.m., January 2, after refueling stops in the Azores and Bermuda. Since the Axis powers had to be kept in the dark as to Allied intentions, the whereabouts of the new Supreme Commander were a military secret. Ike's insignia were removed from his uniform, and he and Col. Butcher arrived at the Wardman Park Hotel in an unmarked civilian car. They entered the building through a rear entrance to avoid prying eyes, carrying Telek's offspring under their coats.

Ruth Butcher occupied the apartment directly across from Mamie's. The two women were awakened simultaneously by their returning husbands, their enthusiasm for the reunion somewhat dampened by the puppies' behavior on the hotel carpets.

Mamie Eisenhower had been fighting her own wars, a war against the boredom that beset so many soldiers' wives, and a war against the rumors about her husband, sparked by Margaret Bourke-White's *Life* article about Kay. What passed between Ike and Mamie on that matter is never likely to be recorded in history books. Some of Ike's wartime letters to Mamie have been published; Mamie's letters to Ike have not. It is known that Kay typed one of Ike's letters, and that Mamie indicated her resentment of receiving typewritten mail from her husband; thereafter, all of Ike's correspondence was handwritten.

Shortly after Ike's return to Washington, General and Mrs. Eisenhower made a secret trip by railroad car to visit their son John at West Point. He was spirited out of class by Col. Frank McCarthy, of Gen. Marshall's staff, to a secret rendezvous with his parents at the railway station. John, like almost everyone else in the United States, thought his father was in England.

Ike then flew on alone for another family reunion. The peaceful, snowbound countryside around Abilene, Kansas, took him back to his childhood; his mother, his brothers, all of the familiar surroundings, made the war and his part in it seem unreal.

The respite was brief. Almost immediately, Ike Eisenhower flew back to Washington for a meeting with the President of the United States.

Roosevelt was not well; the magnificent physique, so long conditioned against the strain of paralysis by daily swimming and exercise, was beginning to crumble under the pressures of age and wartime. Ike was ushered into the Presidential bedroom, where FDR, propped against pillows, his bedside table filled with hated medicines, was fighting off the effects of influenza. The voice was still firm, however, although broken by occasional fits of coughing; the eyes still had their gleam and the brilliant mind was always in command.

"You look naked without your stars, Ike," he greeted his visitor.

"I'm top secret this trip. No one's supposed to know who I am."

"You'll never fool me." FDR flashed the famous smile. "I know exactly who you are. Dwight David Eisenhower, Supreme Commander, Allied Expeditionary Forces, for the greatest amphibious assault in the history of warfare." His voice grew more serious. "Ike, are you as frightened as I am by the enormity of it all?"

"Scared to death, Mr. President."

Ike was determined to press the point he had come to make: the weak link in the invasion plans lay in the scarcity of landing craft which had played such a decisive role in Sicily. It was Eisenhower's belief that Europe was now the Allies' prime objective, that the war in the Pacific would have to take a back seat, and assault craft earmarked for that theater must be diverted to his area.

"What frightens me most, Mr. President, is my inability to persuade anyone in this town that we need much more help in Europe than we're getting."

FDR removed his glasses and polished them with his handkerchief. "Well. I was wondering when you'd get to that."

"We have to double the number of our landing craft or the invasion—"

"Only *double?*"

"Or the invasion will be in desperate trouble! If we can't overwhelm the German coastal defenses and—"

Roosevelt coughed impatiently. "General, would you open the window a bit? I'm about to try my own secret medication." He reached under his pillow and took out his cigarettes and the familiar holder.

"Mr. President, are you sure you should smoke?"

"No. But the pills the doctor gave me aren't working,

177

either." He grinned at Ike, who crossed to the window. "Go ahead, open it," FDR insisted. "We have to blow the smoke out of here before Eleanor comes in. I believe she's home this week."

Ike returned to the bedside, impatient. The President lighted his cigarette and motioned him to sit down again.

"Ike, there *is* another war, you know. In the Pacific. That's that big ocean over there somewhere." He gestured toward the west. "My Joint Chiefs tell me the assault on the main island of Japan will require a force of at least a million men. We can't spare Europe any additional landing craft. Not one."

"Dammit, Mr. President, that's robbing Peter to pay Paul!"

"We're giving you exactly the number of invasion craft you asked for. *You* helped draw up the original plans for the invasion of France across the Channel."

"But I didn't know *I* was going to command it!" Ike stopped short, realizing what he had said. He grinned as Roosevelt burst into laughter.

"Thank you for that moment of honesty, Ike," FDR said, as he caught his breath. "You don't know how few there are like you." He puffed at his cigarette. "I will try to get you everything you need, but in the matter of shipping, my hands are tied."

Ike was on his feet again, pacing, head lowered. "Mr. President, how can I convince all of you here that unless we attack with overwhelming strength, the Germans may throw us back—and gain time! Time to develop the secret weapons Hitler boasts about! Rockets—"

"I know, Ike, I know."

"—that can hit London, and possibly New York. Jet aircraft. Perhaps even some sort of atomic explosive. If we don't overrun them soon, the war in Europe may be lost and the war in the Pacific only beginning! *Give us the landing craft!*"

"No!" The word was sharp, decisive. Ike had a momentary sense of the iron man behind the benign smile and the humbling wheelchair. "You're going to do it with what you've got because you *must* do it with what you've got." Roosevelt started to cough. He put out his cigarette, then turned back to his visitor. His tone softened. "Ike, I do realize the terrible pressures you're working under. I will do all I can to make them easier to bear." He held out his hand.

"Thank you, Mr. President." Ike shook the proffered hand. It felt moist. He was embarrassed to have upset this indomitable fighter when he was obviously not well. "I sincerely hope you'll get over this illness quickly."

"Oh, I haven't felt better in years. I'm just humoring the doctors." FDR smiled.

Ike nodded and turned for the door.

"Ike?"

"Yes?"

"I wonder if you'd do me a favor?"

"Of course."

The President reached over to his bed table and picked up a photograph and a fountain pen. "Would you take this to Miss Summersby for me? I promised it to her in Algiers." He autographed the photo with a flourish and held it out. "I imagine you'll be seeing her?"

Ike took the picture. He hesitated for a moment. "Yes," he said finally.

"There has been a lot of loose talk around Washington, General Eisenhower." FDR paused. "I want you to know I am in no position to cast the first stone." Their eyes met. "Now give them hell across the English Channel. And Ike . . . I'll try to steal some boats for you."

"Thank you, Mr. President."

The two men, so different in background and training, looked at each other for a moment, in mutual understanding. Then Ike turned and left.

He was never to see Franklin Roosevelt alive again.

XIII
Invasion!

The headlight of the approaching train, hooded against the blackout, loomed dimly through a thick, pea-soup fog such as only London can experience. The train seemed almost dream-like as it moved into the huge Addison Street railway station, which was illuminated only by dim blue overhead lights. Kay's heart leaped into her mouth as she watched it arrive; the chug of the steam locomotive and the clanging of the bell seemed to coincide with her heartbeat.

Ike had sent for her. She had been flown from North Africa to London in his Flying Fortress. Gen. Walter Bedell Smith and most of the North African staff had been transferred as well. Ike wanted his family intact for the coming ordeal by fire.

With a hiss of steam, the locomotive came to a halt. *Bayonet,* the Supreme Commander's private railway car, was visible through the swirling fog. The station was almost deserted, except for a heavy security guard; Addison Street was reserved for VIP's, top military personnel, and no chances could be taken with their safety.

The door of the private car opened and Ike peered out, Tex and Mickey behind him. He could barely make out the platform.

"Ike! Ike! Over here!" Bedell Smith, who had come down to the station with Kay, waved through the gloom toward his chief.

"My God!" Ike finally caught a glimpse of them. "This is the worst I've ever seen it."

"There's somebody out there," Tex said. "I can hear breathing."

"It's Beetle here, Ike, but you'll have to take my word for it." He and Kay had made their way to the car. "How are you?"

"Fine, fine. Sorry to drag you out in this soup."

Ike and the other men alighted from the train and handshakes were exchanged.

"We'd never have made it to the station if it weren't for your demon driver." Beetle indicated Kay. "I think she makes little supersonic sounds, like a bat, to keep from bumping into buildings."

"I'm making little supersonic sounds right now, General. It's so terribly good to be back with you."

She held out her hand. He took it.

"You don't know how good it feels to be back with all of *you*," he said. Their eyes met, briefly. "You'll never believe it, but I missed you." He looked around. "Where's the rest of my family? Where's Telek?"

Beetle had taken Ike's arm to guide him through the fog as they headed toward the car, parked inside the huge station near the head of the tracks.

"Poor Telek's devastated," Kay told Ike. "He's been seized by the authorities and must remain in quarantine for six months. British Customs has declared him a dog."

"Oh, no! He must be outraged. Six months? That poor devil. He'll go stir crazy."

"Especially if he finds out the British have given you lovely new housing, right near Berkeley Square. Beautiful townhouse, exquisitely furnished."

"Well. The British are certainly doing their best to be hospitable."

"Not *all* the British, Ike." It was Beetle, bringing them all back to earth. "When the weather grounded your plane in Scotland, we were taking bets General Montgomery had shot you down. He's been trying to take over everything while you were away."

Ike was disturbed. "Monty knew he was in command here only until my return."

"He's been all over England, reviewing troops, making speeches. There's a rumor he's running for King."

"General Smith," Kay put in. "Only we British are allowed to make jokes about the Crown. Our King is sacred to us. You have nothing comparable in America, except your reverence for John Dillinger."

Ike grinned at her. "Thank God you haven't mellowed."

"Not to worry," she smiled back.

"I don't want to alarm you," Beetle continued, "but Monty's got Churchill's ear. He's trying to drive a wedge between you two. On top of that, General de Gaulle feels he's being treated unfairly because Roosevelt is making him stay in North Africa, and he's threatening to pull out his Free French troops. And there's a rumor Stalin is about to make a separate peace with Hitler."

"Damn," Ike said. "Wouldn't it be wonderful if we only had to fight the Germans?"

The drive through the fogbound London streets was hair-raising. Kay peered through the windshield into an absolute wall of mist. Occasionally a London bus loomed up like some huge sailing vessel tacking in the wind, and she had to yank the wheel over hard to avoid it. Once she ran up on a curb and had to bump her way back onto Brompton Road. She found her way to Berkeley Square by

183

instinct and pulled the car to a halt, peering desperately out of the window to make certain where they were.

"I think we're here," she announced. "Of course, there's a chance it's the Thames Embankment. If you hear a splash when I step out of this door, drive on."

"No," Ike said quietly. "I'll dive in."

She looked at him sharply. He was in the back seat. During the drive, she had caught an occasional glimpse of him in the mirror, watching her. Well, then. It was still there. Whatever had been there. What a lovely fog, she thought. What a lovely, lovely night. She threw open the door and almost felt her way outside.

"We'd better be where we're supposed to be," Tex said, leaning out to stare into the dense mist. "You've held up World War II for a solid hour, Kay."

"I'd like to hold it up forever," she said.

"I'm not living in this bordello! I won't see army funds spent on embroidered pillows and pink bed sheets!"

Kay smiled at the sound of Ike's voice, complaining of the luxury. The voice of Abilene, she told herself, as she helped Mickey lay out hors d'oeuvres and drinks in the living room.

Ike and the others appeared from one of the bedrooms. "Tomorrow, we're moving back to Telegraph Cottage, where we can get back to the miserable business of fighting this war," Ike said.

Mickey placed a drink in his hand.

"Thanks, Mickey. You always know just what I need. Now get yourself some rest. We're packing in the morning."

"If you don't mind, Ike," Tex yawned, "I'm going to bed too. I don't know how you do it. We've been traveling thirty-five hours and I'm beat."

"I'll join you, seeing it's past midnight," Beetle said. They started up the stairs together.

Kay crossed toward the front door. "Good night, General. Sleep well."

"Kay, I've been ordered to give you a present by the

President of the United States. Won't you wait a minute?"

Slowly, Kay turned. "I thought you'd never ask."

She came back from the door, placing her uniform cap on a table near the stairway. Tex, who had stopped at Ike's words, turned and whispered to her from the stairs. "Summersby . . . it's no good. Abraham Lincoln can't have a girlfriend. You'll be swept under the rug of American history."

Kay looked at him, her chin lifted defiantly. "I understand I'll have a lot of distinguished company under that American rug." Proudly, she turned to go to the side of the Supreme Commander, Allied Expeditionary Forces.

Ike had found Roosevelt's photograph in his briefcase. He handed it to her.

Kay was pleased. "How kind of the President to remember, and not hold the Revolutionary War against me."

"That's because America won that one," Ike smiled. He handed her the drink he had poured for her.

"Cheers." Kay raised her glass. "To winning *this* one together."

They sipped, neither wanting to say the obvious. Or ask. Finally, Ike crossed slowly to the sofa. "You might as well know that I'd made up my mind to order you back to driving for General Spaatz."

Kay turned quickly to look at him. Ike sat down and leaned back, relaxing at last.

"And then," he said softly, "there you stood on the train platform, waiting for me. Like a lighthouse in the fog."

"How flattering. Two hundred feet tall, solid concrete, and a beacon spinning about my head."

"Shut up. In Abilene, that would be considered poetry."

"I know, General. I do know."

She crossed the room and sat beside him. It was good just to be close together. Barely touching. For the moment, it was more than enough.

Ike propped his legs up on the coffee table and lit a

cigarette, contentedly at home. "Well, did you know the President has heard talk about us?"

"Goodness. Is there nothing better for American Intelligence to do? I'm actually flattered." She kissed him, lightly. "How long will it take for him to find out about *that,* do you suppose?"

"Kay. What I'm trying to say is, I don't want to see you hurt."

"It's too late. You know I'm one of the walking wounded."

"One day I may have to deny you in public. You're going to be scorned, and you're going to be ridiculed. You're going to be disbelieved. My family will refuse to admit you ever existed."

"I can take all that if I'm also wanted. At least, please, let me have that."

"You're wanted."

"My God. The Great Stone Face can speak."

She got up and went to look out of the window. Fog. Nothing but fog.

"I knew that the moment I left North Africa." Ike rose, following her. "I couldn't face coming back to London and not seeing you. It wouldn't really be London." He put his hands on her shoulders, turning her to face him. "But I'm a soldier and a husband. It's a story as old as battle itself. Whatever happiness we have together may only last as long as the horrors of this war. Will you promise to have me on those unfair terms?"

"Good Lord, Ike! They raise a lot of corn in Abilene, don't they?"

"It's honest corn."

"My dear General Dwight David Eisenhower." Gently, she touched his cheek. "I don't know what kind of women have been in love with you before, but this woman loves with all her heart, and that is why she is always hurt—but, oh, the lovely, lovely days between. I can make you any kind of promise you wish, because I am quite certain there is no tomorrow. I don't believe in heaven and I don't believe in hell. What this war has taught me to believe in is *now.*"

She moved away from him, went to the table to retrieve her uniform hat, and placed it firmly on her head. "So you get yourself a good night's rest, because what you have to do from now on is nothing short of saving decency and honor and the England I love, and you go ahead and do your job and I will do mine, which is infinitely less. It only involves loving you so much that I don't give a damn what happens to me."

She started for the door.

"Kay—"

She stopped, but didn't turn.

"Goddammit, Kay."

"Thank you. Shakespeare couldn't have put it better."

And she was gone.

* * *

The news was ominous. Hitler had put Ike's old nemesis, Gen. Erwin Rommel, in command of the Channel defenses. Obviously, the Nazis had been alerted to the huge buildup of men and supplies in England and were preparing to meet it with devastating force. Ike and Winston Churchill held almost weekly meetings at 10 Downing Street. Then one day came the invitation to a full-dress conference of military leaders at Chequers, where Churchill would have the full weight of British history on his side.

The Prime Minister was standing at the medieval entrance, flanked by Montgomery, Field Marshal Sir Alan Brooke, and Sir Trafford Leigh-Mallory, Air Chief Marshal, when Kay pulled Ike's Cadillac to a halt.

"Be careful, he's brought up reinforcements." She indicated the group surrounding Churchill.

"It's all right," Ike reassured her. "I've brought the West Point varsity."

Lt. Gen. Omar Bradley, the studious, brilliant tactician who was to be placed in charge of American ground forces

187

for the invasion, stepped out of the car with Eisenhower and eyed the waiting British officers.

"There shouldn't be any battle," he told Ike. "Even Churchill must realize by now it's too late to postpone the invasion."

Kay shook her head. "Good luck, General Bradley. I'm afraid you'll need it."

"I thought you'd be rooting for an American defeat?"

"No. I hope I've seen the last of those."

Ike smiled at her; then he and Bradley advanced on the British awaiting them.

The tremendous fortifications of the French Channel coast were being inspected by Rommel and Adolf Hitler himself. New concrete was being poured, and huge cannon were being raised into place. "This is official German news film, recently secured through diplomatic channels," Churchill explained to the group seated in the darkened library.

Ike shifted uncomfortably. "The Germans wanted you to have this film, Mr. Prime Minister. Propaganda."

"Perhaps. But those great cannon were not manufactured in Hollywood, General Eisenhower. That really is General Erwin Rommel, not Cary Grant. Those tank traps and those mines are frighteningly real." He motioned to stop the film and rose to his feet.

"We are faced with a final and fateful decision." The Churchillian tones were heightened by the darkness; now the Prime Minister threw open the curtains, admitting the daylight. "The new fortifications make any attack so costly in human lives that we must seriously re-examine the whole question of a massive frontal assault against the beaches of France."

"We've postponed long enough!" Eisenhower was definite, decisive. "The month of June is ideal for amphibious operation. We are going to throw the Germans off balance by striking in two places at once—across the Channel, and into the South of France."

"*Two* invasions at once? Absolutely insane." Montgomery's contempt was open.

"We don't think so." Gen. Bradley spoke quietly. "We can trap half the German divisions in France between the two invading armies."

"And take so many landing craft and men away from the Channel invasion that *both* will be doomed! Lunacy, sheer lunacy!" Montgomery was not one to mince words.

"Not if we can drop enough paratroopers and gliders behind the Channel fortifications to knock them out before the landing!" Ike was angry now, as he realized that Churchill had orchestrated this meeting as he had their first.

Leigh-Mallory, leader of the RAF, was already crossing to a map. "My staff has made a complete study of the American proposals, General Eisenhower. You have selected landing grounds completely unsuitable for glider landings, and targets for your paratroopers impossible to hit in darkness." He indicated the objectives, "Your 82nd and 101st Airborne will suffer seventy percent losses in glider strength, and at least fifty percent in paratroop strength before they even hit the ground."

Ike hesitated. The RAF had been at this business a long time. He looked at Bradley.

"This large an airborne attack has never been tried before," Bradley said calmly. "Nobody on earth can tell us it will or won't work."

Churchill had moved toward them, waving his cigar. "Gentlemen, gentlemen! You will find I am eminently fair. I am perfectly willing to hear everyone out before having my own way."

"And what is your own way?" Ike wanted to know.

"We already have forces on the continent of Europe, in Italy. I repeat my belief that they must immediately strike northward into Germany and enter Berlin through the back door."

"Mr. Prime Minister, the Russian Army is closer to Berlin than we are!"

"That, my dear General, is precisely the point."

"If you want to beat the Russians to Berlin, that's a political decision, not military one, and I'll have no part of it!" Ike's face had flushed red. This was an argument he had met before, one he had felt he had overcome, and now Churchill, with his bulldog stubbornness, was trying to push it through again. "My orders are to enter the Continent across the English Channel and aim at the heart of Germany—not her rear end! You can't fight World War II with World War I thinking!"

"If the Russian Army gains control of Western Europe, we had all better start thinking of World War III."

"Dammit, let's fight this war first!"

"The impregnable West Wall—"

"To hell with the West Wall! There are no longer any impregnable fixed defenses!"

"There are no longer unlimited British lives to throw against them! General Eisenhower, your plan is too risky. It must be called off. *Now!*"

The silence that followed almost crackled. Eisenhower and Churchill stood facing each other on the barricades, the issue clear, the battle drawn.

Ike spoke first.

"Mr. Prime Minister, you made a solemn promise that England would join in the assault across the Channel. My title is Supreme Commander of that operation. Does it mean anything? Is this my military command? Or is it yours alone? If it isn't mine, you British have my resignation here and now."

Churchill surveyed his adversary silently, chewing on his cigar. As last, he spoke. "Are you asking the First Minister of the British Empire for unconditional surrender?"

"I am asking him to live up to his word."

"Sometimes, my dear Ike, that is even more difficult."

190

It was Montgomery who broke the tension. "General Eisenhower, this is a moment for cold logic. We do not yet have the military strength to—"

He had misjudged the moment. Churchill interrupted before he could go further. "Monty, the destiny of man is not decided by material computation. When great causes are on the move in the world, we learn that we are spirits, not animals, and that something is going on in space and time which, whether we like it or not, spells duty." He turned to Eisenhower. "I take no satisfaction in gaining my way if I know my way is inferior. You seem terribly certain it is."

"Don't start being reasonable, Mr. Prime Minister," Ike said. "You're making it tougher."

"That was my intention."

Ike started to pace. This was his opening; he had to exploit it quickly or lose the opportunity. "Okay. This is how I see it. General Montgomery is absolutely right." Monty looked up, surprised. "We don't have the landing craft to conduct two invasions at once. My military consultant, Mr. Churchill, is also right. The West Wall has been strengthened too much for the original plan. We'll take the landing craft from southern France and use them to throw two extra divisions across the English Channel. The time to get off our ass has arrived."

Churchill had been listening with grudging approval. "Ike, you have become a very dangerous man. You have learned my secret of making any compromise which will let you have your own way." He allowed himself to smile. "You are learning to be a politician. Some day, I do not doubt, you will run for President."

"God forbid!"

The Prime Minister did not respond. He knew better than this American general how strong the appeal of power can be. The Presidency of the United States is a magnet which had lured far more reluctant men than Dwight

191

Eisenhower to what they later came to consider their destiny.

"Does this mean the useless invasion of southern France will be abandoned completely?" It was Monty again. "Because if it isn't, I strongly protest against its—"

"Monty, for God's sake!" The Prime Minister had had enough. "It's over. Always test a man to see if he advocates his principles more strongly than you do yours. Then beat a strategic retreat." He turned to Ike. "I am in this thing with you to the end," said the Prime Minister of the British Empire, "and if it fails, we will go down together."

Ike grasped Winston Churchill's proffered hand and shook it warmly.

The massive buildup of American forces in England continued. German wolfpack submarines in the Atlantic frantically redoubled their efforts, but Allied naval forces, aided by information provided by Ultra, managed to smash the U-boat attacks before they could seriously damage the huge supply convoys.

American accents sprouted in the British countryside. GI's swarmed through Picadilly and Soho until they almost outnumbered the ladies of the evening. England's Channel coast, where shipping was massing for the assault, was declared out of bounds even to newsmen and cut off from the rest of the country. Even diplomatic mail to and from foreign embassies was stopped, to prevent the leakage of any information.

Elaborate efforts were made to confuse and mislead the Germans. The Man Who Never Was came into existence, a creation of British Intelligence. He was a British officer who had been killed in battle. His body was allowed to wash ashore on a Spanish beach, in his pockets detailed plans for the coming invasion—an invasion, the plans indicated, which would hit in the Pas de Calais area, the shortest route from Dover to the Continent.

A British actor who resembled Montgomery was elaborately coached to imitate the general and sent to Gibraltar, to make the Germans think Monty was out of England, and therefore the Channel crossing could not be imminent. And George S. Patton, protesting bitterly, was put to work commanding an imaginary army supposedly in training for the attack on the Pas de Calais, while the real army under the real Monty was training for the real attack, which would hit Normandy.

To top it all, German secret agents in England had been captured and turned into allies; they radioed misleading information back to their masters in Berlin.

Adolf Hitler and the Nazi leaders, staggering under the massive defeats on the Russian front, struck back desperately where there could be the least opposition—the underground forces in the occupied countries. Frenchmen by the hundreds were led to the Gestapo's gallows, and the cruel human shipments to the concentration camps from France, from Poland, from Belgium, increased in size every day.

The forces of good were soon to meet the forces of evil on the beaches of France, and the outcome would decide the future of free men for centuries.

It was at this crucial moment that Gen. George S. Patton fouled up once more. He committed a *gaffe* so horrendous it echoed in the halls of Congress.

Ike, fuming, summoned Patton to Supreme Headquarters, now set up at Bushey Park outside London. The day of the meeting, Eisenhower's mood was not improved by Col. Tex Lee, who asked to be released from Eisenhower's staff for a combat assignment.

"Dammit, Tex, I'll give you the same answer Marshall gave me—if I want you, you're going to stay right here! And I want you."

"Ike, I'm a soldier, not an office boy! The whole world's on fire, and I'm sitting here with a squirt gun."

193

"You're part of the family, and I need my family! I don't want to hear another word from—"

Kay opened the door and stuck her head in. "It's old Blood-and-Guts, sir."

"Let him cool his heels a few minutes—it's good for the soul," Ike told her.

Patton pushed his way into the room. "I don't have any soul, Ike, and you know it. Now put me up in front of a firing squad and let's get this whole damn thing over with!"

"George, you put your stupid foot in your big mouth more often than a jackass in a bucking contest!" Ike saw that Kay was still standing in the doorway. "You'd better leave, Kay—we're about to get down to four-letter words."

"Goodness! Are there some I don't know?" But she stepped out, followed by Tex.

Ike crossed to his desk and grabbed a letter from it. "George, let me read what you wrote me last time you were in hot water—after you slapped those soldiers in the hospital in Sicily." He put on his glasses. " 'I am at a loss to find words with which to express my grief at having given you, a man to whom I owe everything and for whom I would gladly lay down my life, cause to be displeased with me.' "

"I apologized to those two lily-livered cowards, didn't I?" Patton growled.

"That's just what I mean!"

"Brave men were dying in the beds next to them—and those two were blubbering with that battle-fatigue bullshit! Brave men don't cry, Ike. I was bringing those two yellow-bellies to their senses."

"What do I have to do to bring you to yours? Take away your pearl-handled pea-shooter?"

"Ike, put yourself in my place. Parading up and down the English coast with my damn bulldog so the Germans will think I'm going to lead the invasion. Know-

194

ing all the time it's Monty, and I'm just a window dummy. I throw up every night! Dammit, I'm ten times the leader that little British son of a bitch is, and you know it."

"That little British son of a bitch has ten times the sense you have, and he's got Winston Churchill and the whole British Empire behind him. All you have is your mouth and the good sense of an orangutan in heat."

"Ike—!"

"How could you make a speech saying the United States and England were going to divide the world up between them after the war? What about Russia?" He picked a dispatch off his desk. "Marshall says Congress is up in arms because you've slapped Joe Stalin in the face just when we need him most. The Russians are thinking of burying you tomorrow in Lenin's tomb. He's agreed to move over."

"I was just talking to a group of women. I didn't know some of them were reporters."

"Women *can* write, you know. We do let them go to school."

"Well, you can't blame that on *me*."

Ike threw up his hands. "George, this couldn't have happened at a worse time. Right now I need all the help God and man can give me, and you foul up like a pig in a parlor."

"Ike, if you'd just give me a command. A battalion. A company. A platoon. One private with a sling shot. Just let me kill Nazis—"

"Don't you realize how serious this is, George? We're talking about *Congress!* They want blood. It's not only your job that's at stake this time—it's mine, too."

"My God, Ike! If I've done anything to hurt your authority as—"

"You have, George. I picked you. I defended you, after that mess in Sicily. I'm responsible for your actions."

Patton turned away. Despite the surface bravado, he was a man of considerable sensitivity and intelligence, a poet, a historian. The thought that his words had in any way undermined respect for Dwight Eisenhower was almost unbearable.

"Ike," he said huskily, "all I wanted was a chance to redeem myself, take a column of tanks and kick the hell out of those obscene Nazi supermen. I wanted to march my boys down Unter den Linden and show those goose-stepping bastards how to win a war!" He turned to face his friend again. "Jesus, Ike, I don't want to sit out the rest of the only war I was born in the right century for. But I'm actually sick at my stomach, thinking of the trouble my big mouth has caused you." Patton took a deep breath. For a career army man, he was about to take the most difficult step of all. "So I'll do the best thing I can to help you. I'm resigning my commission in the United States Army, effective immediately."

Ike's heart went out to this frustrating, unstable, brilliant soldier. Why is genius so often associated with irrationality? Ike knew what Patton's offer of his commission meant. To George Patton, it was the equivalent of hara-kiri.

Ike took off his glasses and placed them on his desk. "George, you taught me everything I know about tank warfare. You wrote the book. Now teach that arrogant son of a bitch Erwin Rommel a lesson he'll never forget, because you're the only man in the world who can." Patton stared, unwilling to believe what he was hearing. "I am giving you immediate command of the United States Third Army."

Shaken, hiding his emotion, Patton turned away. This was so unexpected, yet so typically Ike.

Ike went on. "Just get me some victories, so everyone will think I'm a genius. And remember, if you louse up again, I'll have your balls cut off in public. *Don't let me down.*"

Ike put an arm about his friends shoulders. "You see how wrong you were, George? Brave men *do* cry."

* * *

"His Majesty, the King." Winston Churchill's voice rang proudly through the Eighth Form classroom of St. Paul's School. The old, traditional boys school on the outskirts of London had been chosen for its very incongruity; who would think the highest-ranking officers of the Allied nations would be seated on its cramped benches, facing a schoolmaster's desk and blackboard, for the most secret conference of history's greatest war?

The King rose from one of the schoolboy benches, his innate dignity making it a royal gesture, and crossed to stand before the battered old desk as Churchill settled his ample body into the first row of seats, where generations of British youths had carved their initials into the forgiving wood.

King George VI was a youthful, handsome monarch, whose shyness caused him to stammer painfully; his public speeches were rare and trying efforts. But on this occasion, though his words were hesitant, his manner and force were impressive.

"We are g-gathered here, in old St. P-Paul's S-School —" he paused to gather control "—the leaders of the armed forces of the nations of the free world." He scanned his listeners, in the uniforms of so many nations, a handful of men representing forces great enough to attempt the conquest of Nazi-occupied Europe. "England," he continued, "which once stood alone, greets with gratitude and hope the military commanders of the Commonwealth of Australia, the Commonwealth of Canada, the Commonwealth of India, the Commonwealth of N-New Zealand, the R-Republic of China, the nation of Czechoslovakia, the Republic of France, the nation of Holland, the nation of Poland, the Union of South Africa, the United States of America."

He paused, then, "We are alone no longer."

He waited for the applause to subside and then quietly resumed his place on the bench beside Churchill.

Now it was the Prime Minister's turn to extricate himself from the schoolboy seat and face the audience, which included officers he had worked and planned with for so long: Gen. Eisenhower, Field Marshal Montgomery, Gen. Patton, Sir Alan Brooke, Gen. Bradley, Air Marshal Leigh-Mallory. Churchill had no trouble with words; his problem was limiting his flights of rhetoric to the matter at hand.

"I, for one, long had my doubts about confronting the Nazi military machine along the Channel coast. But, gentlemen, I am hardening toward this enterprise. The fearsome task must be done and it must be done soon."

The piercing eyes beneath the bushy brows inspected the audience. This was the man who had defied Hitler's massed might at a moment when England was almost defenseless, when the rest of the world had given her up for lost, when Churchill's was the only voice to dare the terrible enemy to attempt to cross the Channel. Now the Channel was to be crossed in the opposite direction, and Winston Churchill was preparing to hurl Britain's renewed might and that of her Allies against that same Hitler who had danced a jig after the fall of France.

"We see the Germans hated as no race has ever been hated before in human history, and with good reason. If there is risk now, it is risk we cannot shirk. I repeat what I said in England's darkest hour: let the great cities of Paris, of Rome, of Warsaw, of Prague, of Vienna, banish despair. Their liberation is sure. The day will come when the joybells will ring again throughout Europe, and when victorious nations will plan and build in justice, in tradition, and in freedom, a house of many mansions where there will be room for all."

As the Prime Minister returned to his bench, Ike motioned to Montgomery, who rose quickly and strode to the front, the schoolmaster's role fitting him like a glove. He advanced to the map of the invasion beaches that covered one wall and picked up a pointer from the nearby blackboard.

"Gentlemen, the entire front of our attack will be

over sixty miles long. The Americans will be on the right, at Utah Beach and Omaha Beach. The British and Canadian forces will be on the left, at Gold, Juno, and Sword beaches. We hope by the end of the first day to break out our armored forces in the area beyond Caen, where our British tanks can knock about a bit." He permitted himself to smile at his students. "The initial landings will include 156,000 men, 5,000 ships, and 11,000 aircraft. Participating eventually will be a total force of two million men." He paused. "Good hunting, all."

Now it was Ike's turn. He rose and stretched his cramped legs, then moved to the front of the room beside the old desk, reminded of his days in the red schoolhouse on the outskirts of Abilene.

He spoke—direct, concise. In other words, Eisenhower.

"We must cross the Channel with our convoys at night. We need moonlight for our airborne assaults. We need forty minutes of daylight preceding the ground attack to complete our air bombing and naval bombardment. We must attack at low tide, so that German tank traps and mines can be removed while they are out of water. Only two periods this month have the proper combination of moon, tide, and sunrise—June 5th, 6th, and 7th, and June 19th, 20th, and 21st. There are two other vital essentials. Without the help of the people of France, none of our planning can succeed And, for our paratroopers and gliders, we must have clear skies. The next few weeks will tell if the Lord is on our side."

* * *

The rain fell in torrents. Not the usual English spring rainfall, but horizontal sheets blown by near gales. The canvas tents set up at invasion headquarters at Southwick Manor near Portsmouth shuddered under the downpour; Ike's trailer, hidden away under camouflage and trees, was battered and soaked. The Lord, if He were on the Allies' side, was working in strange ways His wonders to perform.

On June third, Ike ordered advance units to sail so that they would be in position for D-Day on the fifth. The weather worsened. The invasion fleet had to be recalled by radio, and since they could not transmit for fear of giving away their positions, no one knew whether they had received the message.

The "window" of June 5 to June 7 had been narrowed by a full day.

And then a teletype operator for the Associated Press, practicing a message, unwittingly had it go out on the AP short-wave circuits: URGENT A.P. NYK FLASH EISENHOWER H.Q. ANNOUNCE LANDINGS IN FRANCE. This was picked up and repeated by radio stations in Berlin and Moscow, and although it was instantly denied, Ike felt the damage had been done. The Nazis had been alerted that the crucial moment was definitely near.

Through the slashing rainfall, a phalanx of motorcycles roared into stately Southwick Manor, leading a military convoy that escorted an ancient Citroen flying the tricolor of France. The Convoy halted in the center of the tent city. The door of the Citroen opened and a tall dignified French officer unfolded himself from the rear seat and marched through the rain and the wind as if they did not exist. Gen. Charles de Gaulle had arrived.

Under the roofed entryway to Ike's trailer, Eisenhower and Winston Churchill, who was dressed in jump suit and boots against the storm, watched with some apprehension.

"Goddammit, he's right not to want to cooperate," Ike told the Prime Minister, turning up his collar against the biting wind.

"It wouldn't make any difference to Charles de Gaulle if he were wrong." Churchill gave up his attempt to light his damp stogie. "I spoke to him this morning. He will not be swayed by anything so mundane as common sense. Unfortunately, the Almighty, in His wisdom, did not see fit to create Frenchmen in the image of Englishmen."

"But he's *got* to broadcast to the French underground to help us when we start landing. We know he's the only one they'll listen to."

"The problem, my dear General, is that *he* knows it, too."

"He looks as sore as a mule with a burr up his ass."

"Exquisitely phrased. I've done all I can with him. It is now America's turn."

"What do you think I should do?"

"Charm him, my dear Ike. Charm him," Churchill growled. Then his face lit up with his most cordial smile. "Ah! *Mon Général! Enchanté!*" He advanced toward the now thoroughly soaked de Gaulle for the traditional kiss on both cheeks, delivered with little enthusiasm by the savior of France.

"Hitler has been tricked into believing our assault will land here—" Ike's hand pointed to the Pas de Calais area on a map of the Channel coasts. Ike, de Gaulle, and Churchill were in Ike's trailer, reasonably warm and dry, although de Gaulle's hair was still wet.

"We've kept George Patton and a phantom army training opposite Calais, here, in England," Ike continued, "although our real attack will come on the beaches of Normandy, here."

"How do you know Hitler has been tricked?" De Gaulle was not willing to accept one word from either America or Britain without challenge.

"We have broken the German 'Enigma' code and are reading the top-level messages between Hitler and his generals," Ike informed him.

"Why was I not informed of this code-breaking?" De Gaulle's anger had found a point to focus on.

Churchill tried to keep his temper in check. "I believe Mr. Roosevelt thought it was not necessary to inform you, since he felt you received your own messages through divine inspiration."

"General de Gaulle!" Ike interposed quickly. "You will have the honor of making the first broadcast to the French people and the French underground on D-Day, asking them to help us in every way."

De Gaulle regarded him with haughty stare.

"Within forty-eight hours, weather permitting, Allied armies will be on the soil of France!" Ike poured wine into a glass for his guest—French wine, of course.

"By whose authority?" de Gaulle demanded.

"By my authority," Churchill growled, "as Prime Minister of the United Kingdom."

"And by the authority of the President of the United States," Ike added.

"Has anyone bothered to consult the people of France for their authority?" de Gaulle inquired loftily. "Only Charles de Gaulle has the right to give them orders."

Ike was about to offer the glass of wine to de Gaulle, but decided it was the wrong moment. He set the glass down. His visitor continued, his anger growing along with his eloquence. "Until this very day, I have been kept almost a prisoner in Algiers, in ignorance of your plans for my country, because I refuse to allow Franklin Roosevelt to play Louis XIV and choose the leader of France!"

"My dear General de Gaulle—"

"My dear Monsieur Churchill, I have not finished!" De Gaulle turned to Ike. "On D-Day, acting under the instructions of your President, you will proclaim you are taking supreme authority in France. And Mr. Churchill will approve. You expect Charles de Gaulle to cooperate? *Je ne suis pas fou!*"

"How do you expect Britain to take a position separate from the United States?" Churchill demanded.

"How do you expect Charles de Gaulle to take a position separate from the destiny of France?"

Churchill's frustration was growing. He tried to keep his voice even. "This is something you must know: each time Britain must choose between Europe and the open sea, we shall always choose the open sea. Each time I must choose between you and Roosevelt, I shall choose Roosevelt. Those are the facts of life. Will you accept them and use your power to broadcast a message to the people of France urging them to cooperate with the Allied forces? Or will you play dog in the manger and make it impossible for us to bring France the freedom she so desperately desires?"

"Freedom? What sort of freedom is it when the British government is already printing French money to be used in my country by your occupying armies?"

"A temporary necessity which—"

"No! An insult. I shall order the French people not to honor one centime!"

Churchill found his coat and threw it about his shoulders. "General de Gaulle, I never before understood why Joan of Arc was burned at the stake. Thank you for correcting my ignorance. *Au 'voir!*" He turned to his host. "Good luck, Ike."

Churchill crossed to the door, threw it open, and stepped out into the driving rain.

A moment later, an angry de Gaulle followed him. He was just starting through the mud puddles toward the waiting Citroen when Ike appeared in the doorway of the trailer.

"General de Gaulle!"

De Gaulle hesitated.

"I want to speak to you as a soldier to a soldier." Eisenhower's tone was quiet, but he had pressed the proper button. Churchill was a civilian, an outsider. This was a military matter for military men.

De Gaulle turned, the rain dripping off the visor of his képi. Ike approached him and now the two soldiers stood side by side in the rain, oblivious to the downpour.

"On D-Day," Ike continued, "the men of the American 82nd and 101st Airborne will be parachuting in darkness near Ste. Mère Église, on the French coast. Each man carries eighty-five pounds of equipment in addition to his chute. They will be helpless until they hit the ground and untangle their shroud lines. They will be massacred by German fire unless Frenchmen are willing to risk their lives for them. You are the only one who can order the Resistance to do this for us. And for France."

The two Generals walked beneath the weeping trees, barely noticing the rain that sliced into their faces, driven by the wind that was still jeopardizing the entire precarious enterprise.

"You want me to broadcast to the Resistance to open fire on German troops?" de Gaulle said. "Even though, if the invasion fails, they and their families will be murdered instantly?"

"The invasion will only fail if they don't open fire," Ike told him.

They walked in silence. Finally Charles de Gaulle spoke, "First, I must be recognized as the sole authority in my country."

"Goddammit, you don't need *me* to give you that authority, you don't need Roosevelt, you don't need Winston Churchill—you have it! You're the only man who has the support of the French people, and Roosevelt knows it, but he's too stubborn to admit it publicly! What the hell kind of game is this? Lots of brave British and American kids are going to die for France because they've been told their country expects them to. When they find out you won't lift a finger to help them, who will ever convince them that Charles de Gaulle was once a soldier, too?"

De Gaulle stopped short, as if he had been slapped. "I am also a realist," he said. "I must be certain my authority will be recognized before I can agree to *anything.*"

"What do you want? My word I'll defy the President of the United States and see you get what is only your right? I'll put my job on the line right now and tell you I will recognize no French power in France but Charles de Gaulle!"

"You will oppose your own President—your Commander in Chief?" De Gaulle was no fool. He knew exactly what he was demanding, and he wanted it spelled out.

"If that's what I have to do, yes! I have the power under military necessity to recognize your authority, so let's get all that crap out of the way. And I give you my personal guarantee Free French troops will be the first into Paris when we liberate it!"

De Gaulle's eyebrows lifted. This was the heart of the matter: would Frenchmen be allowed to liberate Frenchmen? And would they be de Gaulle's Frenchmen, or the Communist underground's Frenchmen?

Ike pulled a sheet of paper from his pocket and offered it to the man who was the conscience of France. "Here's what I'm going to say in my broadcast to the French people on D-Day. You can change it any way you want to if you think I'm taking your authority by daring to address your people. Now, will you go on the radio too? Will you personally order the French nation and the French underground to help us kill Nazis? Will you give those kids parachuting into Ste. Mère Église an even chance to come out alive?"

Slowly, de Gaulle folded the paper and slipped it inside his uniform pocket. "I shall read this over and make my decision."

It was four a. m. on June 5 when the final meeting was held in the stately old library of Southwick Manor. The storm continued unabated. High winds drove the thin rain through the edges of the blacked-out library windows, making tiny puddles on the wooden floor. The major Allied leaders were all there, for the moment was crucial: if Adm. Kirk's naval forces sailed again the next day and had to be recalled, they would not have sufficient fuel to launch the invasion again on June 7th, and the "window" would have been closed.

Kay and a group of British WRENs were brewing tea over an electric burner, passing the cups around to the chilled officers, who were watching a dour Scot meteorologist at the enormous weather map that extended from floor to ceiling of the library. Ike sat nearby, listening impatiently to the sound of the wind outside.

Group Capt. Jock Burns was reputed to be the leading weather expert in Britain's armed forces, and he took his duties seriously. Slowly, deliberately, he sketched the facts for his worried listeners.

"Wind from the west over the Channel gusting forty miles per hour. Precipitation 2.11 inches and continuing heavy. 'Tis foul weather. The birds are not only walking—a few of them, I do not doubt, are swimming."

"What about tomorrow, Jock?" Ike was in no mood for small Scottish ironies.

"Well, it is no' gude, but it is no' altogether bad. Someone has gone and knocked a bloody big hole in the weather, and were I a church-going man, I might have an explanation. As a scientist, I can only report facts. The rain front over the assault area should begin to clear, and we should have some relatively gude weather lasting perhaps forty-eight hours."

There was a startled murmur from those in the room, so used to hearing nothing but gloomy Scottish predictions. Capt. Burns hastened to assure them there was still room for pessimism.

"But it will then return to its present foul and British nature, as there is another storm over the North Atlantic, on its way in." His audience disregarded that; the excited talk continued. Burns looked annoyed. "Mind ye now," he warned, "meteorology is not yet an exact science. I shouldn't be throwin' away my galoshes if I were you. There is a strong chance I could be wrong. On the other hand, I could be right."

Ike puffed on his cigarette as the tension mounted. The moment of decision could be postponed no longer. "Will our gliders and paratroopers have low enough winds and sufficient visibility to land?"

"Truthfully, I can't say. Possibly aye, possibly nay."

Kay, agonizing for Ike, had reached the front of the room with her tray of teacups. "Will you take milk or lemon, Captain Burns? Or don't you care to predict?" she inquired.

"Milk, thank you, lass," he said, preferring not to notice the acid in her voice.

Ike had risen to his feet, and was chain-lighting another cigarette. He looked drawn, Kay thought; she had never seen him quite this nervous. But then, she realized, she had never seen him with the immediate responsibility for so many thousands of lives.

"Captain Burns, three airborne divisions are going to drop into this uncertain weather of yours," Ike said. "Now, *exactly* what will it be like tomorrow in the Channel and over the French coast?"

There was a long silence. Captain Burns sipped his tea, stirred it thoughtfully with his spoon, and sipped again.

"Dammit!" Ike was losing his temper. "I need an answer!"

Jock Burns set down his teacup. "To answer that question, sir, would make me a bloody fortune teller, not a meteorologist. I have no talent for tea leaves, General Eisenhower."

"Well, you must have a talent for something or you wouldn't be here! Now you tell me this: if this storm is coming from the west, would the Germans know when it will end?"

"No, sir. We have weather stations to the west of the British Isles. The Germans don't."

Ike was pacing now. He ground his cigarette out in an ashtray, then immediately lit another. "What *would* they think?"

Burns shrugged. "If they're watching their barometers, they probably would think anyone who would launch an air or sea attack in the next few days would have to be daft, sir."

Ike paused, considering. There was one more fact to weigh. "If we postpone again, how long before the moon and tides will be favorable?"

"Two weeks."

Eisenhower turned and crossed to the window. He could hear the rain, the sound of the wind, drowning out his hopes. Suddenly he had to feel it, to touch it. No Kansas farmer relied completely on the *Farmers' Almanac* when it was time for the harvest. Ike thrust the blackout curtains aside and threw open the window, letting the rain and the wind blow past his face and into the room.

"Any opinions?" he demanded of the others. "Brad?"

Omar Bradley shook his head. "We don't *know* the weather is going to lift. I'm afraid, Ike, I think it's highly questionable."

"Monty?"

"If I were you, Ike, I would say—go!" General Montegomery leaned back in his chair. "Fortunately, I am not you."

There was one more voice Ike had to hear, the voice of the RAF. "Mallory?"

Air Chief Marshal Leigh-Mallory shook his head gravely. "If the weather blows our gliders and our paratroopers off target . . . if they miss drop zones and don't silence the Nazi fortifications above the beaches . . . we stand to lose half a million lives. And possibly the war. I would say it's much too chancy, General."

Ike stood silently, then turned back to the window. The wind continued to blow. A flash of lightning illuminated his grim features.

Eisenhower slammed the window shut and turned to face the waiting officers.

"Okay. We'll go."

Almost shouting with relief, they jumped to their feet, eager to go about the bloody job. The waiting was over; the biggest battle of the war was about to be fought. The fateful decision had been made.

And *they* hadn't had to make it.

VIX
D-Day

SOLDIERS, SAILORS AND AIRMEN OF THE AL-
LIED EXPEDITIONARY FORCE! You are about
to embark upon the Great Crusade, toward which we
have striven these many months. The hopes and
prayers of liberty-loving people everywhere march with
you. In company with our brave Allies, you will
bring about the destruction of the German war machine, the elimination of Nazi tyranny over the op-
pressed peoples of Europe, and security for ourselves
in a free world.

Your task will not be an easy one. Your enemy is well-
trained, well-equipped and battle-hardened. He will
fight savagely. But this is the year 1944! The tide has
turned! The free men of the world are marching together to Victory! Good Luck! And let us all beseech
the blessing of Almighty God upon this great and noble
undertaking.

Dwight D. Eisenhower.

It read, thought Ike, like the fatuous publicity handout it actually was. But he signed it, because it was the kind of statement expected from a Supreme Commander. As a soldier, he could imagine the reaction to all this rhetoric of some poor GI cooped up aboard a heaving transport—unshaven, frightened, seasick, throwing up into his helmet, on his way to face the huge German cannon embedded in steel-reinforced concrete above the beaches and the tank traps he was supposed to conquer.

Eisenhower could not let it rest at that—a scrap of paper signed with his name.

The night of June 5, 1944, was typical of late spring in the English countryside. Daylight lingered until well after nine p.m. The heavy winds had ceased momentarily and the rain had stopped, but the sky was still filled with angry clouds, turned scarlet by the late sunset, tumbling over each other above Newbury Airfield. A sky the color of blood, Kay thought, as she guided Ike's staff car onto the runway. In the distance, the men of the United States 101st Airborn Division were blackening their faces and sharpening their trench knives. Soon they would be dropping out of the skies into France, hours in advance of the main invasion forces.

It had been Ike's idea to come here; he had wanted to feel the weather on his own face to judge it; he had wanted to actually touch the men who were going into combat so that he could judge them, too.

Kay opened the door for him, and he stepped out of the car, watching the paratroopers across the distant airfield as they clustered about the flimsy, unarmored gliders and small C-47 transports in which they were about to challenge the Luftwaffe and the antiaircraft defenses of the German armies. Tex Lee got out of the car behind Ike's with Red Mueller of NBC, Barr of the BBC, Roberts of the United Press, and some photographers. As Tex approached him, Ike raised a restraining hand.

"Tex, give me a few minutes alone out there. No pictures, no reporters. Not yet. A lot of those boys aren't coming back, and they know damn well whose idea this air drop was. They may not be very happy to see me, but I have to see *them*."

He started forward, then paused as he reached Kay, who stood near the front of the staff car. "Kay, cover up those stars on the license plate. There are no generals here. Not today."

"Of course." She covered the four stars with a tiny canvas hood. Ike started off.

"Sir? . . . Ike?"

He turned.

"It's going to clear. You have my word."

He managed to smile at her, and she at him. The events of the past days had made them lean even more heavily on each other. In their goldfish bowl existence, their affair consisted of a few stolen moments, a few smiles like this—and the knowledge that they were necessary to each other. In the crucible of wartime, love is annealed into a harder metal than that of mere marriage. So they smiled—and without speaking, they spoke. Now Ike turned from her and started across the hard-packed runway toward the young men he was about to send off to an uncertain tomorrow, and he knew that at least one human heart was with him.

Tex stood beside Kay, watching Ike in disapproval. He had held the newsmen back, but they were also watching Eisenhower's progress across the airfield, and what was about to happen between the Supreme Commander and the men he had ordered into battle would be reported in the press of the world the next day.

"I told him this was a mistake," Tex whispered. "I hope he's wearing his bulletproof vest."

Kay ignored this. She kept her eyes on Ike, as he continued his lonely walk.

The paratroopers of the 101st, their screaming eagle shoulder patches belying their fears, blackened their faces with night paint and checked their bulky combat gear. They were too busy to recognize the figure striding across the runway toward them.

Ike felt old, tired. At 53, his age seemed a terrible burden; he was twice as old as many of the men about to parachute, on his orders, into the Nazi firepower. He thought again of the gloomy words of Leigh-Mallory: 70 percent losses in gliders, 50 percent in paratroops, *before they even hit the ground.*

One of the young men, taping an extra bayonet to his boot for an emergency he was certain would occur, caught a glimpse of the face approaching in the glow of the sunset. He thought he recognized it, and straightened up, pointing. Other men turned to stare.

Ike halted, hesitant. Then, determined, he started forward again.

More soldiers had turned, shielding their eyes, to stare in his direction.

"Ike!"

Still more turned, disbelieving.

"It's Ike!"

There was no question now. They had seen that face in photographs a hundred times. The Supreme Commander of all the Allied Expeditionary Forces had come to see them off.

"Ike! Ike! *IKE!*"

It became a shout, a cheer, a chant. More and more voices joined in. They were not forgotten! Someone realized the importance of what they were about to do, someone cared that many of them were about to die! Eisenhower! Eisenhower, himself! They cheered—for themselves, for him, even for America. This was in that golden age when America was a country to be proud of; the kids with the blackened faces and the submachine guns and the trench knives were the same kids who cheered for Notre Dame and NYU and Glenn Miller and Benny Goodman and Rita Hayworth.

"IKE! IKE! IKE!"

The cheering rolled across the field to where Kay and

Tex Lee stood watching. As their eyes met, she gently thumbed her nose at him, then turned proudly back.

Ike had reached the first cheering group.

"Knock it off! *QUIET!*" An officious second lieutenant was trying righteously to restore order in the face of the awesome presence of the Commanding General.

The men quieted down and put out their cigarettes. Their cheers faded into nothingness.

My God, Ike thought, they're all so terribly young.

"This is no dress parade, Lieutenant," he told the officer curtly. And then to the men—the boys—he said, "Break ranks. Anybody got a spare cigarette?"

It was like snapping a chain that had bound them. This was Ike, they remembered, this was the general who spoke to enlisted men. They swarmed around him, talking, lighting cigarettes, cheering. Half a dozen face-blackened paratroopers held out the cigarettes to him. Ike took one, accepted a light from the matches that were immediately proffered, and took a deep puff.

"The best part of my job," he said, "is that I get to shake hands with a lot of brave men."

He held out his hand. It was immediately grabbed, shaken, squeezed, by the hands of these boys about to do battle, at his bidding, against a merciless enemy. The confidence Ike tried to give with a clasp of his hand, the warmth of the Eisenhower smile, and the sincerity of his concern diminished a little the dread clutching at their throats.

"Hey, Ike, would you autograph my short-snorter?" A thin corporal held out a roll of dollar bills. The short-snorter bills were a symbol of World War II; anyone who had flown an ocean was entitled to carry them, with the signatures of those he met. Any short-snorter member who could not produce his roll of bills on demand had to buy a drink for his challenger. Ike signed, with a flourish, then found himself signing a dozen other bills offered by the soldiers crowding around him. One roll of bills unrolled all the way to the ground, and Ike surveyed it with mock astonishment. "How'd you save this much money in the army?" he asked the private who had handed it to him.

"I don't like girls," the soldier grinned.

"Anyone here from Kansas?" Ike wanted to know, when the roar of laughter had subsided.

"Ain't that in Texas someplace?" Another whoop of laughter.

Ike smiled. "Maybe they bought it," he said. "Texas is okay, too. I was born there."

"Ah'm from Waco." A tall, red-headed sergeant spoke up, his accent placing him instantly. The paint smearing his features made him look like the end man in a minstrel show, but he held a submachine gun in his arms.

"Waco!" Ike echoed his accent, "Well, howdy, pardner! Ranch country?"

"You know it. My old man runs six hundred head of ornery longhorn."

"Well, if you can use a ranch hand, I may have to ask you for a job after we win this war." Eisenhower flashed the warm smile again.

The Texan looked him in the eye. "If I'm not there, Ike, ask my old man."

There was a sudden hush. The war had come back, in all its grim reality.

The grin faded from Ike's lips.

Through the shifting clouds, the light of the moon became visible, filtering coldly downward to the earth. The roar of airplane engines began to drown out the wind that was blowing across the sky. A single C-47 appeared, crossing the face of the moon, a black shadow against the silvery brilliance—the pathfinder plane. Soon it was followed by the first formation; then another, and another.

Gen. Dwight Eisenhower stood on the roof of the headquarters building of the 101st Airborne, his hands thrust deep in his pockets, staring upward as the formation became a hundred, two hundred C-47s, sometimes blotting out the sky completely, as they wheeled like an immense flock of birds. It was a breathtaking sight, the beginning of the largest airborne operation in the history of the world, a hint of the overwhelming armadas yet to come.

The others on the roof—officers, newsmen, Kay, Tex —stood back, as if by common consent turning this moment over to Ike, its chief architect and advocate. The huge winged armada turned gracefully in a half-circle, then headed straight across the English Channel toward the guns guarding the beaches of France. The roar of engines rose to a deafening crescendo as more and more squadrons rose from the runways of Newberry and its adjoining fields, some towing gliders.

Ike turned. He found it difficult to speak. "Well, that's it. Only God can help them now."

He started for the iron stairway leading down from the roof, lost in thought, his head bowed.

Kay followed. If ever she were needed, this was the moment.

The roar of engines faded away.

"The tomatoes should be picked." "It is hot in Suez." "The dice are on the table." The little radio in Ike's trailer was tuned to the BBC, but the phrases were being delivered in faultless French. Since the BBC continously communicated with the French underground by means of these cryptic signals, there was nothing about them to alert the German listening posts that something unusual was underway, except for the key phrase that had been decided upon to inform the French that the Allied invasion had actually been launched. It was the second line of Verlaine's *Ode to Autumn:* "Pierce my heart with a dull languor."

German 15th Army Intelligence had wrung the secret from a captured member of the Resistance; they heard and understood.

It was one o'clock in the morning of June 6th. The group keeping Ike company in his vigil included Tex Lee, Gen. Bedell Smith, and Harry Butcher, as well as Kay.

They all knew the coded phrases had a deep meaning. They did not know the enemy held the key.

"Pierce my heart with a dull languor," the announcer repeated, and a German radio operator, listening in his tent near the Belgian frontier, immediately flashed the news to Field Marshal von Rundstedt at his St. Germain headquarters.

Von Runstedt was awakened at once. He swept the report aside as stupid. *Gott im Himmel!* What enemy would announce the launching of a surprise attack by broadcasting it over the British Broadcasting Corporation microphones? Go back to sleep!

"I got you some of your penny-dreadful westerns at the PX the other day." Kay handed Ike a magazine whose cover showed Billy the Kid firing two six-shooters. "I don't know how reading this awful trash can soothe you, but why don't you try?"

Eisenhower tossed the mgazine aside. "What time is it?"

"One-fifteen. Don't you think you should chase us all out and try to sleep?"

Not really hearing, Ike turned back to his desk, where he had been writing on his scratch pad. "I can't understand why there's been no word from the 101st. Leigh-Mallory said he'd phone the moment they had radio contact."

Bedell Smith stretched and yawned. "I'm more worried whether Charley de Gaulle is going to get on the radio to ask the French underground to help."

"He's got to, he's simply got to. I stuck my neck on the chopping block for him and handed Roosevelt the axe." Ike remembered his argument with Giraud, the general whom de Gaulle had long since outmaneuvered for control of Free French forces. "What is it about Frenchmen that makes it easier for them to face a firing squad than a microphone?"

Beetle got to his feet. "To hell with it. Worrying won't

help." He turned to Tex. "I suggest we turn in, as our contribution to the war effort."

Tex nodded. They started for the door, Kay following.

"Kay?" Ike's voice halted her. "Do I have any cigarettes left?"

She turned. Tex exchanged a knowing glance with Bedell Smith, then closed the door behind them. Ike had certainly earned a private moment.

Kay found the crumpled pack of cigarettes and extended it to Ike. "One lonely Camel," she said.

Ike lit it, leaning wearily back in his chair. He ran a tired hand over his eyes. "Tomorrow John Eisenhower graduates from West Point, a second lieutenant, a year before he was supposed to. They're rushing them through because of the war. I hope tomorrow he's still proud of his old man." He shook his head. "If I've miscalculated, tens of thousands of boys like Johnny will have died needlessly."

Kay knelt beside him, taking his hand in hers. "Ike, you didn't invent war. You didn't even start this one. I will not let you take the entire blame for World War II on your shoulders. Leave some guilt for the rest of us."

Ike grinned and patted her shoulder. "Thank you, Kay. You always bring a breath of sanity into the asylum." He tipped her chin up so that he could look at her. "I've been so wrapped up I never noticed how tired you are. How do *you* feel?"

"Me? Very serene. Unbelievably happy." She got to her feet. "When I was helping pull those poor, mangled creatures from the Blitz, I kept thinking, 'You bloody bahstard, Hitler, some day we'll come and get you.' And now we are, and whatever happens, he will know that England is not France, and America is not Poland. And Kay Summersby is not to be trifled with."

"I learned that a long time ago."

"The khaki nail varnish? That was bloody rude of me, wasn't it?"

"So was getting yourself torpedoed."

"I hadn't really planned that, you know."

219

"I hadn't planned to get so upset when I heard the *Strathellen* had gone down with you aboard. It was the first time I knew." Ike stubbed out the Camel in an ashtray, then searched through a desk drawer. "I'm out of cigarettes."

"No, you're not." Kay reached for her purse and took out a full pack. "I've been giving you my ration all along."

He took it from her gratefully. "Greater love hath no woman," he said.

Kay looked at him. "You're ever so right, General." She leaned down and kissed him, very quickly.

Ike said, "What time is it?"

"Good Lord!" She sighed and straightened up. "It is exactly forty-one seconds later than when you asked me the last time."

He rose and handed her the note he had been writing. "You'd better read this."

"What is it? Your last will and testament?"

"Almost."

She looked at the scrawled words. Almost as bad as my typing, she thought. " 'Our landings in the Cherbourg-Havre area have failed to gain a satisfactory foothold—' " She looked up, startled. "Now, you don't know that yet!"

"Just read it, Kay. No editorializing."

" '—and I have withdrawn the troops. My decision to attack at this time and place was based upon the best information available. The troops, the air, and the navy did all that bravery and devotion to duty could do. If any blame or fault attaches to the attempt, it is mine alone. Dwight David Eisenhower, Southwick, England, June 6, 1944.' " She looked up again. "How noble. Burn it."

"Kay, don't you ever bother to beat around the bush?"

"Destroy it. It must never see the light of day. You're Ike Eisenhower, even though you don't really understand yet what that means."

Ike took the note and tossed it on the desk. "Amphibious landings are always risky. And this is the riskiest of all."

"You're to stop worrying about this one. You said yourself it's in the hands of God."

"I hope General de Gaulle will let the Lord handle it. And make that broadcast so the boys of the 101st have a chance to get back to the ranch."

"He will, Ike. Just remember, you've done all one man could possibly do."

"Thank you, Kay. For being here." He reached for her hand. "I can't say things the way I'd like to say them. Don't expect it from me."

"Good heavens, I didn't even expect you to say that you can't say anything." She tried to smile.

Ike turned to the window, snapping off the light as he opened the blackout curtains. Bright moonlight streamed in. Capt. Burns's promised weather had finally arrived.

The pulsing roar of airplane engines could be heard from somewhere in the sky—hundreds, thousands, coming and going, all with their cargo of human lives and high explosives. Never before in history had there been such a sound.

"Do you know how much I want this to go right for you?" Kay moved close to his side, close enough to feel his warmth, for him to feel hers. "So much that I don't even care that when it's all over and the victory is finally in hand, I shall never see you again."

Ike turned quickly. "You're wrong."

"I'm not. You will shake my hand, as you shook the hand of so many of those brave lads today, and send me off to my little death." Abruptly, she moved away. "Good night, General. I'm going to bed. There is nothing further I can do about your tomorrow, or mine."

She left, silhouetted for an instant in the open door against the moonlight outside. The breeze, soft now, blew her hair. Beautiful, Ike thought as the door closed behind her, and he meant the moonlight and the weather and the soft breeze and Kay Summersby, and the triumphant sound of the incredible armada of planes.

Your whole plan is visionary, Gen Marshall had said,

and he had responded that that was its strongest point.

And Kay? That's my weakest, Ike thought. God grant me the right to that one weakness.

"This is the British Broadcasting Corporation. Here is a news bulletin."

Ike turned, galvanized. The voice was tinged with excitement; the game of secret words was over. He turned up the volume.

"Radio Berlin has just announced that Allied paratroops are landing in great force on the continent of Europe. We switch you now to our London studios."

Ike could hear the rustle of papers, the clearing of throats, as the engineers hastily switched from Portsmouth to London. Obviously, with Berlin announcing the landings, secrecy was at an end.

"This is London, the Overseas Service of the BBC, broadcasting to the people of France."

And then, a woman's voice: *"Ici Londres, TSF de la BBC. Citoyens de la France . . . Général Charles de Gaulle!"*

Ike leaned closer, clutching the desk top beside the radio as the ringing voice, the imperial tones, the emotional ardor of Le Grand Charley echoed through the tiny loudspeaker and undoubtedly through headphones in the secret headquarters of the Resistance throughout France.

"Français! La bataille suprême est engagée!"

It was a call to arms, a call to help the embattled Allies who were dropping out of French skies into German guns, a call to Frenchmen to risk everything in this climactic moment of their bloodiest war against their hated Prussian neighbor.

"A bas les boches! Vive la France!" De Gaulle's voice cried out, appealing to the spirit of France to arise from the ashes of disastrous defeat and turn their hidden arms against a merciless enemy.

Ike heard, and understood what this would mean in the sacrifice of French blood. Charles de Gaulle had completed his part of the bargain. The rest was up to the Allied armies, and Dwight Eisenhower's soldier's promise.

The paratroopers dropped out of the skies into the blackness in huge swarms, more like caterpillars descending on slender threads than the screaming eagles of their shoulder patches—and found they had missed the drop zone. Grim-faced young men, clutching automatic weapons and holding their trench knives ready to cut the shroud lines, found themselves splashing into meadows flooded by the Germans against just such a moment. Some drowned under the weight of so much equipment; many survived only to be cut down by enemy machine gun fire. Others managed to move out and form up, signalling each other in the darkness with toy crickets, only to find that the Germans had discovered their method and were using captured toy crickets to lure the men of the 101st to destruction.

Only the utter surprise and confusion of the enemy saved most of the Allied troopers. Dummy parachutists were being dropped inland, near Rouen and Avranches, and the Germans thought they were real. Bombers headed for the Pas de Calais, scattering tinfoil to confuse enemy radar into believing they were the main attack, and the French underground forces burst from hiding places to cut all the telephone lines in Normandy, leaving the hated Germans helpless to mass their armored forces for swift counter-attack.

The 101st and 82nd Airborne Divisions of the United States Army headed from the rear for the key bridges and the concrete bunkers that squatted like prehistoric monsters above Omaha and Utah Beaches, where more Americans were soon to attempt to land from pitching LSTs and LVPs. To the north, the British airborne were having better success. Leigh-Mallory had chosen well; most of the gliders landed on target, and the key bridge across the Orne River, between Caen and the sea, was captured almost without resistance.

Field Marshal Erwin Rommel, commander of all coastal defenses from Scandinavia to Spain, was in his Mercedes en route to Germany for his wife's birthday.

As dawn crept over the horizon, the midget submarine X-23 surfaced a few hundred yards off the Normandy beaches, after lying on the bottom for 48 hours. The X-23 was to mark the exact point for the landing craft to be lowered for the final assault. It was the first vessel to arrive. Soon there were thousands upon thousands, ranging from small boats to battleships, which appeared from the Channel mists simultaneously with a furious air and naval bombardment of the coastal forts, a bombardment timed to precede the paratroop attack being launched from the rear. The seas belched flame, the skies rained tons of mammoth bombs on the Nazis' vaunted West Wall, and 150,000 Allied soldiers prepared to cross the last yards of water separating them from the ring of steel and fire that held Western Europe Hitler's prisoner.

H-Hour. The landing craft headed for the beaches, running into a hail of German artillery and machine-gun fire. The specially prepared amphibious tanks lumbered off the LVTs into rough sea and plunged, most of them, to the bottom. Omaha Beach was a shambles. Underwater obstacles held up many of the boats, jammed with men; they were shattered by heavy enemy fire. But still the troops— the Big Red One, the First Division, toughened in Sicily— kept on, scrambling for the beaches, sheltering behind the tanks that made it before them, forming up, attacking, shoving past the dying and the wounded struggling in the water. The first American combat force to land in France since World War I was on the bloody sands of Normandy.

"Ladies and gentlemen," the announcer said, "the President of the United States."

"Last night, June 5th, when I spoke to you about the fall of Rome, I knew at that moment that troops of the United States and our Allies were preparing to cross the Channel in another and greater operation. It has come to pass. And so, in this poignant hour, I ask you to join with me in prayer. Almighty God: our sons, pride of our nation, this day have set upon a mighty endeavor, a struggle to preserve our Republic and to set free a suffering humanity. Lead them straight and true."

In a few hours, the graduating class of 1944 would march in dress parade across the grounds of West Point Military Academy, and John Eisenhower would be commissioned a second lieutenant, in time to join the war his father had hoped would long ago be over.

She ran through the still-muddy avenues of the tent city, hair flying, dodging the messengers on motorcycles whizzing by in all directions. Southwick Manor, the nerve center of the battle raging across the Channel, had erupted into frenzied activity, and no one had time to bless the sunshine which was flooding down like manna from Heaven.

As Kay reached Ike's trailer, Tex was coming out, carrying a sheaf of forms. "Tex!" she shouted, "oh, my Lord, of all mornings to oversleep! How is it going?"

"Better than expected." He sounded glum as he ticked off the successes. "Every outfit is ashore. Intelligence says we achieved tactical surprise. The Germans were completely fooled. Casualties are light—impossibly light, so far. A few thousand, so far as we know."

"Oh, how wonderful! Of course, not for the poor lads who bought it, but Ike was worried we'd lose twenty times that many! Now, what about the lads of the 101st Airborne?"

"No definite word yet. We understand they missed the drop zone. Communications still jammed up."

Tex turned away, dispirited.

"Good heavens, why are you so gloomy? We're ashore, Tex! We're ashore! In France!"

"Kay, if I ever have kids and they ask what daddy did on D-Day, you know what I'll have to tell them?" He held up two fingers. "With these fingers, daddy typed General Eisenhower's requisition for more toilet paper."

"How terribly stupid of me, Tex. Of course." She looked at him, seeing him almost for the first time. "Why

225

do all men completely unsuited for war want so desperately to get themselves killed?"

"It beats getting your vital organs caught in a mimeograph machine."

"I won't listen to your pessimism on such a historic morning! Oh, just look at this glorious sunshine! I must go in and congratulate Ike on his weather!"

She started to run up the steps, but his next words stopped her.

"Kay! He doesn't belong to you any more. To use an old line, now he belongs to the world."

Kay gave Tex the benefit of her flashing blue eyes. "My dear Colonel Lee, you've missed the entire point. *I* belong to *him*."

And she entered Eisenhower's trailer.

He was seated on his bunk, jubilant, unable to conceal his elation as he spoke into a command telephone. Bedell Smith was pouring coffee as if it were champagne.

"That's the best news you could possibly have given me!" Ike slammed down the phone and jumped to his feet. "That was Leigh-Mallory! He offered his apologies! The kids of the 101st captured the key bridges and then attacked the forts above Omaha Beach! Lots of them missed the drop zones, but they still managed to fight their way through with the help of the French!"

"Oh, Ike! Oh, *Ike!*" Kay rushed to him; then, suddenly aware of Beetle's presence, she stopped short of throwing her arms around him. All she could say was, "You must feel very proud of them. And yourself."

"Kay, I'm so happy I could cry." He was, she noticed, indeed on the edge of tears. "For all of them. For all of us. To top it all, Rome has finally fallen. It's no longer the end of the beginning—it's the beginning of the end!"

Suddenly, devastatingly, she knew for certain.

"You're so right," Kay said. All the happiness seemed to drain out of her. "The beginning of the end."

XV
Aftermath

Adolf Hitler, megalomaniac though he was, did not froth at the mouth and chew the carpets of his Berchtesgaden hideaway at news of the successful Allied landings, although such hopeful stories were widely circulated in the West. Instead, he called upon his armies to die in place rather than retreat or surrender; and he launched a diabolical attack, not against the invading forces, but against civilian lives, with one of the most terrible weapons ever devised by German scientific genius.

In the present age of computerized weaponry, it is difficult to realize the terror that was struck by the first bomb to have no human hand guiding it on its mission of mass murder. Far beyond the heavy toll in blood and fire was the psychological effect on war-torn London of a bomb that flew by itself from far behind enemy lines, across land and water, to deal death by whim of chance wherever it chose, a hundred miles away. Terror was Hitler's favorite weapon, beginning with his Stuka dive bombers which were constructed so that a vertical dive would produce a chilling scream of wind on wing; and he played the same theme in an entirely different way with an English renegade who named himself Lord Haw Haw, and whose clipped British accent mocked his native land.

The first inkling of what was in store came over the powerful transmitters operating in the broadcast band beside the stations of the BBC, where all England would be certain to hear.

"Hello, London. Lord Haw Haw here, speaking to you from Berlin, just one week after your costly and disastrous assault against the coast of France."

Truth was not one of Lord Haw Haw's staples; he believed, with Hitler, that the larger the lie, the more likely it was to be believed. Even as he spoke, a strange weapon of death was being launched from concrete platforms in France, aimed over the Channel. The bomb had wings and a rocket motor, and it was designed by a small group of German engineers who were later to calmly switch sides, when requested, and design the space program for the United States. Dr. Werner von Braun was on his way to becoming an American folk hero. Today, he watched the launching of his brain child on a mission that would spill the guts of Englishmen into London sewers.

"I'm sure you've all heard the good news by now," Lord Haw Haw continued. "Our Fuehrer, Adolf Hitler, has been promising you some secret weapons for a long time, but unlike the bloated aristocrat, Churchill, and the Jew, Roosevelt, Hitler's promises are always kept."

Kay, driving Ike through London's streets to a meeting of military leaders near Whitehall, was unaware of the high explosive headed blindly across the heaving English Channel toward the coast of Britain, too low to be detected by wartime radar. Had the danger come from airplanes with human pilots, flying at normal altitude, the air raid sirens would already have been wailing, sending men and women

228

and children into the stifling safety of underground shelters.

But no sirens sounded now.

"I know how thrilled you must be to watch the first of our lovely new bombs arriving in London without warning. What a lovely surprise on a fine June evening."

The car pulled to a halt outside one of the ministries. Kay opened the rear door for Ike. They exchanged another of their brief smiles; there were always too many eyes upon them. Then Ike entered the building, and Kay leaned against the car, lighting a cigarette, thinking her own thoughts about the two of them.

"It does no good to shoot them down, London. They have no pilots. And you can't tell where they're going to land, because we don't really know ourselves. All we know is they'll land on *you*. They're a barrel of laughs, London."

Suddenly, there were sirens. Kay tossed her cigarette aside. What could this be? No German planes would dare a daytime raid on London this late in the war, with the RAF and U.S. in complete control of the skies.

"Roll out the barrel—" Lord Haw Haw's singing voice was quite good, and he was obviously enjoying himself as he sang the famous *Beer Barrel Polka*.

A strange *putt-putt* sound attracted Kay's attention. She looked at the sky, puzzled and frightened, and saw what seemed to be a tiny bomb flying over the London rooftops, headed in her direction. Flying *horizontally*, not falling vertically from a bomb bay, and giving no indication of when its flight would end. *Putt-putt. Putt-putt. Putt-putt-putt.*

Suddenly the sound of the tiny engine cut off, and the V-1 rocket started its eerie, robot-like dive straight for the ground. Kay threw herself flat on the pavement, seeking the protection of the car, mouth open, hands over her ears, the approved technique to minimize the concussion of an explosion. Nothing would minimize the flying steel, not to worry about that.

". . . roll out the barrel," Lord Haw Haw sang, "for the gang's all here!"

The world seemed to erupt around her. The ground rocked, smoke and dust filled the air, chunks of concrete and plaster and shards of broken glass showered down. The rising scream of ambulance sirens was heard through the shouts and cries of the wounded, and it was the Blitz all over for Kay, the horrible sights and sounds crowding into her memory. She found her hands trembling and her mouth dry, and her whole body was shaking.

I'm alive, she told herself. Somehow I'm alive. What was it?

It became commonplace, if death can ever be commonplace. The buzz bombs kept coming over in unpredictable clusters, and no adequate defense had yet been devised. The RAF tried to intercept them, but it was almost impossible. The machines broke through and killed and maimed and destroyed, day and night, all over London, because London was Hitler's main enemy. London had defeated him once; London must be destroyed.

And on the Continent, the Nazi Panzer Divisions under the brilliant command of Erwin Rommel struck back, again and again, against the invaders and their perilous hold on the beachheads. Ike and Beetle and Tex agonized over the reports at Supreme Headquarters. Montgomery and the British had been stalled near Caen, the city that was to be taken on D-Day, for two whole weeks.

Omar Bradley and his American divisions at Omaha and Utah Beaches had not yet been able to move inland and capture Cherbourg, whose docks and piers were absolutely essential to supply his armies if they were not to be shoved into the sea. And above all, there were the disturbing Intelligence reports: the Germans were preparing something new, the V-2 rockets, which would make the little buzz bombs look like toys. They were said to carry ten times the explosive power of the V-1s, and could be rocketed into the air to fall directly on pinpointed targets in any city in southern England. There was no possible defense. Time, if not God, was on Hitler's side. The V-3 rocket, next in line, could span the Atlantic Ocean. The prototypes had already been built. War was being taken out of the hands of soldiers and placed in the hands of mechanics.

Something had to be done quickly. This was brought home more forcefully by the arrival of Lt. John Eisenhower, ordered to Ike's side by George Marshall for a brief visit, a reward for the Supreme Commander. It was a reward that reminded Ike there was a new generation whose future depended upon what happened next on the continent of Europe. It was time for Dwight Eisenhower, General and father, to go to the battlefields.

The countryside near the ancient Norman city of Bayeux seemed peaceful and pastoral, the apple blossoms blanketing the orchards with a feathery pink cover of fragrance and beauty. Only the boom of distant artillery and the ugly columns of military vehicles hinted at how close the war was. Between the hedgerows, under the lovely trees, khaki tents were hidden beneath camouflage nets, the tents spread out so that no direct hit could kill more than a few men at a time.

The jeep with Ike and Tex passed a hospital tent, where ambulances were disgorging their cargoes of wounded, and pulled up in front of the canvas headquarters of Field Marshal Sir Bernard Montgomery. Ike leaped out and strode toward the entrance.

Maj. Gen. Francis De Guingand, Monty's suave Chief of Staff, came out of the tent and saluted. "General Eisenhower! General Montgomery ordered me to give you a hearty welcome in the name of His Majesty's forces!"

Ike eyed him suspiciously. It was not military practice to send an underling to greet the Supreme Commander. "Cut the bull, Freddie. Where the hell is Monty?"

"Called away, unfortunately."

"Dammit, I sent him a signal I was coming!"

"He was merely following your orders not to let your visit keep him from his military duties."

At the jeep, Tex whistled softly to himself. Insubordination at the four-star level was always interesting. Ike threw him a disapproving glance, then turned back to the imperturbable De Guingand.

"Freddie, he's absolutely right. When do you expect him to return?"

"I suspect he'll be along shortly. In the meantime, would you care to inspect our apple blossoms?"

"No." Irritated, Ike turned and started for the jeep. "Let's go to Bradley," he told Tex. "I don't think there are any apple blossoms on Omaha Beach."

Immediately Sir Bernard Montgomery made a theatrical appearance from the orchard nearby. "Ike, old boy! Dreadfully sorry to have detained you."

Montgomery was carefully dressed in the height of incongruity—a turtleneck sweater, corduroy trousers, and the black tanker's beret which was his trademark.

Ike was not properly impressed. "You timed that entrance beautifully, Monty."

"Thank you, old chap. I knew you'd appreciate it. You do it so well yourself." Montgomery smiled.

"Where can we talk privately?" Ike wanted to know.

"Afraid the headquarters tent is somewhat crowded— shall we walk into the orchard? Just be careful of the cow droppings."

"I don't need a warning. I've had conversations with you before."

Tex smiled as he watched his boss take Montgomery's arm and lead him toward the sheltering apple trees.

"Colonel Lee." Freddie De Guingand, always the diplomat, had approached in an effort to smooth the troubled waters. "In spite of what you may have heard, General Montgomery has a very high opinion of General Eisenhower."

"From what I've heard, he also has a very high opinion of General Montgomery," Tex said. "He's going to need it."

Freddie frowned, following Tex's gaze. The two commanders were stalking together under the blossoms, engaged in heated debate.

"Monty, don't give me excuses!" Ike had flushed beet red. Monty always rubbed him the wrong way, but he had to keep a tight rein on his temper, in the interest of Anglo-American unity. "You've been sitting here on your ass for over a week!"

"The Germans are blocking this sector with everything they've got. Tanks. Artillery. Infantry. I'm simply not going to attack, my dear Ike, until I have enough men to be certain of victory."

"And you want me to steal them from the American forces under Bradley?"

"Why not? He doesn't know what to do with them." Monty flashed his most charming smile. "I visited his sector. He has scarcely moved off the beach. Bradley should sit tight, shut up, and be given only enough supplies for his bare subsistence. He has no reserves behind the front, morale is low—why, his officers seemed delighted when I issued some firm orders."

"You issued orders to Bradley's officers?" Ike said.
"Of course."

"What did Brad do—kiss the hem of your garment?"

"He would have, old boy, but I was walking on water at the time." Again, the Montgomery smile. "Now, what I propose is that you give me complete and permanent command of *all* Allied ground forces in France. Then I shall concentrate the main strength on this front and drive straight for Berlin."

"That isn't the battle plan, and you know it!"

"It should be."

"Would you like my hat, too?"

"Afraid it's too small, old chap." This was said charmingly, of course.

"Monty, the worst thing that can happen to an invading force is to get stalled, and that's what's happened to us!" Ike paused amid the graceful trees to make certain his point was made. "You're supposed to be beyond Caen

233

and halfway to Paris right now! Not smelling apple blossoms and waiting for my job!" Angrily, he pulled a cigarette out of a pack.

Monty raised a warning finger. "I say, old boy—terribly sorry, but you know I don't allow smoking at my headquarters."

General Dwight Eisenhower carefully lit his cigarette. "That's all right, old boy," he said, "I *do* allow it at *mine*."

Omaha Beach was only twenty miles from Montgomery's orchard headquarters, but it might as well have been on another planet. Shattered hulks of bombed-out shipping littered the water near the beaches crammed with tanks, trucks, cannon, and acres of supplies. Offshore, huge concrete artificial harbors, the brain children of Lord Mountbatten and Winston Churchill, had been towed into position from across the English Channel and were now receiving cargo from the flotillas of cargo vessels. A high wind and choppy seas slowed the operation, banging ships against concrete piers. Long lines of wounded were being carried aboard landing craft drawn up on the beach, to be transported to hospital ships offshore and to England itself. And burial crews were still at work, shovelling sand over the silent rows of canvas bags. In the distance, there was the boom of the guns, the crackle of small arms fire. The battle had barely moved inland, after so much time, so much death. The casualties on D-Day had been mercifully light, but God and Rommel were showing no mercy now.

Ike stood on the beach beside Omar Bradley, all his anger drained away by the sight.

"Those poor kids . . . still taking casualties like that."

"Ike, we've tried to break out time and again. The Nazis are holding onto Cherbourg like it was Berlin."

Hitler himself had issued orders to the Cherbourg garrison that there was to be no retreat; every man was to stay at his post until death. The Gestapo and the SS were ready to finish off any German soldier who disobeyed and tried to escape.

"Brad, you were supposed to take Cherbourg by the fifth day," Ike said.

"It'll be closer to the fiftieth. But we'll do it."

"Dammit, we can't wait that long!" At least, with his friend, Ike could release his anger and frustration. "London's going under from the buzz bombs! If the Germans had had them six months ago, they would have destroyed our invasion fleets before they could leave port! D-Day would never have happened!"

"I know, Ike."

"You've got to break out *now!* Get George Patton and his Third Army tanks on the road to Germany! And most of all, knock out the launching pads for those goddam buzz bombs or they're going to knock out London!"

"Why don't you ask Monty to take some risks, too, and help take pressure off this front?"

"Don't worry, I have! I've got to get both of you more men and weapons, or we're going to be shoved back into the water!"

"It's going to take a while, Ike. To get the supplies here. Look at the Channel today."

The wind was increasing. Angry gray waves were breaking against the shoreline. Landing craft were being tossed about like eggshells as they attempted to unload.

Bradley was as gloomy as the weather. "Our meteorologists say the biggest storm in twenty years is going to hit right here on the Normandy coast tomorrow morning."

Ike watched the black clouds looming low on the horizon. The wind was blowing even harder now, tearing at the sand all around them, sending spray inland from the crashing waves.

"Tomorrow," Ike said, "is the 19th of June—the day the invasion would have had to take place if I'd called it off on the sixth. And Rommel would be standing here instead of us . . . waiting."

Antiaircraft searchlights criss-crossed the sky above the British countryside. The mindless, eyeless robots were

235

flying inland from the English Channel, soaring batlike over the moonlit landscape, a hundred Draculas seeking English blood. Air raid sirens screamed an endless warning. Distant ack-ack batteries fired futile salvos. The robots flew on.

Returning from an errand in London, Kay hurled Ike's Cadillac up the driveway to Telegraph Cottage and braked to a halt at the back door. Her hands were trembling as she leaped out. Too much, too much, her mind was saying. How long, O Lord? If there *is* a Lord. He must be a bloody sadist if He does exist, with each side praying to Him for help in killing the other. And He always seems happy to oblige both sides.

She raced into the kitchen where Mickey McKeogh was helping Sgts. Moaney and Hunt prepare a meal.

"Mickey! Why the devil aren't you all down in the shelter?"

"Ike's just back from France—says he's got too much to do to worry about buzz bombs. We're having dinner as usual."

"But when I serve the soup, it's gonna have waves in it," Moaney told her with a grin.

Kay was furious. "He can be stubborn if he wants to —but how dare he endanger all of you?"

She rushed into the study, too distraught even to knock, and surprised Ike and Tex going over radio messages. "Can't you hear those sirens?" She was almost shouting, something Kay never did, and that fact, even more than her question, caused them to look up. "You must get into the shelter immediately and get everybody else down with you!"

Ike returned to his work. "I'm not going to run and hide every time one of those German sausages comes over."

Tex had been growing increasingly nervous as the ack-ack batteries had continued firing. "There's a lot of meat in those sausages, Ike. Two and a half tons of TNT."

"You can go if you want to." Ike was irritated. This

was not an artillery barrage; there was no imminent battle. It was precisely Hitler's intention to immobilize an entire city with a handful of inaccurate weapons. "I can't afford to spend half my time in a storm cellar." He remembered his Abilene youth, the twisters corkscrewing across the plains, spewing dust and debris, the family ducking down below the house to a fragile safety.

"You know damn well I'm not going if you're not going," Tex said.

"Look at you two little boys, trying to outbrave each other!" Kay was contemptuous. "If you'd lived through as many bombings in London as I have, you'd—"

Mickey stuck his head in from the dining room, trying to sound relaxed. "Dinner's ready, General."

And then one hit. Not close, but near enough for the concussion to jar the taped windows and set the lights flickering.

"Hurry, hurry!" Kay's voice shook. "Everyone says they've got this area zeroed in because they know we're here!" She yanked open the door to the kitchen. "Moaney! Hunt! On the double!"

She raced to the door, followed by Tex and Mickey, then realized that Ike hadn't moved an inch.

"Ike!" She screamed at him as the sirens continued to wail. "Dammit, you're not immortal! You and Dick, tramping through your stupid mine fields!"

He understood then and started toward her. Kay grabbed his arm and pulled him outside.

It was a lovely summer evening, the garden in full bloom. Yellow marigolds and white roses glistened in the moonlight, beneath a night sky filled with criss-crossing searchlights. The air raid shelter, constructed for Ike by personal order of Winston Churchill, was buried in the back yard a short distance from the house. It had been carefully planted over with grass, but its curved top made the lawn look pregnant. The sandbags shielding its entrance were ominous and ugly.

The wail of the sirens rose to a crescendo as they

dashed across the lawn. Suddenly Kay slipped on the grass and tumbled down, her leg doubling up beneath her.

"Oh, damn!" She tried to get up, then felt the stabbing pain. "My ankle!" she sobbed, "my bloody ankle!" Tears streamed down her cheeks, and she didn't care, she damn well didn't care who saw. It was too much, all too much, if only those bloody sirens would stop their bloody yelling! She buried her face in the cool grass, trembling.

"For God's sake, Kay, don't be a child!" She felt Ike's strong arms under her, lifting her, turning her over, carrying her. "This isn't like you."

"I'm sick and tired of being like me! I'm sick and tired of false courage! Four and a half years, four and a half years of this filthy killing!"

Something was putt-putting across the sky. And then suddenly the silly noise stopped, and there was only the sound of the wind.

"Here comes one!" Mickey shouted, and dove for the shelter entrance, throwing it open. They all ducked inside and slammed the door shut.

It was invisible, whatever it was. Until it hit the building on the other side of the golf course. Then the flash lit the sky, and the sound arrived, the hoarse thud of TNT exploding. Shouts. A scream. The wail of ambulance sirens.

The shelter was spartan, but polished and clean— cots lined up side by side, telephones, washroom, ventilating fans, bare bulbs. Electricity was furnished by an emergency generator, so that even if London were knocked out, this tiny corner would still operate. The air raid sirens could still be heard, and the barking antiaircraft guns. Shooting at what? Ike wondered as he set Kay gently down on one of the cots.

"Tex, would you get Kay a glass of water?" he said.

She sat up immediately, full of unreasoning anger. "He's not your water boy! He's a colonel!" She flung herself back, face down on the cot, her shoulders shaking. Ike tried to pat them soothingly, but she slapped his hand away. Battle fatigue, he thought. Why would I expect it from a soldier and not from Kay Summersby?

Tex brought a glass of water. "Here you are, General."

"Thank you, *Colonel*." Ike offered the glass to Kay. "Did I do that all right?"

She sat up and tried to smile, taking the water and gulping it down like a child.

"You're learning," she said. It was an apology.

Ike turned to the others. "This may last a while. Might as well prepare to spend the night. Sorry about dinner, Mickey."

"Cake fell anyway, sir."

Ike sat down on the cot next to Kay and started to remove his boots.

"Sorry to have been so bloody unmilitary," she said. "I couldn't help it."

"It's all right, Kay."

She took out her pack of cigarettes and automatically handed one to Ike. There were so many things about each other they took for granted now.

"No, it isn't," she said, allowing Ike to light her cigarette. "But you see, in the Blitz you could do something. Shoot his bloody Stuka out from under him." She lay back on top of the covers, remembering how it had been in those dim, dark days. All of two years ago. Before she and Ike had met. Everything in her life dated from that moment.

"These things," she mused, "they just have a little German engine puttering away. If you *do* knock one down, it simply explodes and kills you. And if you don't, it switches itself off and there's that dreadful silence before it kills you anyway."

Her cigarette had gone out. She lit it again. "I don't think I'll mind dying too awfully much, but I *would* hate to be killed by a *thing*."

Ike had been wanting to reach out for her hand, to reassure her. He knew what other fears lay within her, fears he was powerless to do anything about. Or was he?

"You'll never die, Kay," he said. "I have a feeling if all of England were wiped out, you'd be left standing on the beach at Dover, daring that 'bahstard' Hitler to come across so you could spit in his eye."

"I would, too."

Ike flipped the switch that turned off the main lighting, leaving the dim emergency lamp glowing near the telephone. He lay back on his cot, only too conscious of her presence next to him, her cigarette glowing with his. They listened to the sounds of the air raid sirens and the ack-ack in the distance, enjoying that comfortable wartime feeling of momentary personal safety. *"I'm* all right, Jack," the British called it. *I'm* all right, no matter what happens to *you*. Not very heroic, but human. I'm all right, Ike thought to himself, but what about Kay?

Ike raised up on one elbow. *"Colonel* Lee?"

"Yes, *General* Eisenhower?"

"You're leaving for Washington in the morning."

Tex sat up on his cot. This was news. "I *am?"*

"This war isn't won by a long shot. Our trip across the Channel was the clincher. We need more of everything and we need it fast. I want you to let General Marshall know exactly how I feel."

"Does he have to bring him a glass of water, too?" Kay wanted to know.

"Why don't you wait and see? You're going with him."

"I am *what?"* Now she too sat up. "Why would I want to go to the Colonies?"

Ike stubbed out his cigarette and glared at her. "They're not the Colonies, they're the United States of America, and it's time you found it out! You've earned some R and R and you're going to take it. You need it. Badly. You're going to eat all the unrationed food you can eat, and get some sleep, and forget the war and the bombs."

"That's hardly possible."

"Kay, you're going to go! I've leaned on you long enough. Lean on me for a bit."

She rolled over to look at him. He couldn't say anything that really meant anything, she told herself. Not the slightest commitment. Even if they were alone, which they weren't, although the darkness was a cloak. But there was something in his tone she was supposed to understand—and believe.

"Let me send you out of the battle zone, Kay. Please go. I'm terribly worried about you."

Kay felt goosebumps. For Ike Eisenhower, that was a public declaration of his love. Or something terribly close to it. She waited a moment before she could trust her voice. Then she said, "I'm worried about *you*. If I go, who'll steal cigarettes for you?"

Ike leaned back on his cot. "Shut up and be grateful, Kay."

"Is that an order, General?"

"Goddam right."

She turned away from him then, rolling over to the other side of her cot so he wouldn't see the smile. He knew, though, that she was smiling.

There was another explosion, somewhere in the distance. The ack-ack was building in intensity. The air raid sirens rose in crescendo.

But she felt safe.

* * *

Kay and Tex left for Washington in Eisenhower's Flying Fortress, the B-17 that also carried Lt. John Eisenhower back to the States and more training before assignment overseas. They were all on easy terms and the flight on the luxuriously converted bomber was pleasant.

But Washington, D.C., was another matter. Never having been in the Colonies, Kay hadn't known quite what to expect, but this certainly wasn't it. Here, in the capital of a country at war, such opulence, such waste, so many people doing jobs that had no relation to the conflict going on across two oceans. The shops crammed with goods; a puny rationing system that left Americans with more butter and more gasoline than Britain had ever seen in peacetime; women joining volunteer organizations because they liked the color of the uniforms; petty jealousies and squabbling among officers' wives. No realization that oceans were no longer barriers to modern war, and no real belief in Kay's protestations that Hitler *was* developing immense robot rockets that could hit their favorite beauty parlor if he so chose.

She had almost determined to hitch a ride back to England on some Air Force plane when Tex told her of the invitation. Although she was apprehensive about the whole idea, she permitted herself to drive with him in the car the army had given him.

Since it was the Fourth of July, Tex was determined to combine a little American history with the occasion, hoping also to soothe her nervousness over what lay ahead. They drove past the Lincoln Memorial and there it was, far across the Mall, pointing to the sky like an avenging finger. Tex couldn't resist the opportunity.

"That, my dear Londoner, is the Washington Monument." He slowed the car to a halt so that she could be properly impressed by its height and granduer. "It is dedicated to the American general who beat the pants off the British Army with a little rag-tag group of boys, using muzzle-loading muskets and practically no cannon."

Distraught though she was, Kay could not help rising to the bait. "Not to mention," she reminded him, "the Marquis de Lafayette Baron Kosciusko, and the not inconsiderable strength of the entire French navy."

Tex grinned. "I'd like to read an English history book after this war. I'll bet Ike turns out to have been Monty's idiot orderly."

He started up the car.

"Tex—take me back to my hotel."

He looked at her. She was staring straight ahead, trying not to meet his eye. Very un-Summersby.

242

"That's not being polite. Mrs. Eisenhower was careful to point out that the invitation was for *both* of us."

"I'm sorry. I don't like cocktail parties."

"Kay—"

"It would be all right if I felt terribly guilty. I could brazen it out. But not really having done anything too awful, I'm afraid I'll be terrified of Mamie."

"The worst thing you can do for Ike is run and hide. It will only encourage a lot of vicious talk in this town— and this town is *built* on vicious talk."

"Dammit, I can't, I can't! I could pretend to anyone but you, Tex. But my hopeless little romance can't survive reality for one minute."

She turned to him, and he saw.

"My God, Kay! You're crying. I hate woman who cry!"

"I hate men from Indiana who call themselves 'Tex'!"

"It's real, isn't it? You care that much? I never believed it for a minute."

She found her handkerchief. Stupid, to have let him see. To have let herself be intimidated by such a tired situation. The Jealous Wife. The Other Woman. Good Lord, she ran from exactly that sort of play.

"I'll go," she said firmly. "I couldn't. And if I'm shot down over a liver canapé, you *will* bind my wounds, won't you?"

Tex, understanding Tex, shook his head. "I don't know. It might be kinder to let you bleed to death."

Whatever her feelings, Mamie Eisenhower was the perfect hostess. She greeted Kay graciously and conducted her and Tex to the bountiful buffet table set up in the living room of her hotel suite, smiling and chatting as if nothing existed but the surface of life. Kay was grateful, and honestly impressed by the array of food, from glazed ham to sumptuous desserts.

"Mrs. Eisenhower! I'm trying to recover from the shock. Actually real cream—from cows, I suppose?"

Mamie laughed. "Yes, I believe the Wardman Park

Hotel deals in authentic cream. And please call me 'Mamie'."

"It's the pastry I cannot believe. I'm sure I'll discover I've died and gone to heaven—where none of this is fattening."

Mamie smiled again, then hurried off to greet other guests. Kay had been a little more than she had expected. Young, of course; beautiful, of course; but a strength and a dignity that transcended the stereotype. She could be as formidable as the British Empire.

Kay turned to Tex as Mamie left. "I'm terribly disheartened. She's a lovely woman. I can't find anything to dislike."

"I have confidence in you. You'll manage."

Kay made a face at him over the dish of hors d'oeuvres she had carefully assembled. She debated whether to attack the shrimp or the barbecued ribs first.

"Miss Summersby?"

She looked up. A woman in her forties, fashionably dressed, nursing a martini, stood beside her. "I'm Helen Westerfield. I told everyone I simply *must* meet Ike's lady driver." She eyed Kay with interest. "You are his driver, aren't you?"

Kay took the proffered hand. It was damp and cold from clutching the martini. "Yes. I'm also the General's secretary."

"How convenient."

Kay threw her a murderous look. Mrs. Westerfield appeared not to notice. "You may know my husband. General Paul Westerfield? He has a command under Mark Clark in Italy."

"I've heard General Eisenhower speak about your husband quite often, Mrs. Westerfield."

"Well, we talk about *you* quite often, Miss Summersby. There's *so* much to talk about."

It was to be open warfare, then. Kay drew a deep breath. "How nice. I dare say soon you'll be writing it on the lavatory walls, won't you?"

Tex had been viewing the gathering storm with apprehension. Now he took Kay's arm and made an effort to draw her away. "How about a drink, Kay? Scotch?"

She pulled her arm away, facing her adversary, her chin raised, her eyes flashing. No surrender, no retreat.

Helen Westerfield was conscious of the heads turning to stare. The room was filled with army officers and their wives, each of them with his own idea of who and what Kay Summersby was. Helen was among friends. She smiled at Kay. "It may interest you to know that my husband is a major general in the regular army, while Dwight Eisenhower, although a charming, intelligent man, still holds the permanent rank of only chicken colonel."

"My dear Mrs. Westerfield." Kay's voice was friendly, dangerously so. "The Italian campaign has taken a dreadfully long time, hasn't it? I believe I've heard your husband mentioned around Supreme Headquarters as the chicken general."

"Miss Summersby!" Helen Westerfield snapped. "If I were Mamie, I'd throw you right out of here! If it were *my* husband you were sleeping with!"

There was a shocked silence as her words echoed through the suddenly quiet room. Kay turned white.

"Lovely party," Helen murmured as she moved off.

Mamie had witnessed the incident from across the room, but whether she was embarrassed or jubilant, no one was ever to know. She went on about her duties as hostess as if nothing had happened. After all, what could be said? I hate you for what you are and what I'm not? I hate you for taking advantage of a war to try to take from me the only thing that has really mattered in my life? I hate you for being young and I hate you for being pretty; but most of all, I hate you for being with him? Far better to serve the cocktail shrimp, the cheese soufflé. Far better to smile. The good soldier, always.

Kay had no such inhibitions as she glared after the retreating Helen Westerfield. "That bloody bitch!"

245

"I'd better take you back to the hotel," Tex said apprehensively.

"Don't you dare. The fireworks are just beginning!"

"Kay." Once more, he put a restraining hand on her arm. "That's just what she wants."

"But—"

Tex steered her to a neutral corner and offered a cigarette. There were lighted candles on the coffee table. She leaned over and lit her Camel, still breathing hard, still hurting.

"You've seen Ike's world now," Tex said. "Do you think you could fit into it? Or would want to?"

She looked at him. Poor, worried Tex. What a trial she must be to him. She felt drained, helpless.

"It *was* a hopeless little romance, wasn't it? All on my side, too." She watched Mrs. Eisenhower greeting some late arrivals, on the surface unperturbed, the bangs that were her trademark bobbing as she spoke warmly to her guests. "She is a lovely woman, Mamie. And so right for him. If it weren't that sex is such a dreadful pile of offal, we could be such marvelous friends."

This time, there was no way she would let the tears start. Not here. Not now. Not with Tex watching her with such damn sympathy on his face.

"I hate being a good sport about Ike," she said. "But I suppose I must be. I'll simply fade away." She sighed, seeing the bleak future that had always been there. "And what hurts most is that he'll probably be too busy to notice . . . Take me home, Tex."

Home, of course, was London.

* * *

The war had not stopped, though in America Kay had hardly been conscious of its existence. Finally, the beachhead forces started to move out, grinding down the German resistance; the men and machines and guns of the Allies built to a point where they were militarily irresistible. Cherbourg, Caen, St. Lo, Avranches, the familiar obstacles, were overwhelmed from the air and on the ground. The bombing of Western Europe rose to a new fury, the planes concentrating their attacks on the launching pads for the robot bombs, only to find that the new V-2 rockets were being hurled into the air almost vertically from holes in the ground, holes that could only be reached by direct hits. The Red Army continued to advance, pushing the hated Nazi forces out of Mother Russia and sending them, reeling and bleeding, into Poland and beyond. Germany was beginning to crumble from the inside. An attack was made on Adolf Hitler's life, the bomb in the little briefcase exploding just inches away. He lived; his enemies died horribly, hung from butcher hooks by the Gestapo to writhe their lives away. Erwin Rommel, seeing the handwriting on the wall, put a bullet through his head.

Kay and Tex flew back to England in Ike's B-17, and Kay insisted they pause at the kennel where Telek had been imprisoned since his arrival from North Africa. Six long months had passed; he could now be freed from quarantine. The little Scotty almost went out of his mind when Kay appeared, kneeling down to lift him in her arms and hold him to her as he showered her with kisses. It was so good after Washington, she told Tex, to see a friendly face.

They drove to Telegraph Cottage, and the first person they encountered was Sgt. Mickey McKeogh, coming out of the kitchen door. "Colonel Lee!" he shouted. "Welcome home!"

"Thanks, Mickey." Tex climbed out of the front seat. "It's a relief to get out of the combat zone and back here to safety."

"Telek! You old son of a gun!" Mickey had spotted the dog in Kay's arms. The Scotty leaped to greet his old friend in a fury of joy. Mickey picked him up and petted him as he turned to Kay. "Where've you been? The old man's been having kittens, worrying you'd been torpedoed again."

247

"In a B-17?"

"He said you could manage. Better go right in—he's asked for you at least six times."

Kay started for the cottage, followed by the others.

"Any juicy gossip while we've been away?" Tex wanted to know.

"Well, there's been a lot of loose talk about me and a corporal in the WACs," Mickey grinned. "All of it true. We're gonna be married."

Kay stopped and turned to him. "How lovely, Mickey. How perfectly lovely. And I do mean it."

Ike was on the scrambler in his study, speaking into the telephone that connected him with the code room. He was dictating a message to George Marshall, his mood one of elation, of triumph—the invasion had finally taken the turn he had planned for it. His words to Marshall were uncharacteristically unmilitary. "We're to hell and gone in Brittany and slicing 'em up in Normandy! American troops under Bradley and Patton have broken through on two fronts, and Monty isn't far behind! We've gotten Patton's tanks into open country. We've bombed all bridges over the Seine and are moving toward Paris. I want to recommend Bradley for permanent Major General, and Patton—hell, we can't do anything for him—he's run off the end of the maps and I can't keep up with him!"

Jubilant, Ike hung up the phone just as the knock came on the door. "Come in!"

The door flew open and a furry ball hurled itself across the room, up on the desk, and into his arms.

"Telek! You old Scotch son of a gun! Where did *you* come from?"

Kay stepped in quietly. "He's been a prisoner of war for six months and I was sure no one else remembered, so we picked him up on the way from the airport."

Ike put down the frantic dog and turned. "Kay! You don't know how I've missed you." He crossed quickly to her. "It's such a lousy war without you."

She said nothing.

"I was beginning to get worried. The Germans are sending over those damn V-2 rockets. One hit the airfield last week."

She turned away. "Ike, I think you should know I called General Spaatz from the airport. He can use another driver as long as he doesn't have to toss a coin for her this time."

"Now what's *that* all about? I need a driver, too!"

He searched in his pockets for a cigarette. Automatically, Kay took her pack out of her purse and handed it to him.

"I'm sure you can find another to shout at, General."

"Kay—!"

"I met your wife, Ike."

He paused as he lit the cigarette. "Of course." That was it, obviously.

"She's a lovely person, but I wouldn't hesitate to steal you from her. If I wanted to." Kay reached out a hand, and he gave her one of the cigarettes from her own packet. "It's so terribly strange. I'm not out of love, but the thought of being without you doesn't hurt quite so much any more."

The telephone rang. Ike picked it up and barked, "Tell him to wait!" He banged it down, then put his hands on Kay's shoulders. "Kay, the thought of being without you hurts terribly."

"Then what the devil did you send me away for?" It all rushed out now, the things she was never going to tell him because he should have known them all the time. "Why did you ship me to the Colonies and throw me to the savages? I'm all tomahawk wounds!" She drew savagely on her cigarette. "For once I got a good look at what will become of me after this war. A thousand Helen Westerfields pointing their fingers! All right, Ike. It's time for you to face it, too. Time to give me some proof that I'm not just Telek, or Tex Lee, or the world's worst typist."

"What proof do you want?"

"I don't really know. But *do* something. You stand

249

up tall and straight against the awful buzz bombs, you shout at generals and you shout at Prime Ministers, bu' you dive for shelter when it's a question of my feeling: against your precious reputation. I will not, shall not, cannot love a coward." She turned away from him. "There I've said it, and I suppose not even poor Telek will have a kind word for me from now on." She started for the door

"Kay." She didn't stop. "Kay, if you'd stop yelling a me long enough, I'd like to tell you something."

Now she whirled, expecting another triviality. "For God's sake, Ike, don't try to say anything sweet!"

"You know I don't know how. Maybe this will help say it for me." He picked a letter off his desk and handed it to her. "I've arranged for you to join the American Army."

"Good Lord. Right in character. The Tank Corps, o' course? How romantic."

"Shut up, Kay. You're going to be commissioned a lieutenant in the WACs so I can have you transferred to Washington with me after this damn war is finished, and without—"

"You know very well I *refuse* to join the American army."

"Will you, for crying out loud, let me complete a sentence?"

"Sorry."

"*Without* giving up one iota of your precious British citizenship."

"I believe that's impossible, General."

"Nothing's impossible, Kay, if it's by order of the President of the United States." He indicated the letter "You will note the President agrees with me that he cannot understand your continuing to treasure your British heritage . . . but you are to be excused because, in our joint opinion, you *are* a child."

Kay looked up from the letter, her eyes moist. Something he had said was echoing in her mind, but it had al happened so quickly, she wasn't certain she had actually heard it.

"Transferred to *Washington* with you?"

He nodded.

She *had* heard it, then. "Ike . . . what will people say?"

"In the immortal words of Rhett Butler, frankly, Lieutenant Summersby, I don't give a damn."

XVI
Liberation

Paris! The name leaped from the headlines. The City of Light, soul of the French nation, was within the reach of the Allied armies fanning out toward Germany. General Patton had already sent spearheads across the Seine to the north. But still Eisenhower refused to order his forces into a frontal attack. His plan was to bypass Paris. There was no immediate military advantage in committing hundreds of thousands of fighting men and millions of tons of supplies.

He had figured without the Parisians. Over his express orders to be patient, the French underground rose in utter fury against the city's Nazi captors. Pitched battles raged in the ancient streets as the Germans fought back viciously, slaughtering civilians from the Arc de Triomphe to the Palais de Chaillot. The Place de la Concorde ran with blood as it had in the days of the Revolution.

And still the Allied armies made no move.

It was a moment in history made for Charles de Gaulle. He appeared, imperious as ever, at Ike's forward headquarters in a Normandy apple orchard. The two generals faced each other in Ike's trailer, and neither wasted time on diplomacy.

"Everywhere, Allied armies are pouring across the Seine! But at Paris—nothing!" De Gaulle glared at the one man whose power in France was greater than his own.

Ike rose from his desk, removing his spectacles, and accepted the challenge. "General, I'm trying to bypass the city and save it from being destroyed."

"You do not save the body by cutting off the heart!"

"I didn't tell the underground to start shooting Germans. I warned you to keep the Free French from moving before we could protect them."

"We are free, and we are French. We shall protect ourselves." De Gaulle got to the crux of the matter. "If we don't, the Communist forces in our underground will take over our government."

"Dammit, you're just like Churchill, asking me to make a political move at the sacrifice of military logic!"

"No, General Eisenhower. All I am asking is that you honor the promise you gave as a soldier to a soldier."

His eye caught Ike's, and Eisenhower's was the first to waver. "Things were different then."

"That can only mean you have a direct order from President Roosevelt to keep Charles de Gaulle out of Paris."

"You're getting warm."

"*Eh bien.* I ask you as a soldier to order General Le Clerc's Free French Armored Division to advance on Paris —or *I* will do it!" De Gaulle turned abruptly toward the door.

"General de Gaulle!"

There was no mistaking Ike's tone. De Gaulle paused, his hand on the doorknob.

"You do that, and you won't get one more bullet, one more pound of supplies, one more gallon of gas! Maybe you can part the Red Sea, but you better damn well wear your water wings."

De Gaulle looked at his adversary and recognized the truth. "I represent the Free French, General Eisenhower. I find it terribly sad that you are not a free American."

Kay was crossing to the trailer, carrying a sheaf of correspondence, when de Gaulle stalked out and entered his jeep. She wore her new WAC uniform; she was in the Army of the United States at last. But still, as she proudly pointed out, she was a subject of His Majesty, King George.

Ike came wearily down the steps as de Gaulle's jeep pulled away. "Kay, I'm out of cigarettes," he said, and she extended her pack.

"It hasn't affected your lungs," she said. "You could hear every word quite clearly, halfway to the English Channel."

"I always get mad when I'm wrong."

"You *did* promise, didn't you?"

"Yes."

"If you don't honor your word, no one will believe any of your promises, ever."

She looked at him, hard.

The arrival of Omar Bradley and Gen. Edward Sibert, Chief of 12th Army Intelligence, interrupted the moment. With them was Maj. Roger Gallois of the French underground, who had just escaped from Paris with the startling news that the city was to be blown up, on Hitler's orders. Is Paris burning? was not an idle question; it had been asked by the Fuehrer several times when he telephoned Gen. von Choltitz, German commander of the city.

"I myself," Gallois insisted, "have seen the dynamite being placed beneath the Eiffel Tower."

"How could you be so stupid as to start firing before we were ready to help?" Ike demanded.

"In the hope of dying." Gallois saw Eisenhower's look of disbelief. "Colonel Rol, commander of the Communists in the Resistance, is certain we can take over France from General de Gaulle only if all order in Paris is destroyed. Chaos is his aim. If you parachute arms to him, he means to use them against Frenchmen to gain control of the government, even if twenty thousand Parisians perish. Yesterday evening, I heard him say this."

"I thought you were a Communist yourself?"

"I thought so too, General. Last night I found out I was a Frenchman."

Ike turned to Bradley. "Tell General Le Clerc the Free French Second Armored is ordered forward. Objective, Paris."

The Germans defended the outskirts of the city with such ferocity that the American Fourth Division had to come to the aid of the French tanks. But, true to Eisenhower's word, the forces of Gen. Le Clerc were the first to enter the city when the Nazis retreated. There followed a demonstration of happiness unequalled in this or any other war. The citizens of Paris, by the millions, thronged the streets, laughing, cheering, weeping. Girls climbed on tanks to kiss the liberating soldiers; wine flowed freely. Since the city was Paris, it was a moment of high emotion never to be surpassed.

Kay drove Ike and Bradley through the cheering crowds toward the Gare Montparnasse, the railway station where de Gaulle had set up his temporary headquarters. They were pelted with flowers, and pretty girls, clambering over the jeep to kiss the embarrassed officers, slowed their progress to a crawl, but no one seemed to mind. As Kay pulled the jeep to the curb, Ike called to Bradley, "Let's get out of this thing before we get killed!" and they pushed through the laughing girls to the sidewalk.

Inside the station, Charles de Gaulle greeted Ike as an old friend. He stood with Gen. Le Clerc, backed by members of the Republican Guard in their resplendent uniforms.

"The city is yours," de Gaulle told Ike, "but it's not yet mine. The Communists have refused to recognize my authority."

"So I've heard."

"There will be, this afternoon, a parade of victory down the Champs Élysées. I ask for American troops to participate, so those who doubt the United States supports Charles de Gaulle can see with their own eyes."

Ike understood the political implications. "How many troops?"

"To impress Communists, it will take a full division."

Ike turned to Bradley. "Brad, have we got a division to spare for parading?"

"Hell, no. They're all fighting."

"Where's the 29th?"

"Heading through the city toward the front."

Ike turned to de Gaulle. "General, I'm going to order the United States Army's 29th Division to change their order of march to take them down the Champs Élysées. They'll be in full battle gear and in a hell of a hurry. Don't expect them to salute."

De Gaulle understood the dramatic gesture.

"General Eisenhower," he said, "you are a true soldier. And a man who honors his word. There are not many of us left in this world."

He saluted Ike solemnly with a kiss on both cheeks.

"Now," said Eisenhower, "I've been kissed by *everybody* in Paris."

It was late at night when Gen. Marshall entered the Oval Office. The summons had come suddenly, unexpectedly. The President was waiting, wheelchair drawn up behind the desk, blanket over his knees. He wasted no time with preliminaries.

"I told Ike not to let the Free French into Paris first. Charles de Gaulle, naturally, took all the credit."

"Don't you think he deserved it, Mr. President?"

"That was for the French nation to decide."

Marshall knew that this was the sore point: Roosevelt's belief that de Gaulle was an opportunist, a usurper. More, one who would not do FDR's bidding.

Roosevelt had lit the cigarette in his holder, clenching

it between his teeth. "Ike has gone over my head! He has let General de Gaulle grab control in France over my distinct opposition! Who's Commander in Chief around here?"

Marshall summoned all his abilities as a peacemaker. "Mr. President, Eisenhower informed me he acted only out of military necessity. He had given his promise to de Gaulle that—"

The President cut in sharply. "By what right? That was an act of rank insubordination. Don't you think General Eisenhower should be removed immediately?"

Marshall shifted uncomfortably in his chair. "Sir, what I would suggest is that you reprimand him severely."

"That's all? A reprimand?"

"Yes, sir."

"General Marshall, I am outraged!" The President leaned back to puff at the cigarette in its ivory holder. "I am also a politician."

Marshall looked at him, questioningly. Clearly, Roosevelt was enjoying the moment.

"Ike Eisenhower doesn't realize it, but at this moment he is the most popular figure in the free world. I am recommending to Congress that he be given a fifth star and the title of General of the Army." He permitted himself a Rooseveltian grin. "I have a tough election coming up."

XVII
The Last Christmas

They moved silently through the snow, white camouflage cloaks over their green uniforms. The heavy fog that clung to the ground near the German border made them appear like a line of ghosts advancing, bayonets at the ready. The German monster was alive and marching into Belgium once more. Huge Tiger tanks of the Nazi Panzer Divisions crushed their way through the trees. The snow, the sleet, the fog, the clouds, made Allied airpower useless. Eyeless in the forest of the Ardennes, American troops were shocked and overpowered by the tremendous forces suddenly thrown against them by an enemy they had believed defeated. The American Third Army, under Patton, was already inside Germany near Sauerlautern, after breaking through the Siegfried Line. Montgomery and the British were moving toward the Rhine. The Russians had surrounded Budapest and were advancing toward Berlin. And then Adolph Hitler, madman or genius, ordered the last of German strength thrown into the greatest gamble of the war.

It was the week before Christmas.

Snow fell through the mists shrouding the ancient church in Versailles where the bells pealed the happy tidings of another Catholic wedding.

Supreme Headquarters had been established at the Trianon Palace Hotel near the vast royal gardens because Ike had not wanted his staff exposed to the temptations of Paris. Now, Sgt. Mickey McKeogh and his WAC corporal bride-to-be had arrived at the altar of the old stone church. News of what was happening to the north had not yet reached Versailles.

The Supreme Commander was seated in one of the pews, Kay and Tex at his side. Mickey was a beloved member of the family; his happiness made all of them warm and comfortable.

"Poor Mickey," Tex whispered, "marrying a WAC!"

Ike smiled. "I'll say this for him—he doesn't even look scared."

Kay turned to look at him. " 'The coward dies a thousand deaths; the hero dies but once.' "

Her meaning was not lost on him.

The bridesmaids, in their army uniforms, stepped back from the altar. Somewhere the bride had secured a wedding gown; she was marrying as a woman, not as a soldier, and the filmy whiteness of her lace emphasized her femininity.

"Dearly beloved, we are gathered here—"

The rear door of the chapel flew open, and Gen. Bedell Smith hurried down the aisle, his uniform flecked with snow from the storm outside. Every head turned as he knelt beside Eisenhower.

The conversation was hasty, whispered. A slight penetration of our lines in Belgium, Beetle reported. Instantly, Ike's soldier's instincts were aroused. The Allies should be penetrating German lines at this stage of the war, not the opposite. He got to his feet. Kay watched, hopelessly; they were mucking up Mickey's wedding.

By the time Beetle and he had reached the outdoors, snow swirling about them, Ike had formulated his plan. "I want everyone for a meeting, at once. Bradley, Patton, Tedder. The Nazi armies are on the ropes—we can't let them off, not now."

"I'd say Bradley and the others are too busy at the front to come here."

"I don't want them to come here. I'll go to them."

Verdun. A name from the past. In World War I, a million lives were lost on both sides here, clawing over a few thousand yards of shell-torn earth.

At Verdun, in the grim, gray fog of a December dawn, Ike convened the hasty meeting of his front line commanders: Air Chief Marshal Tedder, Gen. Bradley, Gen. Patton, and Lt. Gen. Jacob Devers. The meeting was in a cellar command post, illuminated by a few bare bulbs. Only 40 miles to the north, across the Belgian border, the battle was raging in such utter confusion that no one on the Allied side had any true idea of Nazi objectives or Allied losses.

George Patton, for once in his lifetime, seemed truly disturbed. The usually neat uniform was creased, the stubborn chin bore a stubble of beard. He hadn't slept in 24 hours.

"Ike, I've never seen such a goddam foul-up! The Germans are using captured American jeeps and uniforms. They've got a whole battalion of Krauts who must have escaped from Brooklyn, speaking perfect English."

"Who speaks perfect English in Brooklyn?" Ike was trying to ease the atmosphere of tension and defeat. Kasserine, he kept saying to himself, Kasserine again. He chain-lit another cigarette.

Patton continued. "They're infiltrating behind our lines, raising hell, cutting wires, turning road signs around, spooking whole divisions, shoving a bulge into our defenses."

Tedder spoke up. "Newspaper chaps are already calling this the Battle of the Bulge."

"First Army captured a German officer at Liège, carrying American papers. This ought to interest you, Ike." Patton leaned forward across the bare table. "He said he was part of an assassination squad assigned to get *you*. Commander is Ubersturmbanfuehrer Otto Skorzeny."

"Skorzeny?"

Patton nodded. "The clever bastard who rescued Mussolini from that mountain."

"I wish I were in better company." Eisenhower dismissed it with a wave of his hand.

"This is no penny-ante game, Ike," Patton insisted. "Hitler's playing for the whole pot. He's thrown in all the divisions he was saving for the defense of Germany."

Ike turned to the careful tactician, the soldier who could be counted on for calm appraisal of any situation. "Brad?"

Omar Bradley shook his head. Under the pale light bulbs, his complexion seemed almost green. He was weary, unshaven, shaken by the events of the past hours.

"Can't give you an exact picture, Ike." He shrugged. "Most of my communications are completely shattered, wires cut everywhere. Whole units have been wiped out. The Germans have driven a wedge between my Eighth and Ninth Armies—a hundred thousand men are cut off from the rest."

"Tedder?" All eyes turned to the Air Chief Marshal. Without planes, the Allies were blind, ignorant.

"Flying conditions are simply impossible," Tedder said grimly. "Nothing can get off the ground in this fog. I feel bloody helpless."

Ike got to his feet, stubbing out his half-forgotten cigarette. "This is no time to feel helpless. It's time to attack."

They looked up.

"Ike, we've got to stabilize our front lines first. St. Vith . . . Bastogne . . . maybe half a dozen other pockets with cut-off units. They may not be able to hold out." This from Jacob Devers. Solid, conservative Devers.

"Damn it! They have to hold out!" Ike was pacing now, hands clasped behind him. "I made another stupid mistake, pushing too fast for the German border, but now Hitler has opened the door to Germany for us. He's throwing in the only reserves he has left. If we can smash back fast, this could be the last big battle of the war!"

Patton was on his feet. "Smash back" was a language he understood. "You're damn right, Ike! We got them out in the open at last! You get me back the gasoline and the supplies you gave Monty, and Third Army will blow their Nazi asses off!"

"Thank you, George. I knew I could depend on you for the calm, reasonable approach."

They all smiled at that, Ike noted. Some semblance of clarity, of proportion, was returning. He turned to Bradley. "Brad, you're going to have to hit with whatever you've got left, but your Eighth and Ninth Armies are out of your control. They must go under Montgomery's command."

Now Bradley was on his feet, instantly. "I'll never get 'em back!"

"Monty will use them to take India for the Queen!" That was Patton, of course.

The generous supplies he was furnishing Montgomery's armies had resulted in Ike's being called, "The best general the British have," and Eisenhower knew it. He had to scotch that right now.

"This is an Allied operation, and I won't stand for that kind of talk!" Ike snapped. "We've got to coordinate our actions and stop the German spearheads before they split us in two, not split ourselves up before we start!" He turned to Tedder. "Arthur, somehow, some way, you've got to get planes up in this soup." He crossed to the wall, plastered from floor to ceiling with a huge operations map

263

of the area. His fingers traced the highways between Libramont and Houffalize. "The key to the whole operation is right here—Bastogne." He indicated the strategic road junction. "It controls all the major roads in central Belgium. We've got to hang onto it at all costs."

"Ike." Tedder stood beside him at the map. "We sent the 101st Airborne in to hold it, but a German Panzer Division has them completely surrounded. They can't hang on much longer."

"I know. That's where you come in, George." Ike pointed to Patton. "I once shook hands with those kids in the 101st and sent them off on a desperate mission. They came through for me. It's time I returned the favor. I don't want all those boys to die in the snow."

Everyone in that command post knew what Eisenhower meant. The day before, in Malmedy in Belgium, 150 American soldiers, cut off, had surrendered to the Germans. An SS unit had tied their hands behind them and machine-gunned them to death.

"Bastogne is 130 miles from here—that's **a** real hike!" Patton, the commander, was thinking about his men. "But you get me air support, and I'll get there."

Tedder shook his head. "Not a chance. Won't have anything in the air for at least forty-eight hours."

"That'll be too late." Ike crossed to his old friend. "You've got to do it without air support, George. You're going to have to put your men under forced march and send them into battle without sleep. Maybe without food. Will they do it for you?"

"Third Army will do it." Patton was grim, but certain. No one knew the odds better than he. "They hate my guts, but they'll do it. They know I'm a son of a bitch, but I'm *their* son of a bitch."

"You're mine, too, Georgie."

"I know, Ike. This is the one I owe you."

Hitler's plan was becoming clear. His beefed-up Panzer Divisions were striking through Belgium for the

264

port of Antwerp and its mountains of supplies and ammunition. Oil was the Germans' greatest need; as the mammoth tanks blasted their way forward, they refueled on what they could capture. Only Antwerp could support their war long enough to prevent the Allies from making good their aim of unconditional surrender; Hitler could make that too costly, strike a bargain for a separate peace with the Americans and the British, and use that as a means to halt the Russians.

Bastogne was the key; without the use of the highways it controlled, von Rundstedt's Panzers could not move swiftly enough. The Ardennes forest was a formidable opponent—jagged mountains, underbrush, huge trees. Time was the issue; if the weather cleared, if the Allied air forces got off the ground in force, the German advance could be bombed out of existence. The 101st Airborne had been rushed into Bastogne by land; the fog prevented parachuting. The paratroop division had been completely surrounded, but still it held out, denying Nazi armor the use of the main highways. On the fourth day of the seige, the German commander had demanded surrender, and Maj. Gen. Anthony McAuliffe had given him his classic reply: "Nuts!" His eloquence carved him a place in American history.

George Patton personally led his tanks into combat. For six solid days, in snow and fog and sleet, Third Army battled forward against the ferocious Panzer Divisions surrounding the city. The 101st Airborne, with even the wounded pressed into action, held out and held out against the ceaseless German artillery fire and tank attacks. They were cold, hungry, sleepless, freezing in their snow-filled foxholes. Somehow, Tedder managed to get Dakota transports up into the soup to drop supplies by parachute and glider, but only enough for bare subsistence.

The grim soldiers with the screaming eagle on their ragged uniforms heard the approach of another tank attack on their defense perimeter and swung their guns around to meet it. Almost unbelieving, they saw the white stars on the front of the lead tanks. Third Army! Third Army! They climbed wearily from their foxholes into the snow, waving their arms, shouting with what strength was left, dragging themselves forward to be greeted by American voices, American cigarettes.

George Patton rose to his feet in the open command car behind the line of tanks. The shouting paratrooper headed past him toward the truckloads of supplies bringing up the rear. Patton shoved his goggles up on his head and turned to the staff officer standing beside him.

"Now," he said, "everyone will think Ike is a genius."

It was the day after Christmas, 1944. The sun was breaking through.

The headline read, "MONTY SAYS BRITISH SAVING U.S. TROOPS FROM DISASTER."

Ike hurled the newspaper down on his desk in the Trianon Palace Hotel headquarters, beside the tiny Christmas tree with its pitiful decorations made of gilded Spam cans.

"Damn Monty! He's going to get a Christmas present he doesn't expect—me!" He turned to Bedell Smith, "Can I fly to his headquarters in this weather?"

"To Hasselt?" Gen. Smith shook his head.

The weather had closed down again. Hasselt, in Belgium, with its minimal air strip, was out of the question. Even though this was the last straw—Montgomery had issued a series of uninhibited statements to the press—it didn't warrant risking the Supreme Commander's life. Eisenhower was already fretting over having been confined to headquarters for two days, because of the rumored Nazi assassination squads out to get him.

"If we can't fly, get that fancy private train ready for me," Ike ordered. "I'm not staying here one more minute."

"You're not leaving this hotel, Ike," Beetle told him. "Day or night."

Ike snorted. "The krauts aren't trying to assassinate me. They're letting Monty do the job."

Kay came hurrying in, breathless, happy, waving a dispatch that had just arrived. "Ike! It's from 101st headquarters in Bastogne, and all it says is 'Merry Christmas!' "

This was the first direct word, and Ike snatched the message from her hand.

"From the signature, I would say it's from Cry Baby," Kay added, smiling.

Ike put down the dispatch. "Patton. He's made it. Who ever thought old Blood-and-Guts would turn out to be Santa Claus?"

The gamble had worked. Brave men had rescued brave men. The battle of the Ardennes was tipping in favor of the Allies. An old friend had paid off an old debt.

"Ike," Beetle said quietly, "shall we forget Monty now?"

Eisenhower came instantly out of his momentary reverie. "No! He'll take credit for *this,* too. Find out about that train."

"You're not to leave this hotel!" Kay was horrified.

Neither Kay nor anyone else doubted that Adolf Hitler could order the murder of the Allied Commander. The world had not yet been asked to credit the gothic tale that Hitler had ordered six million human beings cremated in the ovens built by efficient German industry for the specific purpose of gassing and burning Jews. It would be months before the West believed the existence of Buchenwald and Auschwitz. On the other hand, Skorzeny and his tough commando paratroops were already proven kidnappers, having snatched Benito Mussolini right out of an Allied prison on top of an Italian Alp. They might well be outside the Trianon Palace, a dozen Nazi SS assassins masquerading as GI's, waiting for the precisely correct moment.

"There could be Germans out there with orders to kill you!" Kay insisted.

Ike crossed to the little Christmas tree and searched among the packages still there until he found the one he wanted. "You've been seeing too many Hollywood movies," he told Kay.

"Ike!" Beetle warned. "Stay away from the windows. They may have sharpshooters."

"Can I go to the bathroom?"

"Use your own judgement."

"Beetle, use yours. I'm going to Belgium to have it out with Monty, and I don't care if the Germans are sending Frankenstein himself to knock me off! Now get that train ready."

There was a point beyond which Eisenhower could not be pushed, and Beetle Smith recognized it. He left to carry out Ike's orders. And to order a full company of Military Police to guard the train of the Supreme Commander.

"Kay, let's get some fresh air for a few minutes." Ike was holding open the forbidden doorway, the one that led to the terrace. "I've been cooped up in here for two whole days because of those foolish rumors."

"Ike, please. Don't go outside. This bloody war is getting too close for comfort. General McNair bought it a while back." She hesitated. "I'd hate to lose another friend. I have so few left."

It was the first reference she had made to Dick Arnold in months. Ike could see the fear in her eyes, as if her life were a continued story that had come around again to where it had begun. These last two days, necessity had forced them to live in close proximity, day and night, neither being allowed to leave the hotel. Kay herself might be a target for kidnapping, she knew so many classified secrets.

So Ike understood—and understanding, cared. He held up the little box he had found under the Christmas tree, as you would tempt a child. "It's a little late, but don't

268

you want your Christmas present?" And he stepped out-side, letting feminine curiosity do the rest.

Kay followed him out onto the snow-covered terrace, where armed sentries eyed them with displeasure, but did not dare order the Supreme Commander back to safety.

It was a cold night. Somewhere in the distance, a phonograph was playing Christmas carols.

"God, fresh air smells good" Ike said, his breath forming little clouds of vapor as he exhaled. He broke an icicle from a tree branch, as he had in Abilene as a boy, and tossed it idly at a snow bank. "We're going to smash them this time, Kay. I'm not going to let Monty muck it up."

"Well, you've learned one British word." Kay shiv-ered, arms clasped about her. "Now let me have my diamond tiara quickly, so we can get back into the warm."

"Not diamonds, Kay. Not for you, ever. Not in character."

"Well, *I* think they're in my character. It's yours they're not in." She took the small package and tore at the wrapping, unable to wait any longer.

"Kay, the other day I got a message from Roosevelt that says I'm to get my fifth star."

She looked up from her unwrapping. "Oh, Ike, how marvelous for you! Five stars; Like Wellington!"

"Like *Marshall*."

"If you want to be provincial . . . you've certainly earned it."

"So have you." Ike reached into the tiny box she had just opened, and removed one of the two identical gleam-ing pins. He held it up for her to see.

Kay stared. "What is it?"

"The only one in the world."

It was. Five stars on a blue shield, topped with an American eagle.

"Kay, you are no longer to drive my car. You are no

longer to type my letters. Badly." Ike took the emblem and pinned it to her lapel. It wasn't easy to surprise her; she was in the middle of everything that happened in his office. He was happy as a schoolboy to have accomplished it. "You are now, officially, First Lieutenant Summersby, aide to General of the Army Eisenhower, and entitled to wear his five stars yourself. The first woman in history, if history interests you." He pinned the second emblem to her other lapel. "Merry Christmas, Kay."

She wanted to tell him she understood. Dwight David Eisenhower did not indulge in sentimental gestures. This one had a deeper meaning. This was something for the world to see; it meant, so was Kay Summersby.

"It's not diamonds," she said, "but it will do. It will certainly, beautifully do."

She put her arms about him to kiss him, unmindful of the watching sentries, and then it happened—four sudden, sharp explosions. Instinctively, she hurled her body over Ike's, knocking him down into the snow, expecting Skorzeny's paratroopers to burst over the wall and finish the job. She clung to him.

"It's okay, General!" a sentry called. "Jeep in the driveway backfired!"

Ike rose. He helped Kay to her feet, smiling at her, and brushed the snow from her uniform. "Thank you, Lieutenant," he said.

"I was so happy for a moment," Kay said softly.

He looked at her, questioningly.

"It flashed through my mind we might die together," she said.

* * *

Hasselt lay at the northern, or British, end of the lines in Belgium, beside the frozen King Albert Canal. Ice and snow still blocked the roads; only the silver ribbon of the railway lines kept the lifeblood of war moving into the forward Allied positions. The fog was everywhere. At any moment the tanks and shock troops of another Nazi surprise might loom out of the swirling mists.

The railway platform where the Supreme Commander's train had pulled in was under heavy guard, MP's questioned even those in Allied uniforms, because of the everpresent threat of Skorzeny's assassins.

It was a moment made for Wagnerian music: two of the strongest personalities on the Allied side were about to clash head-to-head with each other. Only a few miles away, on the German border, the death throes of Hitler's empire were suggested by the forces being mobilized there. Not the dread Panzer Divisions which had slashed their way into American lines; there weren't any more of these left. The majority of troops that remained behind to protect the Third Reich were the Volksturm, the Home Guard, old and infirm men, and the Hilter Youth, children as young as twelve, clutching rifles. Even the children were supposed to stand and die, rather than shame the Fuehrer by surrendering.

And Adolf Hitler crouched in his bunker in Berlin. The thunder in the east was the advancing Russian Army, an army bent on vengeance. The crimes of the Nazi SS troops, the horrors of the concentration camps, still only rumors in the West, were spelled out to the Russians in the names of wives and mothers and fathers and sons who had been mowed down by Nazi bullets on the soil of Russia. To the leaders of the Third Reich, surrender to the Russians meant surrender to responsibility for their own actions. Hitler could never allow himself to fall into the hands of Truth.

The climax of the opera was being played out on the snowbound station platform of the little Belgian town of Hasselt; the only twist of the plot remaining to be unravelled was who was to assume the role of Allied hero. The cocky figure of Field Marshal Sir Bernard Montgomery, striding through the fog and drifting snow, left little doubt as to his own choice. Once again, as in North Africa, he had come to rescue an inept Kansas soldier from his own military incompetence.

"Halt! Show your I.D., sir."

Monty was brought up short. An American MP at the entrance to Eisenhower's railway car was blocking his path, pretending not to recognize Britain's greatest soldier.

"You know very well who I am," Montgomery told him curtly. "If you don't, you should be courtmartialed." He turned to Freddie De Guingand, at his elbow as always. "I suppose this is a put-on show for me by Eisenhower."

"Sir, I must have identification." The MP was insistent.

"Better show him your papers, General." Freddie, much more of a realist than his commander, was nervous about the meeting. "The Americans are afraid the Germans are trying to assassinate Ike."

Monty snorted. "Good Lord, they'd never do that. They want to *win*." Grumbling, he handed over his papers for inspection.

The door to the railway car's vestibule opened and Ike stepped out onto the platform, followed by Bedell Smith. Ike's mood was as grim as the weather.

"Hello, Monty. Come right in."

Montgomery looked up at him and smiled. "Step into my parlor?"

"Interpret that any way you like."

"It's to be open battle, Freddie," Monty said to De Guingand. "I prefer no witnesses." To Eisenhower, he added, "Don't you agree, General?"

"I'm not going to say anything these officers shouldn't hear."

"Well, *I* may. You'll excuse us, General Smith?"

Beetle looked questioningly at Ike. Eisenhower shrugged. If Monty wanted secrecy, he was not as sure of himself as he pretended. "Wait on the platform," he told Beetle.

Ike took out his pack of Camels, selected a cigarette,

and lit it slowly as Montgomery came up the steps. Then he opened the door for his adversary. "After you," he said, noting with satisfaction Monty's horrified glance at the cigarette as they entered the railway car.

On the platform, Beetle and De Guingand had been watching this bit of byplay.

"Giving odds, old boy?" Freddie wanted to know.

Beetle nodded.

"Abilene by forty points."

Bayonet was a luxurious railway parlor car that had been gutted and redecorated for the use of the Supreme Commander. Even after the installation of the tables, desk, and upholstery for its military duties, *Bayonet* still sported solid mahogany walls and a fretted ceiling with indirect lighting. The car behind it contained dining and kitchen facilities, including three coal-burning stoves.

Squared off against each other in *Bayonet* were two of the most dissimilar personalities ever to have the misfortune to find themselves on the same side. Bernard Montgomery was a product of the British system—the old school tie, caste and privilege, stiff upper lip. Dwight Eisenhower was an American dirt farmer who had attended West Point only because he was too old to get into Annapolis; all he was seeking from either school was a free education. Monty was studied in his deshabille—old mackinaw over old sweater above old trousers, beret tilted to one side. Ike's shoes were shined to perfection, his new trousers had a knife edge; he wore the trim jacket that had been given his name: Eisenhower.

Two other men were in that railroad car, both invisible. Behind Montgomery, Churchill. Behind Ike, FDR.

The prize at stake was the heavyweight championship of the greatest war in history.

Montgomery began by taking the offensive, all pretense aside. "It would be sheer folly, my dear Ike, to continue the present battle plan. Von Rundstedt almost broke through to Antwerp because your American generals are

273

terribly overmatched. I'll be brutally frank. General Bradly and General Hodges should be removed. Immediately."

"And replaced by?"

"Your humble servant."

"I'll be brutally frank. They won't be."

"That is idiotic. You need, immediately, one single commander to run the entire land battle for you, or you still face the prospect of devasting defeat."

"I don't need anybody to run any battles for me! I've taken full command and I don't intend to be unemployed!"

Monty toyed with a loose button on his mackinaw. "You have made rather a botch of it, Ike, haven't you? Surprise, confusion, division. Retreat. What you must have now is a single, massive assault, which I will be happy to lead directly to Berlin."

"*Your* assault has been so swift nobody's been able to see it these last few days." Ike puffed angrily at his cigarette. "Your forces haven't moved one inch."

"When I'm ready, I will move." The button came off in Monty's hand, an indication of the tension beneath the quiet smile.

"No, dammit, you'll move when *I'm* ready!"

Ike Eisenhower's patience was at an end. The issue was larger than either of them; Montgomery was questioning the chain of command, the basis of military discipline. Right or wrong, the commander must be obeyed.

Ike's voice was firm.

"If you don't want to do it—well, goddammit, Monty, there isn't room enough for both of us in this command!"

"You may be right, dear boy."

Ike crossed to the mahogany desk and grabbed a carbon copy of a message. He waved it at his imperturbable opponent. "I've drafted a cable to send to the Combined Chiefs, saying that this tug of war must end right now! They must either fire you or fire me!"

Montgomery read the cable carefully. He looked up. "Does the Prime Minister know of this effrontery? Going over his head to recommend the removal of a British commander?"

"If he doesn't, I'll be glad to tell him!"

"No, my dear Ike, leave that pleasant task to *me*. Winston and I are dear friends. I am certain he will see that the proper choice of commanders is made." He rose calmly to his feet, and crossed to the door, then turned. "Next time we meet," he said, "please don't smoke."

"Monty, for an intelligent man, you're pretty damn stupid," Ike said.

Field Marshal Sir Bernard Law Montgomery had made the fatal error of underestimating an opponent. Eisenhower had worried that there might be some hidden purpose, some British plan with Churchill's crafty backing, behind Montgomery's intransigence. Politics had always been Ike's Achilles heel. But this had turned out to be a straightforward, knock-down-drag-out fight. And his opponent didn't even realize he had been knocked down. Eisenhower felt almost sorry for him.

"You never attack unless you have overwhelming forces," he reminded Montgomery. "I *always* attack when I feel the other fellow is bluffing. Take another look at your cards."

Monty, mystified, shrugged and took his leave.

Ike breathed easier, and crossed to the mahogany sideboard. *Bayonet* had a well-stocked bar.

"I know exactly what he meant." De Guingand was accompanying his superior across the snow-covered tracks toward the command car waiting to take them back to British headquarters. "You don't think for one minute Winston Churchill is going to bite the hand that feeds England?"

Montgomery shook his head. What nonsense! Winston Churchill, who had defied the might of Germany, would certainly back his own British general.

De Guingand pressed his point. "The United States

275

is pouring twice as many men and machines and ten times as much money into this war as poor old Britain can afford. Churchill *must* do whatever Roosevelt tells him, and in military matters Roosevelt will do whatever Marshall says. To coin a phrase, Monty, you're batting on a sticky wicket."

"Nonsense!"

Montgomery refused to accept reality. Military strategists still argue the merit of his battle plan over that of Eisenhower; Monty may well have had logic on his side. But this is seldom enough, in war or peace.

"Britain must have its best military brains in command," Montgomery insisted now. "Who would they ever get to replace me?"

"Field Marshall Sir Alan Brooke or General Sir Harold Alexander," De Guingand answered promptly.

Monty stopped short. He had come to think of his little world as consisting only of Montgomery and the Western Front. De Guingand had instantly ticked off the names of two men who had outranked him in the British Army from the very first, and who had impressive victories of their own to lay on the scales.

"You know, I'd forgotten all about them?" he said, honestly shaken.

"No, Monty. You'd forgotten all about Ike."

It crashed in on him. Genius is not enough. Not even being British is always sufficient. That cablegram in his pocket was addressed to Washington, not Whitehall. Washington meant George Marshall, Eisenhower's greatest friend. And George Marshall and the United States were calling the plays for the remainder of this war. By directly opposing Eisenhower, Montgomery had made it impossible to secure acceptance of his battle plan by indirection. Or to secure acceptance of himself. He might indeed, if Eisenhower ever sent that cable, have forced Marshall to have Bernard Law Montgomery removed from command of his own troops.

"I've put my foot in it, haven't I, Freddie? What the

devil shall I do?" Snow was drifting inside his shoes, and he realized they had been standing in a snowdrift.

"Might I make a small suggestion?"

Freddie De Guingand's suggestion, which was acted upon, consisted of a short telegram signed by his proud and brave superior:

"MY DEAR IKE. YOU WILL HEAR NO MORE ON THE SUBJECT OF COMMAND FROM ME. ALL OF US UP HERE WILL WEIGH IN ONE HUNDRED PERCENT TO DO WHAT YOU WANT. YOUR VERY DEVOTED AND LOYAL SUBORDINATE, MONTY."

XVIII
Welcome to Germany

For the first time since Franklin Roosevelt had given him the title of Supreme Commander, Ike felt it belonged to him. He personally supervised the smashing of the German armored forces in Belgium. The Panzers ran out of gas, literally and figuratively, and were cut off and decimated by Allied power. With the return of good weather, Allied bombers by the thousands were sent to pound and destroy the centers of German industry. And Ike ordered a three-pronged drive to isolate and conquer the Ruhr, Germany's industrial heart, despite Churchill's vehement protests that the first target should be Berlin. It was Eisenhower's soldierly decision that Berlin was too expensive a souvenir for the toll it would take in lives. Leave it to the Russians, who counted it well worth whatever price had to be paid.

At forward headquarters in Rheims, France, Ike was at dinner with some of his airborne commanders,

Ridgeway and Taylor and Gavin, when the sudden phone call came from Omar Bradley.

"My God, Brad, that's absolutely great!" Ike turned to the others, jubilant. "We've captured a bridge across the Rhine at Remagen before the Germans could blow it up! Our troops are already crossing to the other side!" Then, into the phone, an instant command decision: "Pour everything you've got across it as fast as you can, to hell with the battle plan, to hell with everything—we've got to hold that bridgehead! I'll give you everything you can use as fast as you can use it!"

He hung up. Triumphant, sensing the final kill, he said, "It's like that old spiritual I used to hear way back when I was a kid in Kansas. 'One more river to cross, O Lord, One more river to cross.' Now it's been crossed, and Judgment Day is at hand."

Ike ordered the driver to stop the command car. He climbed out from beside George Patton, his guide for this part of the journey, and looked at the huge billboard at the side of the narrow road:

WELCOME TO GERMANY
COURTESY
OF
THE UNITED STATES THIRD ARMY

Some GI had painted a broad white line across the road.

The air was brisk this April morning, and the smell of victory was in the air. The German retreat was becoming a rout; the passenger list to Argentina, through neutral Switzerland, was crowded with Nazi elite. The Red Army had entered Vienna.

Dwight Eisenhower stood silently, drinking in the moment. Then, deliberately, he stepped across the white line. It had been a long, long time since an Eisenhower had returned to Germany. Ike, himself, had never been there.

For the first time he was on the soil of his fathers; and now it no longer belonged to Adolf Hitler.

Kay, seated up front beside the driver, could only imagine his feelings. She rejoiced for him, and was saddened for him. And saddened, too, for herself.

Ike turned back abruptly and jumped into the rear seat of the car. "Let's go,"

The car bumped forward into the Third Reich, whose Fuehrer had boasted his empire would endure for a thousand years.

Already, there were ruts in the road.

Their eyes were smiling, their hands reached out to him. They were trying to tell him of their joy, although most of them were marked by death; their ragged clothing revealed the skeletons that were all that was left of their bodies.

We are Jewish and so we will die, was their message, but you have given us the word of God that we are not forgotten, that His retribution is inevitable, and we have been allowed the happiness of seeing our torturers captured by your avenging angels, young and bearded and tough, wearing the uniforms of your triumphant armies. Blessed is the Lord, the Lord is One.

The stink was terrible, overwhelming. Certainly the German farmers, plowing the gentle green countryside in the vicinity, could not have been ignorant of what had caused it.

Ike felt the revulsion in the pit of his stomach when the next courtyard revealed bodies stacked like cordwood —naked, thin, white. There was no blood, no mark of torture. These men and boys had died, and very recently, of starvation. He heard George Patton retch. Old Blood-and-Guts, hardened by the most savage and brutal warfare, could not face this proof of the truth of the terrible rumors they had been hearing since the advance into Germany began. Patton turned away and was very sick. He could not go on.

Only Omar Bradley found the strength to continue with his commander. Ike spared himself nothing: the gallows where the body of a prisoner still hung, swinging in the slight breeze, putrefying, dead for at least a week, no one paying the slightest attention; the table in the open air where prisoners had been stretched and beaten in view of the entire camp; the barracks where emaciated human beings lifted themselves on bony elbows, trying to emit some sound to indicate life was still here, though ebbing fast, amidst the smell and the filth; the pitiful piles of shoes on the path to the gas chambers, shoes of grown men and women, shoes of little children. The Nazis had wasted nothing but human beings.

When Ike had sufficient control of his voice to speak, he gave orders to his official photographer. "Take pictures. Pictures of every goddam thing. I'll see they get printed. The world has to rub its nose into this, or it may forget."

This was Ohrdruf, Germany, the first concentration camp to be overrun by Allied troops. It was incontrovertible evidence of what the German psyche was capable of— orders had been given, orders had to be followed. *Heil Hitler*.

Ike turned to one of the local officials who had been forced to accompany him. "I want every German in this town, from the mayor on down, to march through this camp within two hours, and no one is to turn his face away. I never want it said they didn't know." He took in his breath sharply. When he spoke again, it was with the deepest sorrow. "You have made me ashamed my name is Eisenhower."

His orders were carried out that afternoon. The entire town paraded through the camp, and no face was allowed to turn away.

That night, the mayor of Ohrdruf and his wife committed suicide.

Ike and Patton were at Third Army headquarters that evening, unable to sleep, hoping a glass of soothing Scotch whisky would take the taste and the memory away. It didn't.

Kay came running in, upset. It was April 13, 1944. To many who remember, it was only yesterday.

"Ike!" She ran to him, dropping to her knees to take his hand. There was little pretense between them now, but considering the company, this was a bit unusual, Ike thought. Then he saw her tears.

"I was listening to the BBC." The words rushed out of her. "Franklin Roosevelt died last night at Warm Springs, Georgia."

"Damn!"

The sudden shock he felt, the shock so much of the world felt, made it impossible to say more. It was a death in the family.

"It isn't fair, is it?" Kay clung to his hand, as if to take some of his strength.

Ike's emotions had been torn almost too much that day. This, now, was the final tragedy. Characteristically, he tried to assume some measure of fault. "If I'd done a better job, the Nazis would have surrendered in time for him to see it, Kay." Then he shook his head. "But at least, he never had to look at what I saw this morning."

Kay rose to her feet and offered Ike a cigarette. The moment was shared between them; Patton might as well not have been in the room.

"He called me 'child'," she said. "I never told him that, very secretly, I thought of him as 'father.'"

Ike took her hand and pressed it between his. "Very secretly," he said, "so did I."

Joseph Goebbels telephoned Adolf Hitler in his bunker headquarters, where he had been waiting for a miracle to save him. "My Fuehrer," Goebbels shouted, bubbling with happiness, "I congratulate you! Fate has laid low your greatest enemy. God has not abandoned us!"

Two days later, the Russian Army stormed the outskirts of Berlin. Hitler killed himself.

Their faces were drawn beneath the grim swastikas of their uniform caps. Their eyes burned in their sockets from sleeplessness and humiliation. Forcing themselves to stand proudly erect, they got out of the cars and approached the red schoolhouse. The Allied sentries, reacting automatically to the flashing gold braid, saluted. The salute was returned, stiffly, properly—the German Army salute, not the Hitler salute, observers noted.

Through the glass doors of the schoolhouse at Rheims where generations of young French children had learned their lessons, Gen. Alfred Jodl and his aides on the German General Staff entered to learn theirs.

From an upstairs window, Kay watched, holding Telek up so that he too could have a view of this historic moment.

He was not impressed.

"General Jodl says he has complete authority from Admiral Doenitz, new head of the German state, to sign the unconditional surrender, but he requests a two-day delay."

Ike looked up sharply from his desk in the office on the second floor of the schoolhouse. "What the hell for?"

Bedell Smith shrugged. "He says German communications are in such bad shape it will take him that long to get word to all German army units."

"No, goddamit! They're stalling so that they can move as many soldiers as they can to the west, and avoid surrendering to the Russians."

"What do you want me to tell Jodl?"

"You tell him that unless he signs the surrender immediately, I'm going to close the entire Western Front to all German soldiers. Then every one of them will have to give himself up to the tender mercies of Marshal Zhukov and a Red Army that has seen exactly what the Nazis have done in Russia."

Ike was furious. To be treated as if he were ignorant of the political realities, by an enemy whose armed forces had been blown to pieces, was an affront only a German General Staff could have had the insolence to attempt.

"If Jodl agrees to sign right away, will you come down and be present at the ceremony?" Beetle was anxious to preserve the military amenities.

"No!" Ike's blue eyes glared angrily. "Not until the last Nazi officer has signed the surrender document, admitting that their armies have been beaten thoroughly, completely, and beyond all pretense, on the holy soil of Germany itself, will I look one of those goose-stepping sons of bitches in the eye."

Cameras whirred; flash guns went off like giant fireflies. Seventeen Allied war correspondents were the audience; one lone microphone recorded the sounds for posterity.

The pale blue walls of the schoolhouse were covered with battle maps and casualty lists, but looming larger than all of these to the members of the German General Staff at the table was a huge thermometer against a background of swastikas. The thermometer showed the number of German prisoners now in Allied hands, and the top of the red line was well into the millions.

Bedell Smith, Freddie De Guingand, and French and Russian officers representing their armies sat across the table from Field Marshal Alfred Gustav Jodl. "Tooey" Spaatz was there, and Col. Harry Butcher, and representatives of Allied sea and air power.

But not Gen. Dwight D. Eisenhower.

Jodl's pen scratched as he signed the document into history. Then he rose. Standing erect and defiant, he spoke unexpectedly in English. "I want to say a word."

Startled, Beetle nodded to Maj. Gen. Kenneth Strong, who served as official interpreter. Now Jodl spoke in German, holding up the surrender document. Strong dutifully translated his chilling words—chilling because they indicated that nothing had been learned.

"With this signature," Jodl announced, "the German

people and the German armed forces are, for better or worse, delivered into the victor's hands. In this war, which has lasted more than five years, both have achieved and suffered more than perhaps any other people in the world."

"Jesus Christ!" One of the photographers almost dropped his camera. Then there was utter silence. Jodl glared around the room and continued. "In this hour, I can only express the hope that the victor will treat them with generosity."

He bowed, stiffly, and sat down.

The war was over.

Waiting, Ike paced from his office into the adjoining cubicle, where Kay stood near her desk, holding Telek. She put the dog down and lit a cigarette, handing it to Ike as he passed. He waved it away.

"My God," she said, "a first." She ground the cigarette into an ashtray.

Ike paced back into his own office. It was 2:41 a.m., British Double Summer Time.

Heavy footsteps sounded on the stairway, slow, deliberate—the footsteps of defeat. Kay snatched up Telek and shoved him under her desk.

"Just stay there and look fierce," she admonished. "Remember your proud Scottish heritage."

Now General Jodl and the German delegation appeared, striding stiffly through the office. Kay stood, thanking God for having allowed her to be present at this moment of retribution, hearing again the screams and moans she had heard at the back of the ambulance she had driven through the streets of Lambeth after the fire-bombing, on that long-ago Christmas when she had almost lost belief in the Prince of Peace.

Then came Beetle and the other officers, and the correspondents, each one feeling and remembering his own times past.

How like Ike, Kay thought fondly, to have refused to be part of the play-acting downstairs. He had forced the

286

General Staff of the most vicious army of modern times into this humiliating parade. She stood with Tex in the doorway of her office, on the fringe of history, and watched the drama taking place at Ike's desk.

The German officers came to a halt, clicked their heels, and saluted the Supreme Commander. Ike did not return the salute. Coldly, he addressed Field Marshal Jodl, and Gen. Strong translated his words into German, the language of Dwight Eisenhower's ancestors.

"Do you understand the terms of the document of surrender you have just signed?"

"Ja." Jodl was curt, military, glaring resentment at the American who had refused to recognize him as a fellow soldier.

"You will, officially and personally, be held responsible if the terms of this surrender are violated." Ike leaned forward now, resting his hands on his desk. There was a bitter elation within him, for this moment was the indication of his own military thinking, a strategy that had begun back in the days when he was shunted behind a desk in the War Plans Division. "Including," he went on, "its provisions for German commanders to appear in Berlin at the moment set by the Russian High Command to accomplish formal surrender to that government."

He waited a moment for the import of this to sink in, remembering his own bold statement as a junior officer: "If the Russians are knocked out of the war, gentlemen, we had all better start learning German."

Well, they hadn't been knocked out, partly because of Dwight Eisenhower's tenacity. And now a lot of Germans were going to start learning Russian.

"That is all," Ike concluded sharply. The Germans snapped to attention and saluted him again. They waited. He did not return the salute.

Field Marshal Jodl and his group of naval and air commanders turned in unison. In perfect step, they marched out of the office.

Suddenly, the tension broke; the cheering, the laugh-

ing, the shouting, began. Men who scarcely knew eac'
other pounded each other on the back, newsmen an
generals alike.

Ike Eisenhower exhaled, the sound of it almost lik
a whoop of exultation, and got to his feet, arms extendec
the Eisenhower grin so large it dominated the room. Flash
bulbs popped, and everyone jockeyed for position for
photograph with the Supreme Commander.

"Ike! Ike!" Tex called, holding out a pair of gol
fountain pens. "These are the pens that signed the sui
render! Hold 'em up for the cameras, please!"

Ike took them in one hand and formed them into a '
for Victory. "How's this?" he called out.

"Great! Great!" The photographers were shoving eac
other aside in their effort to get the final pictures.

Ike realized suddenly that something important wa
missing. "Just a minute!" He turned and looked for Kay
who was still standing in the doorway, her eyes mois
savoring his triumph but staying well off the stage.

"Kay, I want you in on this," he said.

She hesitated. This is history, she thought. I don
belong in history books, not even as a footnote.

Ike was waving to her. "You come here, Kay, or I'
come and get you. We started together, we're finishin
together."

Slowly, she made her way through the throng abou
him, the others looking at her curiously. Proudly, she too
up a position somewhat behind Ike. He smiled at her.

"Now," he said. And the flashbulbs popped ami
more cheers and shouts.

Only later did the Signal Corps censors black Kay'
face out of the picture.

"Ike!" Tex shouted. "How about a victory statemer
for the press?"

"Yes! Yes!" The reporters clustered around, and Ka
saw the triumph fade from Ike's face as he considered th
true meaning of the moment.

At last, he said, "I'm not much in the mood for tha

now, but I'll try." He hesitated, then continued. "Just a few minutes ago, in this building, Germany surrendered unconditionally its forces on land and sea and in the air. Germany has been thoroughly whipped."

They waited for the glorious words, the fancy phrases that embroider the volumes of the world's histories. They should have known their man better.

"That's all?" one of the reporters asked finally.

"That, gentlemen," said the Supreme Commander, "is plenty."

They cheered wildly then. It was a moment made for cheering. The end of the most destructive and horrible war Europe had ever endured had been summed up by Dwight Eisenhower in characteristically brief and pointed American.

XIX
Duty, Honor, Country

The cheering continued on a scale even Kay could not have envisioned. Ike was wined and dined and honored with huge parades all over Western Europe.

And then, finally, London. Hundreds of thousands lined the sidewalks as Dwight Eisenhower, in the traditional open carriage, was cheered through the streets of Kay's favorite town, the heart of her precious Empire, to the entrance of the ancient Guild Hall, still forbiddingly impressive although its entire roof had been blown off by Nazi bombs.

City aldermen in wigs and robes, Members of Parliament, generals and royalty, even some fortunate commoners, jammed the antique, roofless building for the ceremony that dated back seven centuries.

Kay sat beside Tex in the audience, brimming with pride as Winston Churchill's voice rang out over the hall.

"I can think of no man more deserving than General

Dwight D. Eisenhower to be granted the freedom of London. His are the shoulders on which fell some of the most awesome decisions of this terrible war's most crucial moments. . . ."

On and on, the felicitous phrases, for the man he had once thought of as a clerk, Kay remembered. And now, to England, Ike was almost St. George.

Eisenhower rose, embarrassed as the applause thundered in waves over him, and stepped forward to receive the ceremonial sword from the Lord Mayor, a symbol that he was now a citizen of London.

Then there was quiet, as they waited for him to speak. Kay crossed her fingers. Ike had not wanted to wear glasses for this occasion; he wanted to present a military figure. Carefully, she had prepared a series of cards with his speech in large letters and placed them for him on the lectern. Now he began to read.

"Humility must always be the portion of any man who receives acclaim earned in the blood of his followers and sacrifices of his friends," the familiar voice began.

As Ike continued, Tex nudged Kay. "Your lips are moving," he whispered.

"We rehearsed this for hours," she whispered back. "If he's becoming part British, I don't want him to miss a bloody word."

Ike didn't.

"We Americans who at first doubted the tales of British sacrifice soon changed our opinions when we saw your scarred streets and avenues. We saw your women manning flak batteries and driving ambulances." He was looking directly at her, and Kay realized suddenly that he wasn't reading from her cards any more. The words they had gone over and over so many times had a different meaning, in this place, at this time.

"Gradually we grew closer until we became true partners in war." Yes, yes, not only America and Britain, Kay said to herself. Americans and Britons. Ike and Kay. So dissimilar, so alike. "My most cherished hope is that now that this struggle is over, we shall not be separated, but shall go forward together to a prouder future, a happier time. . . ." Of course, it was foolish; he was speaking to England, not to her. "Knowing in our hearts that neither London nor Abilene, sisters under the skin, will sell her birthright for physical safety, her liberty for mere existence." Mere existence? Liberty? Whose?

She rose with the others in tumultuous applause. Ike was smiling and waving to the vast throng, not even looking in her direction. Well, she asked herself, did you expect him to blow you kisses? She knew now what she had to do, must do; there was no doubt in her mind. Ike *had* meant what she had heard. Now it was her turn. She wished desperately that for once in her life, she could be weak, mean, and selfish. But no. She had to be British.

They were standing in a little group around the Supreme Commander, aldermen, some Members of Parliament, an admiral or two, unwilling to end the moment. The rest of the crowd in the Guild Hall had left to join the celebration outside in the streets of London. Kay made her way to Ike's side, carrying his greatcoat and Telek in her arms.

"You've got to hurry," she reminded him. "You're due at Mansion House in thirty minutes for the luncheon the Prime Minister is giving you."

"Now that I'm a Londoner," Ike grinned, "I suppose it'll be fish and chips."

"You could do worse. Hamburger, for instance."

He laughed as she helped him into his coat, then made his apologies to the others. "Sorry—my slave driver says I have to run."

There were final farewells as Kay waited, impatiently and a little apprehensively, until she could have him to herself. And then the others were gone, and they were, incredibly, by themselves for a few moments in the vast hall.

"Remember, General, tomorrow you go back to Occupation Headquarters in Frankfurt for a day, then it's

293

off to Paris, where they will give you the Champs Élysées for your key chain." She handed him his uniform cap. "And then, you leave for Washington. Alone."

She hadn't meant that to be a signal. But it was.

Ike turned to her immediately. "Have you got a cigarette?"

She fished in her pocket, found a pack, and extended the last lonely cigarette to him. He took it gratefully, smiling at her. Or possibly, she thought, at Telek.

"I never thought I would be sad to see the end of this awful war," she said quietly. "It's to be the end of us, isn't it?"

"The hell it is!"

She turned away from him. They had begun to sing in the streets outside. It would probably go on all day. Outside.

The words did not come easily, but she had made up her mind that they must be said.

"Ike, I want you to know I hold you to no covenants. You have signed no surrender." She faced him again. "I would never ask you to keep any promises made in the heat of battle."

"Kay—!"

"You are free of me. I went into this with my eyes wide open, knowing I was to be swept under the rug when this moment came. I shall mind, of course, but it's been— oh, such a lovely rug."

He took her by the shoulders, forcing her to look at him. "Kay, I'm not the simple soldier boy from Abilene you drove to the Connaught Hotel. I've been through too much. *We've* been through too much. You helped me keep my sanity during the most terrible moments of this terrible war. I need you to keep helping. You're coming back to Washington with me."

She looked at him, so serious, so determined, so unaware.

"Poor, darling Ike. Don't you know yet who you are?

294

Hitler blew his brains out and Rommel killed himself—all because of a Kansas farm boy."

"With a little help from some friends."

"You stood up to Franklin Roosevelt, and you stood up to Winston Churchill—and Abilene, Kansas, came out on top. I don't know what the future holds for you, but I'm certain it's something marvelous." She smiled now, and touched his face with the tips of her fingers. "I'm a big girl, Ike. I know when I'm out of my class."

"Kay . . ." He tried to find words, but couldn't. "Goddammit, Kay."

"Thank you, General." She linked her arm in his. "Now we'd better go. There is so much more cheering to come."

History records part of what happened next. Gen. Dwight Eisenhower took Kay Summersby to the London theater that night, and sat her at his side in full view of the startled audience. The photograph exists. Ike and Kay. Kay's mother and Gen. Bradley. Ike's son John, in uniform, with his date. A highly unusual family portrait.

There is no photograph of something else that may have happened after that.

A president of the United States, Harry Truman, is reported to have said, "Why, right after the war was over, he wrote a letter to General Marshall saying that he wanted to be relieved of duty, saying that he wanted to come back to the United States and divorce Mrs. Eisenhower so that he could marry this English woman . . . Well, Marshall wrote him back a letter the like of which I never did see. He said that if he . . . if Eisenhower even came close to doing such a thing, he'd not only bust him out of the Army, he'd see to it that never for the rest of his life would he be able to draw a peaceful breath . . . I don't like Eisenhower . . . I never have, but one of the last things I did as President, I got those letters from his file in the Pentagon, and I destroyed them."

Harry Truman had made honesty the cornerstone of his political career. Late in life, when he made the statement, it is possible his memory was faulty. His daughter, Margaret, said more recently, ". . . I think he suggested that it might be better if General Eisenhower's letter about divorcing his wife be taken out of General Eisenhower's file. I think that's true. I have always thought that was true."

Others, many others, have thought differently.

What *is* known beyond doubt is that Dwight Eisenhower went back to Washington after the end of the war. And never returned to his position as Military Governor of a divided postwar Germany.

* * *

She came running along the sidewalk, the wind whipping her auburn hair, her cheeks pink from excitement. She was late again, as she had been on that long-ago afternoon in London when she had run from the Connaught to the Embassy to meet that dreadful American general.

The setting was different now, the signs here were in German, and gutted buildings sagged into the pockmarked street. Kay was hauling a startled Scottie by his leash; in another moment she scooped him up in her arms and headed for the building across the street.

The building was huge, concrete and steel and glass that had survived the war almost without damage; within its walls, green trees and gardens made this a pleasant place to work. I.G. Farbenindustrien had manufactured chemicals—never mind what they were to be used for— that were important to the Reich war effort, and its offices had been made large, airy, attractive. The Frankfurt building had been chosen to be the site of Supreme Headquarters for the occupation forces headed by Gen. Eisenhower.

The main space inside the entrance, three stories high, had been turned into a reception area. When Kay entered, Col. Tex Lee was standing on a desk surrounded by dozens of American officers and WACs. He had almost finished reading from the sheet of paper in his hand. It was a tableau Kay was to remember for the rest of her life. Breathless, clutching Telek, she stopped to listen.

"Wolinsky, Sergeant T.J.; Youngblood, WAC Lieutenant Eleanor; Ziffrin, Captain F.E." Each responded with a happy wave of a hand. Tex looked up. "All of you are to report to Frankfurt Airport at 0800 hours Friday for transport to Washington, D.C., and the office of the new Chief of Staff of the United States Army, General Dwight D. Eisenhower." Cheering, whistling, those who had been named hurried off to collect their belongings, to get out of defeated Germany with its platoons of ghosts and memories, to go back home where wars were something that happened only to foreigners.

Kay pushed her way to Tex's side as he climbed down from the desk. "Sorry I was late," she said, still trying to catch her breath. "It was Telek's morning at the vet, and he was impossible." She tried to keep her voice steady. "Should I ask?"

Tex, her good old Tex, looked at her. "What do you think?"

"I don't think. I know, don't I?"

He nodded. "Not on the list."

Her throat tightened. Naturally. Of course. It was exactly what she had told him she wanted. Nothing. For a long moment, she petted the dog in her arms. She hadn't expected him to believe it.

"Any message?" she asked finally.

Tex busied himself straightening the papers on his desk. "Not a word."

"Strange, I thought there might be a message." Cut off, as if by an axe. She hadn't thought it would be quite this way. She turned away from Tex's gaze. "I didn't think it would hurt, really. It does, dreadfully."

"Can I buy you a drink?"

297

"Thank you, Tex, no." She hesitated. "No message?"

"Not a damn word. It's not like him. It's not fair. Even though I warned you, long ago."

Tex took her by the arm, and they walked through the half-empty headquarters toward the daylight beyond the glass doors. Kay was still clutching the dog.

"What am I to do with dear Telek?"

"What do you mean?"

"He's the General's dog. I gave them to each other."

Tex shook his head. "Not on the list."

"You looked under the T's?"

"Sure."

"Dear Lord, I don't know how being kind to a poor little dog could tarnish the name of the United States of America. But then, I'm not a bloody Yank." She started to open the huge glass door.

"Kay?"

She turned.

"I'm so goddam sorry."

"Sorry? Sorry for Kay Summersby? Why, I fought this whole bloody war, didn't I? We British gave you everything we had. *Every*thing we had. And we're still here. Me. England. We'll muddle through, thank you."

She yanked the door open, went out of the building and set the dog down on the German pavement.

"Come on, you little Scotch bahstard," she ordered, "hold your head up high."

They crossed the alien sidewalk, pushing past passersby until they reached the street and then a pitiful patch of grass beyond, the Scottie hurrying on his short legs, his head held high by the leash in her hand. Then Kay stooped, picked him up in her arms, and kissed him.

The last Tex saw of them was when Kay set Telek down and went off with him proudly along the crumbling street of the shattered city in the once powerful, terrible land they had both helped to conquer.

In America, the victory parades continued—unceasing, interminable. Thousands in Abilene. Millions amid the ticker tape of New York's Wall Street. Cheering crowds along Pennsylvania Avenue. Cheering for Ike.

For Ike and Mamie.

* * *

Afterword

The cheering and the images have faded into yesterday. This is a tale of a time and of people seen only through a glass, darkly. But there will always be those who will seek for something called Truth, and they are entitled to know where the photographer has retouched his portrait.

What was in the letter Ike wrote to General Marshall, I do not know. That it was ever written is still in controversy. On the record is only the statement of crusty old Harry Truman.

What is truth? I do not know. And not knowing, I will not hazard a guess. Some of it lies, perhaps, in the wartime letters of Mamie Eisenhower to her husband, letters that have never been published. Or it lies, more exactly, in her heart. Both are her property, and deserving of privacy.

I would not have gone back into my own past to recreate how things seemed to me if I did not honestly believe that Dwight Eisenhower was human being enough to have felt what any of us might have felt, given that war and that time and that woman. By those who were there, I have been told that he did feel, deeply and honestly; and so did Kay Summersby.

Both Ike and Kay have now gone on. The truth, the absolute truth, if such a thing ever can exist, died with them.

THE BEST OF BESTSELLERS FROM WARNER BOOKS!